IT'S A DRAG

IT'S A DRAG

CROSS-DRESSING IN PERFORMANCE

JANET TENNANT

APPLAUSE
THEATRE & CINEMA BOOKS

Guilford, Connecticut

APPLAUSE
THEATRE & CINEMA BOOKS

An imprint of Globe Pequot, the trade division of The Rowman & Littlefield Publishing Group, Inc.
4501 Forbes Blvd., Ste. 200
Lanham, MD 20706
www.rowman.com

Distributed by NATIONAL BOOK NETWORK

British Library Cataloguing in Publication Information available

Library of Congress Cataloging-in-Publication Data available

ISBN 978-1-4930-5905-8 (paperback)
ISBN 978-1-4930-5906-5 (e-book)

♾™ The paper used in this publication meets the minimum requirements of American National Standard for Information Sciences—Permanence of Paper for Printed Library Materials, ANSI/NISO Z39.48-1992

For Keith, with love and thanks

CONTENTS

CONTENTS

INTRODUCTION

Years ago, as a taller-than-average teenager at an all-girls' school, I played King Menelaus in a Greek tragedy. I loved the sprayed-on silver hair and kept it for the week of the play, insisting to the teachers that it was impossible to apply nightly. I also took various male roles in Shakespeare, acted Tony Lumpkin in *She Stoops to Conquer*, and played policemen. Principal boys in the local Christmas pantomime were also my forte. I took to the stage in shorts, fishnet tights, and high heels and attempted, rather badly, to sing of my love for Cinderella, Red Riding Hood, Snow White, or whoever was the heroine of the current production. Rather naively I didn't realize then that the Principal Boy role was the most glamorous one in any panto, and one year I rejected it and pleaded for a "girl's" part. My best friend Carole, a petite and pretty, curly-haired blonde, always got to wear a crown and a pink ball dress, and I wanted one, too. The astute director smiled and gave me my female part—an old hag with blacked-out front teeth. I think it was Red Riding Hood's grandmother. I learned my lesson. The next year I was back in the shorts and high heels as the prince! I even reprised the role in my forties, playing, rather bizarrely, Principal Boy to my teenage daughter's Principal Girl.

Britches roles are familiar to me—and most likely what started my interest in cross-dressing for performance.

Cross-dressing, defined as the taking on of clothing and accessories commonly associated with the opposite sex, has been used throughout history by people for many reasons: for disguise, comfort, and self-expression—and sometimes as rebellion. In most societies, there are expected norms for gender (historically only two) relating to the type of clothing that is appropriate. In some cultures, there are guidelines and even laws that guide and restrict what a person of any gender wears. Many people have chosen, and still choose, to ignore such constraints.

But this book is not about why people in their ordinary life cross-dress. It is all about performance.

There are many reasons why those who present themselves to audiences and those who write or compose for them have chosen to depict their characters as being of a gender different than the one they usually claim. Such reasons are varied and complex. They include cultural and religious norms, expediency (e.g., a shortage of those of the "right" gender at the time), comedy, and titillation. But political control, social rebellion—or, increasingly, experimentation to bring new dimensions to a role—also play their part. As this century progresses, the push toward equality has resulted in more demands, from both women and men, to shrug off convention and to play roles previously assigned to another gender. So, too, is there a growing trend for previously "male" or "female" roles to be reconfigured as being gender neutral.

This book looks briefly at the early history of cross-dressing but moves on to concentrate on how and why performers in the Western world have used such devices up to the present day. It is about gender imitation and not primarily about sexuality, although inevitably the latter plays a part in the choices some performers—but by no means all—make. The late twentieth and now our early twenty-first century have seen much experimentation in the performing arts. Cross-dressing has become increasingly used on stage but less to make the audience aware of gender difference than to convince them of its unimportance. Perhaps also, as more stage productions are set in the present where much of our clothing is gender neutral, even the term may be outdated. "Color-blind" casting—giving actors roles irrespective of their racial origin—is already regarded as routine in theaterland, although black actors would argue the change is too slow. "Gender-blind" casting, however, is still comparatively novel.

The book ends with a look into the future.

At the time of writing, the whole theatrical profession is in crisis. It has been one of the hardest hit sectors of Western economies with many venues still dark and little work for the vast array of people who work in the industry—from directors and actors to stage staff and those who care for the buildings. Many theaters and concert halls on both sides of the Atlantic are bravely struggling to get back to some sort of normality, with smaller productions, reduced seating, and social distancing for their audiences, and looking forward to when such measures will no longer be necessary. It seems that the way to survive is likely to be choosing the productions and the well-known performers that are the safest box office—the ones that will reduce debt and eventually restore economic stability. Let us hope that this is temporary. I hope that, when you read this, new innovative theater, opera, musicals, and dance will once again become the norm. And let us hope that all the talented individuals and groups, including those of all genders and color who have yet to find their rightful place in our marvelous performing arts, are once again fully employed in entertaining us.

Just a note: I know that it is now usual to refer to all actors as just that. However, to avoid confusion, and the use of too many adjectives, I hope I will be forgiven for reverting to the use of the terms *actress*, *actor*, and *ballerina* where necessary.

1
OVERTURE AND BEGINNERS

Have I not suffered? Doth it call
No tears? . . . Ha, ye beside the wall
Unfathered children, God hate you
As I am hated, and him too,
That gat you, and this house and all!

—EURIPIDES, *MEDEA*[1]

Medea, the title role in the play by the Greek writer Euripides, is a peach of a part. It has everything that a female actor who enjoys tragedy could ever want in a theatrical role; it is one that she can get her teeth into. Euripides puts the character at the center of his play, and she has all the best lines. Any actor who plays Medea has to demonstrate feelings of bitter disappointment, abandonment, rage, anger, and vengeance and to participate in murder and infanticide; it is one of theater's meatiest women's roles.

Medea, a former princess of the barbarian kingdom of Colchis, leaves her homeland to marry Jason, the famous leader of the group of adventurers known as the Argonauts and the hero who led them in their quest for the Golden Fleece. Medea bears Jason two children. When he leaves her for a political marriage to a Greek princess of Corinth, she is understandably enraged. She takes vengeance on her ex-husband by murdering Jason's new wife and, horrifically, her own children. She then escapes to Athens to start a new life.

The play, written and first performed in 431 BCE, was rediscovered in sixteenth-century Europe, and since then, it has been a classic of the repertoire of the Western canon and the most frequently adapted and performed Greek tragedy, popular throughout the nineteenth and twentieth centuries and into the twenty-first. Famous female actors in Europe and across the Atlantic have played the part, and it has been of great interest to the feminist movement, which has interpreted it sympathetically as a portrayal of Medea's struggle to take charge of her own life in a male-dominated world. The play holds the US Tony Award record for most wins for the same female lead character, with Judith Anderson winning in 1948, Zoe Caldwell in 1982, and Diana Rigg in 1994. There will probably be more.

Many actors recall playing Medea with real passion for the role. Fiona Shaw, who took the role in Dublin, London, and New York between 2000 and 2003, thinks it is because Euripides expertly manipulated his audiences' emotions. "He's absolutely meticulous about cornering her," Shaw says.[2] Not long into the first act, the audience is aware that Medea has already defied her father, executed her brother, and abandoned her home, all for the love of her husband, Jason. This makes her sense of betrayal so hard to bear when Jason chooses to secure his political future by abandoning her and marrying the Corinthian, King Creon's daughter, Glauce. In this situation, says Shaw, "there is absolutely nowhere for her to go. That is brilliantly, mathematically set up. Thereafter, the audience feel sympathetic, right until the moment when she says: 'I must kill the children.' It's not surprising she's infamous for killing them—but we should be infamous for agreeing to it." Far from being a willing infanticide, Shaw argues, Medea forces herself to kill her children so that no one else can. It is, like everything else she does, an act of selfishness driven by sexual passion. "What she's really on to is the terrible myth in our society, whereby we tell children that they are the primary source of love, and the cruel truth is that they're not: the passionate partner is. People will not give up their lover for their children."

If such a part unleashes such deep analysis by women who take on the role of Medea, how amazing it is to think that the part was originally written to be played by a man impersonating a woman. Women were not considered as potential actors until many centuries later.

Although one of the best known, *Medea* was not the first of the Greek plays. The earliest were tragedies and dated from about 530 BCE. There had been a performance tradition before this time, but Aeschylus was a tragedian who for the first time wrote what we would recognize as plays, those in which his characters interact rather than communicate only with a chorus. From around 487 BCE, Greek playwrights began to write comedies as well as tragedies, and such plays were often given their first airing at festivals to celebrate the gods. The most important festival featuring such drama was the Dionysia, a large festival in ancient Athens in honor of the god Dionysus. People from all over Greece would converge on Athens to celebrate the Greek god of wine, theater, and revelry, and playwrights would compete for prizes. The festival included a theater competition in which playwrights would present one comedy and three tragedies, which occupied the whole day. Euripides was one of the winners as were Aeschylus and Socrates. The sources of their material were the legends of Greek heroes such as Hercules, but they also put famous Greek women at the center of many of their plays. Such women were not at all the disenfranchised wives and mothers of Greek society but strong women who often defied convention and took unexpected actions to pursue their own ends. Aeschylus's Clytemnestra takes awful revenge on her husband Agamemnon and the woman he had taken as a war prize. She kills them both. Sophocles's Antigone hangs herself rather than die imprisoned, and in Aristophanes's comedy *Lysistrata*, the heroine encourages the women of the warring city states of Greece to withhold sexual privileges from their husbands to force the men to negotiate peace.

All such plays required the playwright to write and then the actors to demonstrate deep emotions and characteristics of feisty women. Presumably the perceptions of both writers and their audiences of how the female mind worked and how women reacted to major events in their lives was from imagination and from observation of their wives and daughters, but it is also likely that conversations with hetaerae played a part. These were women in a special class in ancient Greece who served as companions to wealthy men. They were freer than the men's wives who were carefully secluded at home. They had special training and were very influential, serving as social arrangers, advisors, entertainers, and even as courtesans, and they would probably have accompanied rich men to some festivals and plays.

Despite the female roles being written in a way so that even now our best actors need to study the characters in depth to play them with real conviction, women were barred from the stage, and all the famous female characters in ancient Greek drama were originally played by men dressed as women. Although women were not slaves and did take part in many of the other religious rituals associated with the gods, they were not allowed to perform in these plays, which were a tribute to Dionysus—the god of grape-harvest, winemaking and wine, ritual madness, religious ecstasy, theater, and fertility. In Greece, only citizen landowners were allowed to act, and since women and slaves were not permitted to be citizens, there could be no women actors in this paternalistic society. Male actors, on the other hand, were regarded as respected professionals; they could own land and were granted citizenship in Athens. Although because of these cultural norms women did not perform speaking roles, it is generally accepted that they did occasionally take to the stage in Greek theater. They most likely acted female characters who remained silent and were walk-on roles in support of a main character.

There were usually only three actors in a play, each one playing multiple roles. The actors did not, as would be appropriate today, try to "get into" the role. They represented the character rather than became it and wore costumes and helmet-like masks to do so. They donned a different mask each time they took on a new character role and also within each role to show different emotions or moods. As theaters increased in size, the masks were constructed with more exaggerated facial expressions so that the audience members sitting at a distance from the stage could recognize the change. The mouth size, originally quite small, became bigger to allow more of the voice to be heard by everyone in the amphitheater. None of these masks have survived, but the pictures of them on pottery from different periods indicate the move to unrealistically large mouth apertures.

Pollux, a rhetorician writing in the second century CE, lists seventeen female masks used in Greek theater. They include fat and thin, old women, two matrons, one virgin, a bawd, a mistress, three courtesans, and a lady's maid. No masks have survived as they were probably made of organic materials like stiffened linen, leather, wood, or cork, but on the pottery of the period, they are often shown in the hands of actors waiting to perform. These vase decorations show that wigs often had a quantity of hair. The actors would be limited in what they could see through the eye-holes while wearing the masks, so it is thought that the ears were covered by substantial amounts of hair and not by the helmet-like mask itself. The ability to hear what was going on was necessary so that players could orientate themselves and move more naturally about the stage area. Masks for men and boys in female roles have large mouths, long tresses of hair with decorations, and big dark eyes: stylized women, but not the real thing.

Actors wore full-length chitons (gowns), which differed from those worn in everyday life; they were longer and incorporated sleeves of different colors and patterns. Female roles required the actors to wear long white sleeves, possibly part of an undergarment, to show femininity. To suggest a womanly figure, the male actors wore a wooden *prosterneda* in front of their chest to imitate female breasts and a *progastreda* on the stomach to emphasize curves. The backstage dressing process must have been very complex.

This early depiction of women's roles in Greece by cross-dressing men was mirrored by that in early Roman theater, which began some two centuries later, influenced by the extensive contacts between the Romans and the Greeks. Roman theaters were originally temporary outdoor structures erected in temples, arenas, and the forum (central square), and it was 55 BCE before Pompey the Great had the first permanent theater built. In such large performing areas actors had to have stamina and agility for exaggerated physical acting and for projecting their voices in the open air to be seen and heard by the many thousands who filled such theaters. They too were masked to demonstrate differences in gender and character.

Juvenal,[3] the Roman poet active in the first and second centuries CE, wrote bitterly about the rich newcomers to Rome, and particularly he describes the incoming Greek actors:

> *They go into ecstasies over some shrill and scannel [harsh] tenor who cock-a-doodles worse than a rooster treading his hen. We can make the same compliments but they're the ones people believe. Who can beat them in any performance of female parts, as courtesan, matron or slave girl?*
>
> *No mantle, either; you'd swear that what you saw and heard was a woman, not an impersonator; no bulge beneath the belly, all smooth, with even a suggestion of the Great Divide. Yet, back home, even the most famous of these tragedy queens and dames will pass unnoticed.*
>
> *They're a nation of actors. Laugh and they'll out guffaw you, split their sides.*[4]

There was no love lost by Juvenal for such actors, but he knew their performances. Unlike in Greece where actors had long been considered professionals and accorded the rights of citizens, the men who first appeared in

Roman performances were considered of low social status, akin to prostitutes and criminals, and were denied the same political and civic rights that were afforded to Roman citizens. Juvenal obviously considered the incomers as threats to Roman society as he knew it. As sexual predators.

> *Besides, nothing's sacred to him and his randy urges, neither the housewife, nor her virgin daughter, nor her daughter's still beardless fiancé, not her hitherto virtuous son—and if none of these is to hand, he'll lay his friend's grandmother.*[5]

Many were "foreigners" from Etruria, an area to the west and north of what is now Italy. Other actors were slaves and could be beaten by their masters if they were thought to have acted badly. However, while acting slaves had few rights, they did have the opportunity to win their freedom if they were able to prove themselves as successful actors. Although there was a big difference between Greek and Roman theater in how actors were regarded, they were alike in having no female actors. As in Greece, there is the possibility that women may have played some nonspeaking characters. However, all historical evidence suggests that men performed all the speaking roles.

As the Western Roman Empire decayed during the fourth and fifth centuries CE, the center of Roman power moved to Constantinople (now Istanbul) and to what is now called the Byzantine Empire. The Byzantines preserved many classical Greek texts, and there was theater in Constantinople until the fifth century. But from this time on, Western Europe was mostly unstable until the tenth century. During this period, referred to as the Dark Ages, it is likely that there were small traveling groups of players performing wherever they could find an audience but, unlike their predecessors, only producing crude scenes. Such performers were denounced by the church as dangerous and pagan, so it seems unlikely that women would normally take part in such acts. However, in troupes of entertainers throughout the centuries, men and boy entertainers do not travel alone. They are accompanied by wives, sisters, and daughters. I find it hard to believe that there was never a woman who, in the absence of a necessary male actor, did not don a mask, climb on to the temporary stage to masquerade as a man playing a woman. And do it well.

But, out of the so-called Dark Ages a theatrical woman's voice was heard. In the tenth century, in the convent of Gandersheim in northern Germany, an intellectual center at this otherwise barbaric period, lived a nun, Hrosvitha, known as the Nun of Gandersheim. She lived a short life (ca. 935–973), but during her time at the convent, she wrote down accounts of Christian stories, verse, and six or seven prose comedies, all in Latin. From her work (not published until 1501) it is clear that she was familiar with the Christian legends and philosophy as well as classic authors. But she also knew the work of Publius Terentius Afer, better known as Terence. He was a playwright of North African descent who was born around 195 BCE in Carthage (in what is now Tunisia) and was initially taken to Rome as a slave. His writing abilities led to his freedom, and he wrote six separate plays. Hrosvitha admired Terence's ability and his style—but not the way he wrote about women, which she thought was pagan and lacked morality. Her own comedies were moral dramas based on Christian principles and she substituted the dissipation she found in his work for stories of "pure virgins." Her aim was to elevate the moral standards of the drama.

There would have been no point in Hrosvitha choosing to write plays if they were not to be performed. That is what plays are for. Most likely they were performed in the convent by young nuns before an audience, including the bishop of Hildesheim and possibly high officials of the empire and members of the imperial family who founded the convent and from which most early abbesses were drawn. All the plays had both male and female characters, so the nuns at Hildesheim were probably the first women to act and to take on roles of a different gender. Whether or not the young nuns used masks is lost in the mists of time. However, since the tradition of Western drama thus far was to use masks to define gender and mood, it was most likely that the women devised such ways to disguise their young faces.

For the long centuries of the later Middle Ages, from the tenth to the middle of the sixteenth century, there were wandering players, jugglers and minstrels, rude country folk-plays, traditional mumming plays, and secular pageants, all of which helped satisfy a popular demand for entertainment. However, the real drama grew from the regular services of the church. The church needed to convey the Christian story to a mostly illiterate population with little or no education who would not understand the Latin used in the churches. This led to the appearance of religious dramas used to illustrate key religious ceremonies such as Easter and Christmas. These were performed and acted in the churches, and were mostly visual. The actors would use minimal dialogue in Latin, which was slowly replaced by French and later English. As before, the men cross-dressed to play female roles. At Easter, for example, one priest would be the angel and others the three Marys at the tomb of Christ. They would speak responses to a choir. At Christmas, a priest might play the Virgin Mary in the stable. Equally slowly but surely the priests were replaced by lay actors, and the performances took place away from the churches in town squares and at fairs. An element of coarse comedy was introduced to Bible scenes with stock comic characters. Herod always appeared as a blustering tyrant, and the wicked characters, particularly the devil, were placed in ludicrous situations. Noah's wife was regularly represented as a shrew who had to be beaten before she would enter the ark. Townspeople began to be more involved in the plays, and particularly where the trade guilds or handicraft unions were prominent in the town governance, they took over control of performances. Usually, but not always, each play was presented by a single guild, and often there was a special fitness in the assignment of scenes to be played by each guild, as when the shipwrights represented the building of

Noah's Ark or the bakers acted out the Last Supper. The scenery was basic, either a doorway to represent a house or a tree for a forest. The costumes and props, on the other hand, were often detailed and accurate to demonstrate the skills of the guild. Although it is very likely that women would have been involved with some part of creating the costumes and properties for these Mystery and Miracle cycles, they never acted. Men and boys took the women's parts.

The popularity of such religious cycles waned from the fourteenth and fifteenth centuries until by the seventeenth they were rarely seen; however, there are some places in Europe, notably Oberammergau in Bavaria, where they exist to this day. Growing up alongside them and slowly replacing the religious plays were the Moralities, adaptations of allegories and with stock characters such as Gluttony, Pride, and Every Man. These too began to wane in popularity, and by the end of the fifteenth century, they had slowly merged into the Interludes, which, as the name suggests, were often used to fill the interval in a festival or court entertainment. These were merrier and more farcical than preceding plays and meant as entertainment rather than illustrations of the Bible or exhortations to a moral life.

But it was a man's world, both in the writing and acting of such theatrical entertainments and in the way that they portrayed women. A flavor of how women were regarded is seen in a play by John Heywood, an entertainer at the court of Henry VIII. One of his plays, The Four Ps, concerns a dispute among a Pedlar, a Pardoner, a Palmer (pilgrim), and a Poticary (apothecary). They are challenged to tell the greatest lie. Eventually after a lot of unsuccessful attempts, the Palmer says that he has never seen a woman out of temper. He wins the contest!

Most of these dramatic forms from the tenth to the mid-sixteenth century are no longer much in evidence. But they demonstrated the persistent taste of the public to be entertained. Above all, they strongly affected performance traditions in the burgeoning drama of the Elizabethan period and to some extent into later times. These traditions included the disregard of unity of time and place, the mingling of comedy with tragedy, the use of some stock figures such as the Clown, a lack of all but basic scenery, and the presentation of women's parts by men and boys.

They laid the foundations of what was to come.

2
BOYS WILL BE GIRLS—WILL BE BOYS?

But there is, sir, an eyrie of children, little eyases, that cry out on top of question, and are most tyrannically clapped for't.

—WILLIAM SHAKESPEARE, *HAMLET*[1]

After dinner on August 18, 1660, Samuel Pepys and a friend went to the Cockpitt theater to see *The Loyal Subject*, a play by John Fletcher. Late that night, in his diary, Pepys recorded his impressions of actor Edward Kynaston. When the young man took to the stage as the Duke's sister, Pepys thought he "made the loveliest lady that ever I saw in my life, only her voice not very good." On January 7, 1660–1661,[2] he saw Kynaston again. "Tom and I and my wife to the Theatre, and there saw *The Silent Woman*. The first time I ever I did see it, and it is an excellent play. Among other things here, Kinaston [*sic*] the boy; had the good turn to appear in three shapes: first, as a poor woman in ordinary clothes, to please Morose; then in fine clothes, as a gallant, and in them was clearly the prettiest woman in the whole house, and, lastly, as a man; and then likewise did appear the handsomest man in the house."

By the time Kynaston was admired as both a beautiful woman and a handsome man by Pepys, he was already about twenty years of age, although still termed a boy actor. One story about him at this time tells how the start of a play had to be delayed while he shaved. Although he was probably the most celebrated of the young men playing female roles, his days as such were brief. His last role as a woman was as Evadne in a 1661 production of Beaumont and Fletcher's *The Maid's Tragedy* with Thomas Killigrew's King's Company.

Charles II had succeeded to the throne in 1630, and after the long period of theater closure by the Puritans, a more liberal atmosphere prevailed. Only women were permitted to act female parts on stage, and boy actors were no longer needed. Kynaston went on to a long career playing male roles and retired as a successful adult actor thirty years later; however, many other boy actors disappeared from the theatrical scene when they reached adulthood and made their lives elsewhere.

Boy players have been part of theatrical history since records began. The use of prepubescent boys to play female parts in companies of adult players can be traced back to their use in medieval theater. This tradition of using boys continued, and by the time of Henry VIII's reign in England, small companies of players, possibly a half dozen men and boys, performed for the nobility. Some noble houses maintained their own troupe, and Henry himself had a small company, the "Lusores Regis." They could not be fully employed at court, so some of these actors toured the country to earn money. As more groups began to work for others than their patrons, the move toward commercial entertainment for those who could pay gathered momentum. These were touring companies, but the origin of what we would recognize as modern theater—the time when playing companies established themselves in London—dates back to the 1572 Acte for the Punishment of Vagabondes. This was an early precursor to the modern welfare state, which made communities rather than the church take responsibility for poor citizens. Until this time, independent troupes of traveling male actors and players had toured country inns, but with the passing of the act, they were regarded as vagabonds and made unwelcome. They were also suspected, probably unjustly, of being responsible for bringing plague to the communities through which they traveled. The Acte deemed that such companies could no longer exist on their own; they needed a nobleman to provide patronage (a form of sponsorship). To some extent, the playing companies that existed from 1572 until

Cromwell closed the theaters in 1642 were independent, although as the names suggest, there was a loose patronage that allowed them to function, among them the Earl of Derby's Men, the Admiral's Men, and Worcester's Men. Some companies were based in London; others were chiefly provincial. Some changed locations at different times of their existence. All of them, wherever they performed, used men—but more often prepubescent boys—to play women's roles. Women were not permitted to act in public.

This was very different in other parts of Europe. In the early part of the sixteenth century in the reign of Charles V (king of Spain, Castile, and Aragon, 1516–1556), a woman appeared on the stage in Spain for the first time. Such appearances were then suppressed by royal edict, but soon actresses became the norm, especially in the higher-class theatrical troupes such as the Farandula and the Compania. Men and boys continued to act female roles in the less prestigious groups. Sometime later, around the middle of the century, women made their debut on the Italian stage. Pope Innocent IX forbade their appearance; however, his edict was ignored, and women quickly took over the female parts from the men. Mixed-gender acting troupes from Italy and Spain began to travel in Europe, and in September 1548, a tragi-comedy performed by Italian actors and actresses entertained the king of France and his wife at the residence of Cardinal de Ferrara, the bishop of Lyons. It was another fifty years, however, in 1594, before a French woman appeared on stage in her own country. This was Marie Vernier, the first French actress to be known by name, who acted under the stage name of La Porte. She was leading lady and codirector of Valleran-Lecomte's theater company, which performed in Paris and toured France and the Spanish Netherlands. It soon became usual for women to be seen as actors both in troupes of strolling players and in more established touring companies. In *Don Quixote*, published in 1605, Cervantes describes how Don Quixote encountered a cart driven by "a hideous demon" and "loaded with the most varied and extraordinary personages imaginable." When asked who they were, the devil replied, "Sir, we are strolling players that belong to Angula's company, and it being Corpus Christi-tide, we have this morning acted a tragedy, called *The Parliament of Death* in a town yonder behind the mountain and this afternoon we are to play it again in the town you see before us, which being so near we travel to it in the same clothes we act in, to save the trouble new dressing ourselves. That young man plays Death; that other an angel: this woman, sir, our poet's bed-fellow, plays the queen."[3] In Europe, women players were becoming a common sight. But in England, the sight of women on stage was still a long time in the future.

The later part of the sixteenth century was a turbulent period in English theatrical history. Many theatrical companies—groups of actors (sharers) who both acted and managed the company—were set up. The members acted the principal parts themselves but hired minor actors, including young boys, to play other roles. These boys were also expected to help with all the backstage jobs. Some companies succeeded; some failed. The most successful established themselves in permanent buildings in London, while others were forced to tour until they received permission to perform in the city. And most changed their patronage and their names quite frequently. By the beginning of the next century, William Shakespeare's company—the King's Men (previously during Elizabeth I's reign known as the Lord Chamberlain's Men)—and the Admiral's Men were the most prominent acting companies in London, and they were very successful. Shakespeare's company had the open-air Globe in the summer and then used the Blackfriars Theatre for the winter season. The Admiral's Men were based in the Rose Theatre in the 1590s and the Fortune in the early 1600s.

These established companies employed young boys, often prepubescent with unbroken voices, to play female and children's roles. The boys apparently served legitimately as apprentices in the same way as those who were taken on in other guilds and trades at the time; however, they were employed for shorter terms, two or three years, lasting until their voices broke. Depending on the guild that sponsored the apprenticeship, the time could vary. Alexander Cooke, who acted in the Lord Chamberlain's Men and the King's Men, was indentured in 1597 for seven years under the Grocer's Guild, although he was not freed until 1609. He was probably introduced to the theater by John Heminges who had himself been a grocer's apprentice in London, had married an actor's young widow, and become involved in the theatrical life by 1593. After a year with Lord Strange's Men, Heminges became an actor with the King's Men, the playing company for which William Shakespeare wrote. He coedited the *First Folio*, the collected plays of Shakespeare, published in 1623; he also was the financial manager for the King's Men. His protégé, Cooke, performed female roles (and, of course, roles of children if required) alongside adult male actors. It seems strange to us now that such young boys could really play the complex female roles that Shakespeare and his contemporaries devised—and be acceptable as such. But from occasional diary notes made by audience members about their visits to the theater, it is clear that the acting by such boys was of a quality to convince them of its authenticity. When one spectator saw the King's Men perform *Othello* at Oxford in 1610, he wrote of the cast's Desdemona, "They also had their tragedies, well and effectively acted. In these they drew tears not only by their speech, but also by their action. Indeed Desdemona, killed by her husband, in death moved us especially when, as she lay on her bed, her face alone implored the pity of the audience."[4] Although he knew that Desdemona was a young boy, he was sufficiently convinced to refer to the boy as "she." There is slight evidence that adult males sometimes played the roles of young women, but never leading roles. It is likely that the three witches in *Macbeth* were traditionally played by men, and there is a story, found in many accounts of that play's early days, that Shakespeare himself once performed as a woman, cross-dressing as Lady

Macbeth. The story goes that at the original performance of the play, a private one for King James I and his brother-in-law King Christian IV of Denmark, the boy actor Hal Berridge who was to play Lady Macbeth was taken ill. Shakespeare, with no other option, took over the part. However, the story is almost certainly fictional. There is no record of a boy called Hal Berridge as a child actor, although this in itself is not unusual. We do not, by any means, know all the names of the many young actors at the time. But the story was almost certainly made up as a pastiche of the English antiquary John Aubrey, by Max Beerbohm in a theatrical review of *Macbeth* in 1898.[5] A pity. It is a nice story.

Alexander Cooke went on to play adult male roles in the company as did many others, and he became a shareholder of the King's Men in 1604. More than fifty years later, Edward Kynaston, who, in January 1661 played three roles (one female and two male) in Ben Johnson's *Epicene*, moved smoothly into playing adult male roles after the Restoration. But not all boy players in the big companies were able to make such a transition. John Honyman (or Honeyman), christened in 1613, was apprenticed to John Shank, a noted comedy actor with the King's Men. Shank played an important role in training the company's apprentices to act in female roles, using his own experience in playing women to guide them. He had more than one apprentice and claimed to have spent £200 in total on his apprentices. Boy actors were coached to maintain their high voices, put on special diets, and given exercises to keep their petite figures. A considerable part of the spending on costumes for a player's company went on those for the boys. Wigs and dresses with whalebone were important in making young male figures into imitations of women.

Honyman was a successful boy actor. By his mid-teens, he was playing leading roles in many of the plays by playwrights such as Phillip Massinger and Lodowick Carlell as well as Shakespeare but graduated only to rather minor roles as a young adult. In 1633, he became a Groom of the Chamber in the service of James II (VII Scotland). Many young actors left the profession when they became adults, and there were many reasons. Perhaps John Hony-man's voice broke too low for him to continue to be credible as a woman, or maybe he was too short. (He did play a role, Domitilla in Massinger's *The Roman Actor*, in which the text emphasizes the character's small stature.) It is possible that his acting skills did not extend to playing lead male roles.

There was an obvious need to use boys to act female roles on stage. Women were banned. Shakespeare and his contemporaries would have no idea when, or indeed if, their plays would ever be acted with women and men in their defined gender roles. When Shakespeare died in 1616, the Puritan banning of all theaters lay more than a quarter century into the future, and there would be no women on stage in the legitimate theater until after the Reformation. Feminist writers have tended to define cross-dressing in the Elizabethan theater as an episode always within a patriarchal structure and as reaffirming patriarchal power. And, of course, at that time, there was a patriarchal structure underpinned by state and religious laws, first Catholic and then Puritan. Women had limited rights. They could not own property and were not allowed to be part of many professions, including acting. In the context of our own times, attributing what happened in the theater to that patriarchal structure may be a credible view; however, I believe that looking at how women were portrayed and at how cross-dressing was used in performance in such a way is more nuanced when looking back at the society of four hundred years ago.

In the sixteenth and early seventeenth centuries, transformation was a fascination, and there was a strong belief in religious mysteries and in the supernatural. Witches were thought to be able to fly and to change their gender as well as, mischievously, their form. People believed in fairies and spells. There were a number of witch trials in England during this period, the most notable being the Pendle witch trials of late 1612 when nine women and two men were accused. Ten were found guilty and hanged. It was as late as 1712 when the last "witch" in England was tried, and it was 1735 before the law was changed to try to eradicate a belief in witches. In 1692 and 1693, in colonial Massachusetts, the notorious Salem witch trial of more than two hundred men and women resulted in many hangings.

This then was the context in which playwrights wrote their plays. There may have been the beginnings of sophisticated theater in London, but for Shakespeare and his contemporaries, cross-dressing and transformation would be seen as attractively risky but familiar devices to encourage audiences to see their plays. They were, after all, not writing intentionally for posterity, but as businessmen with bills to pay. Banquo's ghost, the witches on the heath in *Macbeth*, the transformation of Bottom the weaver to the beloved ass of Titania in *A Midsummer Night's Dream*, and the invisible Ariel in the magic-filled *The Tempest* all reflect what was believable in Elizabethan England.

As actors, Shakespeare and his contemporaries were associated with two Renaissance obsessions, the one with change and changeability, the other with the world as a stage. The character Jaques in *As You Like It* gives Shakespeare's voice to this thought:

JAQUES: All the world's a stage,
And all the men and women merely players,
They have their exits and their entrances,
And one man in his time plays many parts,[6]

Cross-dressing and impersonation of all kinds—the capacity to be deceived by appearances—was a common concern[7] and caused anxiety among courtiers, diplomats, soldiers, and tradesmen. The nature of acting is by definition deceit, and because on stage this deceit is stated publicly, actors were exposers of such in the world at large. Sensitivity about the idea of impersonation meant that playwrights and actors at the time walked a tightrope between acceptance and giving offense, and they were bound to come up against criticism at times. Cross-dressing was seen as transgressive. Such sensitivity accounts for the quantity of abuse heaped on Elizabethan actors. But the playwrights who were aware of where political, ecclesiastical, and monarchical power lay, and who were prepared to create their characters accordingly, ensured the success of their plays. Shakespeare, for instance, wrote the tragedy *Macbeth* in 1606 to ingratiate himself with the Scottish king, James I, who had succeeded Elizabeth three years earlier. Risking criticism in order to expose the innermost characters of kings, queens, politicians, and the urban sophisticates who made up much of their audiences, as well as the bourgeois and servant classes, the writers used the interest in impersonation to secure enthusiastic audiences.

The fact that boys were the only actors available to play female characters on stage gave these writers other opportunities to put scenes of transformation into their plays. Boy apprentice actors were often at puberty, the stage where externally the physical features of boys are not unlike those of young girls who have not yet fully developed. Both can have smooth skins, rounded features, long limbs, and slim waists, and their growing chests have not developed a male musculature or fully formed breasts. This borderline sexuality could be used as part of the story line: to have them play both young men and young women interchangeably with simple stage costumes converting boys being girls back to "play" boys to enrich the plot. Shakespeare's comedies are full of such devices. At the beginning of *Twelfth Night*, Viola dresses as her supposedly dead twin brother Sebastian and takes the name Cesario to work as a page boy for Orsino. The boy actor is thus able to spend most of the play dressed as a boy although supposedly playing a young woman.

VIOLA: (to the Captain)

I pray thee—and I'll pay you bounteously—

Conceal me what I am, and be my aid

For such disguise as haply shall become

The form of my intent. I'll serve this duke.

Thou shall present me as a eunuch to him.[8]

She is pursued in this guise by Olivia who is attracted to the "young boy." Eventually her brother is convinced that Cesario is his sister Viola, and she tells him where her woman's clothes are. But she does not re-dress as a woman.

VIOLA: The captain that did bring me first on shore

Hath my maid's garments.[9]

In *As You Like It*, Rosalind, exiled by her uncle, dresses a a boy, Ganymede, to deter possible assailants. She then has her lover pretend that she, as Ganymede, is Rosalind to practice wooing—all very complicated. Portia, in *The Merchant of Venice*, dresses as a clever young lawyer to save her husband's best friend. In Shakespeare's early play *The Two Gentlemen of Verona* (1589–1591), Julia, against the advice of her maid Lucetta, decides to dress as a boy to travel to Milan to find her true love, Proteus, and there contrives to become his page boy. Julia becomes amusingly exasperated with Lucetta when discussing how she shall be dressed as a boy:

LUCETTA: But in what habit will you go along?

JULIA: Not like a woman, for I would prevent

The loose encounters of lascivious men,

Gentle Lucetta, fit me with such weeds

As may beseem some well-reputed page

LUCETTA: Why then, your ladyship must cut your hair.

JULIA: No girl, I'll knit it up in silken strings

With twenty-odd-conceited true-love knots. . . .

LUCETTA: What fashion, madam, shall I make your breeches?

JULIA: That fits as well as "Tell me, good my lord,

What compass will you wear your farthingale?"

Why, e'en what fashion thou best likes, Lucetta.

LUCETTA: You must needs have them with a cod-piece madam.

JULIA: Out, out Lucetta. That will be ill-favoured.[10]

When we see Shakespeare's plays produced now, it is rare, unless the production is one by a school or youth theater, to see adolescents playing the parts of lead actors who are supposed to be in their teens. At best, Viola, Rosalind, and Julia are played by professionals in their mid-twenties and often by mature women who are not always fully convincing in their transformations to young men. This would not be the case in Shakespeare's time. His young lovers approaching marriage or newly wed would quite normally be supposed to be in their mid to late teens, the same age as the actors. With parental consent a girl could marry at twelve and a boy at fourteen years of age. John Heminges, one of Shakespeare's fellow managers in the King's Men, married a girl who was already a widow at sixteen. Thus, the interest of audiences in transformation and the availability of boy actors, still in the transitional stage between boy and adult, allowed the creation of memorable double cross-dressing scenes in contemporary plays.

Although the main adult playing companies of the Elizabethan and Jacobean periods used indentured young boys as actors in their plays, perhaps the most overlooked theatrical development for these companies was the appearance of troupes composed entirely of very young boys who played both male and female roles. They were keen competition for the established companies. These "children's companies" were extremely popular, and for a time their success threatened that of adult companies. In *Hamlet*, first performed by the

Lord Chamberlain's men in 1600 or 1601, Shakespeare referred to such children's companies and to the fact that the adults in playing companies, such as his own, saw them as rivals. The actors who come to visit Hamlet had been driven out of London by competition from boy players, and they were to act a scene that parodied *Dido, Queen of Carthage*, by Christopher Marlowe, a play that was written specially for a children's company. Hamlet queries why the actors are in Elsinore when he supposed they would be better off financially as a resident troupe in a theater.

> HAMLET: How chances they travel? Their residence both in reputation and profit, was better both ways.
> ROSENCRANTZ: I think their inhibition comes by the means of the late innovation.
> HAMLET: Do they hold the same estimation they did when I was in the city? Are they so followed?
> ROSENCRANTZ: No, indeed they are not.
> HAMLET: How comes it? Do they grow rusty?
> ROSENCRANTZ: Nay, their endeavour keeps in the wonted pace. But there is, sir, an eyrie of children, little eyases [young eagles], that cry out on the top of question, and are most tyrannically clapp'd for it. These are now the fashion, and so berattle the common stages—so they call them—that many wearing rapiers are afraid of goose-quills and dare not come hither.
> HAMLET: What, are they children? Who maintains 'em? How are they escotted? Will they pursue the quality no longer than they can sing? Will they not afterwards if they should grow themselves to common players—as it is most like if their means are no better—their writers do them wrong to make them exclaim against their own successions?[11]

At the time of writing *Hamlet*, Shakespeare would have good reason to comment about the rise of children's companies. They had grown out of the choirs of boy singers that had been connected to cathedrals, schools, and other institutions since the early twelfth century. In the early sixteenth century, some of these choirs had become acting companies; the most well known of these is the Children of Paul's, attached to St Paul's Cathedral in London. Other groups of boy actors were connected with Eton and the Merchant Taylor's School and with an ecclesiastical college at Windsor. They were in demand at court, and between 1558 and 1576, the year that James Burbage built The Theatre in London, and the date from which popular Elizabethan theater is said to date, they played far more times there than did adult companies.

Puritan opposition in the 1580s saw a lull in the use of the children's companies, but in the first decade of the seventeenth century, the Children of the Chapel, which became the Children of the Queen's Revels after the accession of King James in 1603, were performing at Richard and Cuthbert's private Blackfriars Theatre. They were in competition with Shakespeare's company at the Globe, the other theater belonging to the Burbage brothers. The Children of Paul's were acting publicly, too. It seems strange to think that young boys, many prepubescent, acted successfully in satirical comedies by Ben Jonson, John Marston, and Thomas Middleton as well as serious tragedies and histories by George Chapman. But the duration of boys' companies was short. By 1608, due to the production of controversial plays, the Children of the Revels company were evicted from the Blackfriars Theatre to be replaced by Shakespeare's King's Men. By then, the last of the boys' troupes continued to act and sing at the Whitefriars Theatre until 1613 when they were merged with the Lady Elizabeth's Men and ceased to exist as a children's company. There was a short revival of children's companies in 1637 when Christopher Beeston gained a royal warrant for his King and Queen's Young Company, known as "Beeston's Boys." These boys tended to be older than in previous troupes, and with varying success they performed under Christopher, and later his son William, until the Puritans closed the theaters in 1642. Beeston's Boys briefly re-formed at the Restoration in 1660. But of course, by 1661 women could act, and boy actors in female parts were redundant.

But there was a questionable side to the practice of using young boys as actors. Traditionally, the child choirs had acted religious plays for the royal court, and thus the choirmaster was given the power, by royal authority, to impress children into service.[12] For many children and their parents, this may well have been acceptable. The children were talented, well educated, and well disciplined. But by the early seventeenth century, the links with religious services had been all but severed. Although technically the warrants were designed to allow the master of the children to "take up" boys for service in the Chapel Royal, ostensibly as choirboys, the reality was that the Children of the Chapel was an acting company, a moneymaker for the adults who ran it. Documents of the time, researched by Dr. Bart van Es for his book *Shakespeare in Company*,[13] shows that Queen Elizabeth herself signed warrants to allow theater bosses to kidnap boys and force them to perform under threat of whipping. The children's companies were very popular and needed a plentiful supply of young talent. Nathaniel Giles, who had become choirmaster of the Children of the Chapel, had the power to impress up to twelve boys into service, although the plays he produced often needed more. He would send his henchmen to kidnap likely looking boys from the street, haul them back to the theater, and threaten them with a whipping if they didn't quickly learn the lines that he gave them. Perhaps most parents felt impotent to recover their stolen children; after all, the power to impress boys for choirs came, in theory, from royal authority. But on December 13, 1600, Giles came up against a parent who was not prepared to lose his child and who was determined to fight for his return.

That morning Giles sent a James Robinson and perhaps another man to kidnap Thomas Clifton, a thirteen-year-old who was on his way to Christ

Church grammar school. His father, Henry Clifton, tried to get him back from the theater but was unsuccessful until he contacted a powerful friend, Sir John Fortescue, the chancellor of the Exchequer and a member of the Privy Council. Thomas was returned to him, but Henry Clifton didn't leave it there. In December 1601, he put forward a Bill of Complaint against Giles and his colleagues "Evans, Robinson and others" stating that his boy had been unjustly taken, along with seven others around the same time. Clifton was angry at the treatment of his only son. He protested that the child was being made to "learn a base trade." The result of the court action was that just one of the men accused, Henry Evans, was found guilty of "taking up of gentlemen's children against their wills and to employ them for players."[14]

There is no evidence that the other boys' parents were party to the complaint, probably because they were not "gentlemen," and at least two of these boys were known to have stayed in the company. Evans had to resign, but Nathaniel Giles was not reprimanded and continued in his post. The Children of the Chapel continued to perform plays; however, the publicity accorded to the case had a positive effect. From that time, the children's troupes began to apprentice their young actors in the same way as the adult playing companies.

While most of the children's troupes produced serious plays or comedies and the boys acted sufficiently well to cause the adult companies some concern, there was a darker side as Dr. van Es discovered. In contrast to those groups who performed in mainstream theaters for a diverse, mixed audience, others acted plays that took place in seedy, dimly lit locations and before a predominantly male clientele. The exploitation of such boys was explicitly sexual. Playwright Thomas Middleton described one children's company as "a nest of boys able to ravish a man." Some plays at the time contain scenes bordering on pedophilia. Dr. van Es cites the example of Marlowe's *Dido, Queen of Carthage*, perhaps cowritten with his younger contemporary at Cambridge, Thomas Nashe, and performed by the boy actors of the Children

of the Chapel company. On the one hand, it is a learned play adapted from
Virgil, and on the other, it is mock-heroic; as Frank Romany describes it, it
is "the Aeneid in falsetto voices."[15] In the opening scene, the boy Ganymede
is "dandled" on Jupiter's knee, and called a "female, wanton boy" and "the
darling of my thoughts." He is asked to indulge in sexual "play" and offered
jewelry to comply. The Ganymede to whom the god's bribes are offered is
"delectable, a tarty, petulant Elizabethan page boy." Presumably, Ganymede
was played by a very young, prepubescent boy with an older youth as Jupiter,
intended to titillate the voyeuristic audience.

Such boys were used as instruments by the writers and stakeholders in the
children's companies. The work they did had nothing to do with the religious
beginnings and everything to do with the commercial gain that motivated
their controllers. In contrast, the main adult companies at the time stood
aloof from such practices. Their boy actors, although worked extremely hard
with the often-dizzying number of roles they had to master in a season, were
legitimate apprentices, housed, fed, and paid. Many went on to become adult
actors.

But the closure of the theaters by Cromwell in 1642 saw all actors out of
work, and by the time the ban was lifted, things had changed. Women had
taken their place on the stage.

CHAPTER 3
RESTORATION—A NEW WORLD

FLORIMEL: Save you, Monsieur Florimel! Faith, me thinks you a very jaunty fellow, poudre et ajuste, as well as the best of 'em. I can manage the little comb; set my hat, shake my garniture, toss about my empty noddle, walk with a courant slur, and at every step peck down my head: If I should be mistaken for some courtier now, pray where's the difference.

—JOHN DRYDEN, *SECRET LOVE, OR THE MAIDEN QUEEN*[1]

When, December 8, 1660, a woman played Desdemona in Shakespeare's *Othello* for the first time, an added prologue to the play left the audience in no doubt that things had changed. The most likely candidate to have been this actress was Anne Marshall who took leading roles for Thomas Killigrew's company between 1660 and 1682 in both tragic and comic roles. It is also possible, however, that this first professional actress was Margaret Hughes, an equally talented performer. Whoever it was, as the prologue to the play written by Thomas Jordan made clear, actresses were not only on stage to portray characters but also were sexually available. This was 1660, not pre-1642. No longer would spectators be watching young boys impersonating women on stage; these were real women.

> I come, unknown to any of the rest
> To tell you news; I saw the Lady drest;
> The Woman playes to day, mistake me not,
> No Man in Gown, or Page in Petty-Coat;
> A Woman to my knowledge, yet I cann't
> (If I should dye) make Affadavit on't.[2]

It is obvious from these lines that the speaker of the prologue is claiming to have seen the actress dressing—to have seen her body—and is guaranteeing that she is a real woman and not a boy. The sexual connotation of the word *knowledge* would also not have been lost on the audience. From this very first entrance of a woman on to the public stage, actresses are being defined as sexual beings, to be admired and enjoyed by their audience.

The prologue continues:

> *Do you not twitter Gentlemen? I know*
> *You will be censuring, do't fairly though;*
> *'Tis possible a vertuous [sic] woman may*
> *Abhor all sorts of looseness, and yet play; . . .*
> *But Gentlemen you that as judges sit*
> *In the Star-Chamber of the house, the Pit;*
> *Have modest thoughts of her; pray, do not run*
> *To give her visits when the play is done.*[3]

Although this part of the prologue claims that some actresses may be virtuous, by definition it follows that others may not. It draws attention to the fact that gentlemen may have thought about visiting the women backstage. The coded messages were read correctly, and throughout the Restoration period, the audience, predominantly male, socialized with actresses, visited them while dressing, and took some of them as mistresses. Right from the start, women on stage were seen as sexual objects. It was many years before they were seen as professional actors, and even in the mid-eighteenth century, it was still common for men to visit them in their dressing rooms. Dr. Johnson famously refused to go backstage at Garrick's theater. "I'll no more come behind your scenes, David; for the silk stockings and white bubbies of your actresses excite my genitals."[4]

Until the Restoration, the theater had been thriving in Europe, unlike England. In Italy and Spain, women played a full part in the theaters, both acting and sometimes managing their own troupes of actors. In France, women had been performing on stage since at least 1606 when, it is recorded, Marie Vernier acted with Valleran-Lecomte's players at the Hotel de Bourgogne in Paris. French actresses appeared regularly in the seventeenth century in plays by writers such as Jean Racine and Molière. At least one troupe of players containing women had visited from mainland Europe and performed in London. They had, however, been attacked with thrown apples. And women regularly acted and danced in private masques. These were just as roundly condemned by Puritans as were boys dressing as women on stage. In his *Histriomastix* of 1632, a critique of professional theater and actors, Puritan William Prynne "condemns most aspects of dramatic performance in its era, from the practice of boy actors representing women to the 'obscene lascivious love songs, most melodiously chanted out upon the stage.'"[5]

During the English Civil War (1642–1651) and the period from the execution of Charles I in 1649 to the Restoration of Charles II in 1660, there was a ban on the theater, an "Order for Stage Plays to Cease." Although it is true that the ban catered to the extreme Puritanism of some Parliamentarians, it was primarily for public safety. Playhouses, where large numbers of people gathered, were possible sources of political ferment. There was public tension before the second civil war in 1648, and according to Peter Thompson, "army raids on illicitly operating playhouses in January 1649 were designed to eliminate possible sources of trouble in the days before Charles I's trial."[6] Plays were still performed in smaller venues, but since they did not accommodate large gatherings of potential troublemakers, and since they were illegal anyway, they employed both women and men, although little detail is available as to the individual players.

Things changed in 1660. Charles II, while in exile in Europe, had been a keen patron of the theater and was eager to continue being so in London. When, as the new king of Great Britain and Ireland, he ascended to the throne, Charles gave two royal patents to theater managers Sir Thomas Killigrew and Sir William Davenant. The former established his King's Company in a converted indoor tennis court, and Davenant began to put on plays in the old Salisbury Court playhouse. Killigrew's company outgrew his premises and was soon housed in a splendid new theater on Drury Lane. Davenant headed the Duke of York's Men and produced highly successful theatrical seasons at Lincoln's Inn Fields. Their warrants confirmed that women's parts could be performed by women, and in 1662, a royal warrant was issued that decreed that only women should play female roles. Ostensibly this was to quieten those who had objected to men cross-dressing in female roles, considering it sinful. But this was definitely not the motivation of the increasing number of theater managers for introducing women. Actresses were moneymakers, and morality was discouraged as being bad for business. The warrants from the king also stated that the companies "do not at any time hereafter cause to be acted or represented any play, interlude, or opera, containing any matter of profanation, scurrility, or obscenity."[7] He was not serious. Those last three words would apply quite accurately to most of the plays written in the Restoration period. This was what the monarch and the new types of people that flocked to the theaters really wanted. These audiences differed significantly from those in the old playhouses. In Shakespeare's day, everyone who could get to the theater went to see plays; it was a cheap form of entertainment. And Shakespeare's Globe could accommodate about three thousand people at a time. At the Restoration, playgoing became a pastime restricted to the more prosperous citizens of London. The theaters could take only hundreds rather than thousands of people, admission costs were high, and the start time of plays, certainly in the early days, was often three o'clock in the afternoon.

This suited the court, the leisured classes, and their hangers-on rather than those who worked for a living. Even when performances started later, audiences included more of the middle class. Post-theater social activities were important for the more wealthy groups and often included actresses. In his diaries, Samuel Pepys often refers to visits to the theater—seventy-three visits in the first eight months of 1668—and his attraction to the women on stage.

Up to this point, the number of major female roles for women in plays written in the English language had been limited. Even now, in the twenty-first century, women complain that Shakespeare, for example, wrote few meaty parts for women. Playwrights of the late sixteenth and early seventeenth centuries knew that their female roles would, by necessity, be played by boys and adolescents, so it is not surprising that they concentrated on major male roles. But in 1660, there were actresses, and plenty of them. At first the theater managers scrambled and vied with each other to secure the rights to stage plays from the Elizabethan, Jacobean, and Carolinian eras; however, new plays were urgently needed, and the companies competed for these new plays and for the most popular actors and actresses. The number of playwrights expanded hugely. They wrote plays that rejected the satire predominant earlier in the seventeenth century and replaced it with the new genres of heroic drama, pathetic drama, and Restoration comedy, all of which had crowded plots with plenty of characters, both male and female.

The new writers include Thomas Otway, William Congreve, John Vanbrugh, George Farquhar, John Dryden, and—for the first time writing for the professional stage—women; the most well known are Aphra Behn and Mary Pix. Early Restoration comedy is essentially amoral. Dramatists did not criticize the accepted morality about love, sex, pleasure, gambling, or drink. In their plays, they wrote about such matters as though they were normal and acceptable parts of life. They said exactly what they liked and freely used gross and improper situations and language to entertain and often titillate their audiences. There were fewer theatergoers compared to the early part of the century, but they went often. Fashions in drama changed almost weekly, and audiences wanted to see new plays. A run of ten performances was considered a smash hit; playwrights were kept busy. Dramatists created bustling multi-plot action and stole plot lines and characters from earlier plays, freely adapting them and adding sexual themes and obscenities. Even Shakespeare's plot lines were changed and adapted, sometimes with new characters. In 1681, Nahum Tate rewrote Shakespeare's *King Lear* as *The History of King Lear* and gave it a happy ending with King Lear regaining the throne and Cordelia marrying Edgar.

Suggestive comedy scenes involving women became common. Plots and costumes were designed to titillate men. Rape scenes were common, and the act of intercourse was emphasized even if it was behind drapes or just offstage. The actress reclining center stage, on a couch and in a state of undress, was a regular sight. Dresses were cut low in the bodice to show a substantial amount of bosom, and the cleavage often figured as a place to "post" letters or to hide secret messages. Aphra Behn, the most famous of the Restoration woman writers did not pull her punches in writing women's roles. Her heroines were just as sexually enticing as those written by the men, although her plays did highlight her interest in the institution of marriage and its often-negative effect on the lives of women.

Women on stage were sexual objects. Remaining chaste was almost impossible for Restoration actresses. They were not considered respectable. Respectable women would not usually consider a career in the theater; however, the first actresses came from varied social backgrounds. Moll Davis was the illegitimate daughter of an earl; Anne Marshall and her sister Rebecca came from a clergyman's family; and Nell Gwyn, although her early life is obscure, claimed to have been raised in a brothel. Samuel Pepys's diary for October 26, 1667, reports:

Mrs Pierce tells me that the two Marshalls at the King's house are Stephen Marshall's, the great Presbyterian's daughters and that Nelly and Beck Marshall, falling out the other day, the latter called the other my Lord Buckhurst's whore. Nell answered them, "I was but one man's whore, though I was brought up in a bawdy house to fill strong waters to the guests; and you are a whore to three or four, though a Presbyter's praying daughter!"[8]

Because the playbills changed so often, actors who could read and memorize lines quickly as well as perform them on stage were much in demand. Plays written at the time often required dancing and singing, too; the new actresses, like those of today, were expected to be multitalented.

There were some, like Anne Marshall, who attempted to maintain respectability in private life. She specialized in tragedy, particularly in rape scenes, and delighted Restoration audiences in her many roles as a grandiose heroine. She managed to stay in the business for a long time, and to marry, although her life was not without scandal. Anne Bracegirdle, who as a young girl was put into the care of actor Thomas Betterton and his wife, enjoyed a reputation for virtuous character. This was extraordinary in an actress of the period. In fact, she was probably the mistress of playwright William Congreve and certainly one of his closest friends. She started acting as a very young girl and played many key parts, including cross-dressing roles in Restoration comedies, and was also known for her Shakespeare roles. She retired at the height of her career and is buried in Westminster Abbey. But many actresses were expected to play parts in which their sexuality was advertised to an audience and to entertain men in their dressing rooms after performances. Many became mistresses, sometimes serially, of important and rich men. Peg Hughes was famous as the mistress of Prince Rupert of the Rhine, the English Civil War general, and Nell Gwyn was the longtime mistress of Charles II.

From our perspective in the twenty-first century, we see this as rampant exploitation. Whether the most successful Restoration actresses, having chosen a career on the stage, saw their financial success and fame, which often came from the patronage of peers and royalty, as exploitation or personal success, we don't really know. I suspect it depended on the personality and strength of character of the individual woman, and whether she felt that she was in control of her situation or being controlled and exploited by the men in her life. There must certainly have been actresses lesser known than Nell Gwyn who were used as commodities by theater managers to attract clientele and who had little control over their professional lives.

And cross-dressing by women playing male parts was a significant part of such commodification. Almost as soon as actresses were able to play female parts on stage, they started to dress as men, too. But this was very different from boys dressing as women in previous times. In early theater, cross-dressing had been a necessity. Young men and boys had tried to impersonate women as best they could, using costume, movement, and voice. Although audiences had been well aware that they were watching males—what else could they be since women were banned from the stage?—they suspended belief and accepted the characterizations. But cross-dressing in the Restoration theater meant women putting on male garments to emphasize their femininity and to draw the attention of spectators to it. The earlier comedies abounded in such breeches roles; of the roughly four hundred new plays written between 1660 and 1700, there were eighty-nine breeches parts.[9] Actresses wore tight-fitting breeches (knee-length pants) to emphasize their hips and buttocks, as well as silk stockings to draw attention to shapely calves. Written into the plot, these "breeches parts" were clearly female roles, but they required the actress to disguise herself as a boy either to hide her gender or to engage in some sort of boyish escapade. The disguise would later be abandoned, often with a tantalizing view of bare bosom or a cascade of long hair escaping from a cap. The roles were designed to be erotic and in no way impersonations of men.

There were a few true travesti roles, where actresses were acting supposedly male roles and wore male dress throughout the play, drawing even more attention to their sexual identity, but most cross-dressing was as a disguise. Among Shakespeare's characters were those who dressed in clothes of a different gender to complicate the plot. Viola in *Twelfth Night* and Rosalind in *As You Like It* are probably the best known of these roles. But many of his plays did not give such opportunities. This did not deter the Restoration dramatists. One of the most successful plays was Davenant and Dryden's version of *The Tempest*, titled *The Tempest, or The Enchanted Island*, which included several new roles for women, such as Hippolito, a travesti role. Just in case you might miss the nature of the figure in tight breeches, the prologue to the play tells the audience that Hippolito was a woman, but would not be revealed as such during the play. It warns the audience that they should not:

> Expect in the last act to find
> Her sex transformed from man to Woman kind
> What'ere she was before the Play began,
> All you should see of her is perfect man,
> Or if your fancy will be farther led,
> To find her Woman, it must be abed.[10]

An invitation, indeed! Many of the new actresses played cross-dressing roles at some time. The young Nell Gwyn, one of the first actresses to act in the legitimate theater, was famous for playing young and witty roles, often requiring her to dress as a man. On March 2, 1667, Samuel Pepys, by then an inveterate theatergoer, went to the Kings House to see a new play by Dryden, *The Maiden Queen*. Nell Gwyn, probably only seventeen at the time, was cast as Florimel, the gay and witty maid of honor who cross-dresses as a disguise. Pepys was entranced by what he saw. That night he wrote the following:

> But so great performance of a comic part was never I believe, in the world before as Nell do this, both as a mad girl, then most and best of all when she comes in like a young gallant; and hath the notions and carriage of a spark the most that ever I saw any man have. It makes me, I confess, admire her.[11]

He went to see the play eight more times. Many of Aphra Behn's plays, like those of her male contemporaries, had roles where women dressed as men. She dedicated *The Feigned Courtesans*, performed by the Duke's Company at Dorset Gardens in 1679, to Nell Gwyn (or Mrs. Ellen Guin as Behn calls her) with a fulsome introduction. The role of Marcella, one of the two sisters who pretend to be courtesans, also requires the actress to dress as a boy. Mrs. Currer, who specialized in playing prostitutes and mistresses, took the part. Nell Gwyn would have appreciated the cross-dressing element in the dedicated play, but her reputation and preference was for witty comedic roles.

Pepys also enjoyed—along, no doubt, with the many men who ogled the actresses in their tight breeches—the scenes containing dances. At a time when the swift movement of a woman's body, especially when arms and legs were freely visible, was thought unseemly, a girl in breeches doing a jig was especially enticing. On August 28, 1667, Pepys wrote the following:

> [A]fter dinner, he and my wife and I to the Duke of York's house, and there saw Love Trickes, or the School of Compliments, a silly play, only Miss (Davis's) dancing in a <u>shepherd's</u> clothes did please us mightily.[12]

Moll Davis was most likely playing the role of Selina, who disguises herself as a shepherd. Perhaps part of Pepys's comment that the play was silly was because the play contained a rare male-to-female cross-dressing role. The actor playing Selina's brother cross-dresses as a bride and takes her place at the wedding. This results in a good deal of knockabout humor. Actresses often danced in boys' clothes after the end of a play to tell the audience about the next day's performance, no matter how irrelevant was the dance to the play just concluded. After the end of a "melancholy" performance of *The English Princess, or The Death of Richard the Third a Tragedy* on March 7, 1666–1667, Moll Davis danced a jig. Pepys compared her dancing favorably with that of Nell Gwyn. He hadn't enjoyed the play; there had been "nothing eminent in it, as some tragedies are," but

> *only little Mis. Davis did dance a jig after the end of the play, and there telling the next day's play, so that it come in by force only to please the company to see her dance in boy's clothes; and, the truth is, there is no comparison between Nell's dancing the other day at the King's house in boy's clothes and this, this being infinitely beyond the other.*

Susanna Mountfort, later known as Susanna Verbruggen, was one of the most successful comedians in breeches roles. By the 1680s and 1690s when her career was at its height, there were more mixed audiences, and both men and women enjoyed the way she portrayed a woman disguised as a roistering, swaggering Restoration rake. Her greatest success was as the main character Lucia in Thomas Southerne's *Sir Anthony Love*, where Lucia enjoyed the freedom, then only available to males, by disguising herself as "Sir Anthony." There is some debate as to whether such roles really did empower women who dress as men or merely emphasized patriarchal power by assuming that freedom was obtained only by impersonating them. Whatever Susanna's feelings were on that topic, she chose to play many roles as a Restoration dandy.

Cross-dressing to titillate became less popular as a new century dawned. Between the Restoration and the early 1700s, there were significant social and political changes in the country. The plays produced by theater companies reflected these changes. The earlier comedies of the period were mostly "hard" comedies and reflected an aristocratic—frankly, macho—lifestyle with abundant sexual intrigue. But things changed after the "Merry Monarch," King Charles II, died in 1685. After the short, turbulent reign of James II, with conflict between Catholics and the established church, William of Orange invaded the country in 1688. Protestant William and Mary, no lovers of theater, ascended the throne as joint monarchs in 1689. In the decade after 1680, there were fewer plays written, and there was a swing away from comedy and toward more serious political drama. Changes in social power, and the increasing significance of bourgeois values in opposition to the aristocratic world of the Restoration, saw pressure on the playhouses to produce plays emphasizing the newly emerging dominant morality.

In the resulting second wave of Restoration comedy in the 1690s, the playwrights set out to appeal to more socially mixed audiences with a strong middle-class element and to female spectators. John Vanbrugh's *The Provoked Wife* (1697) examines the legal position of women, then an issue in the courts, and particularly the possibility that an ill-treated wife could have both divorce and financial security. In 1698, Jeremy Collier, a dissenting clergyman, published a vitriolic attack on the stage. Dramatists responded by writing plays that could deal with serious subjects. *The Beaux Stratagem* (1707), one of the last truly Restoration comedies, could be seen as immoral as it tells the tale of two young men on the lookout for heiresses to marry. Yet it tackles the difficult subjects of both loveless marriage and the legal system, which did not allow divorce based on incompatibility and, even if granted, left women disgraced and penniless. Farquhar's very popular *Recruiting Officer* (1706), although a comedy, scathingly satires military recruitment. But yet again, there is cross-dressing. Sylvia dresses as an attractive young man, Jack Wilful, and has two captains competing to recruit him.

(Enter Sylvia, in man's apparel)

SYLVIA: Save ye, save ye! Gentlemen.

BRAZEN: My dear, I'm yours.

PLUME: Do you know the gentleman?

BRAZEN: No, but I will presently—Your name, my dear?

SYLVIA: Wilful, Jack Wilful, at your service.

BRAZEN: What, the Kentish Wilfuls, or those of Staffordshire?

SYLVIA: Both, sir, both; I'm related to all the Wilfuls in Europe.[13]

The eighteenth century saw growth in entertainment of all kinds. When the century began, theater was largely a metropolitan and aristocratic pastime; by the time it ended, it had become, once again, a genuinely popular form of entertainment. British theater in the eighteenth century, as in the early sixteenth, was socially inclusive. People from all walks of life attended, although now they sat in different parts of the auditorium, according to wealth and social status. From the 1720s, many more theaters were built in London and in towns throughout the country. Traveling companies took plays and other entertainment to the new venues, and the demand increased exponentially for performers of all kinds—and not only on stages, however makeshift. Cross-dressing performance was popular in Georgian London. At weekly carnivals known as Midnight Masquerades, partygoers would disguise themselves: men as witches, nursemaids, or shepherdesses, and women as sailors and hussars. An infamous "star" of such entertainments was Princess Seraphina, an early drag queen. Most likely a man named John Cooper, he was able to cross gender lines at a time when same-sex relationships were strictly taboo.

But in 1737, Robert Walpole's government attempted to put a halt to the expansion of theatrical entertainment by passing the Licensing Act, which renewed the monopoly of the patent theaters when it came to spoken drama. The act decreed that every play script had to be approved before performance by the Lord Chamberlain, who was also given the power to close down shows entirely. Managers did find legal loopholes, avoiding the controls stipulated in the act on "serious" drama, and kept their theaters open by offering melodrama, pantomime, dance, opera, and music instead. But censorship was inescapable. It would not be until 1968, 231 years later, that censorship of the stage in the United Kingdom was abolished. One result of the new act was that more classics came into the repertoire. Theater managers chose such safety rather than take the risk of staging new plays that might fall foul of the censor. The less salacious works from the late Restoration era and the plays of Shakespeare were popular. Plays such as Farquhar's lively comedies, *The Recruiting Officer* (1706) and *The Beaux' Stratagem* (1707) stayed in the repertoire, as did William Congreve's *The Way of the World* (1700). Sentimental dramas also gained in popularity, partly in reaction to criticism from commentators that theater was inherently immoral. Many playhouses offered mixed bills with serious plays, including Shakespeare, followed by burlettas (burlesque operas) or elements of pantomime. Dancing and singing were incorporated into drama. The English version of the Italian commedia dell'arte was pioneered by John Rich at Lincoln's Inn Fields in 1716, and such pantomimes, especially at Christmas, are still popular three hundred years later. Italian opera, exclusive to those who could afford the high prices, was performed at the King's Theatre in the first decade of the century.

Another outcome of the Licensing Act, which outlawed many groups of "strolling players," was the enhanced dominance of the official theaters, those in which women could seek careers as actresses. The acceptance of women in the profession allowed them to demonstrate their acting skills. They were no longer expected to play roles that advertised their sexual availability to the men in the audiences, and there was less cross-dressing as the eighteenth century progressed. Although it took time for actresses to be considered respectable, and many had unconventional lifestyles, their characters (and morals) on stage were no longer assumed to be those of the real woman. To be sure, some of the revived Restoration comedies required women to dress as boys and young men. So too, the popular Shakespearean roles of Viola, Rosalind, and Julia were performed partly in male attire; however, the actresses acted in such roles primarily to represent the characters and not to draw attention to their sexuality. They also began to play serious male characters on stage.

Susanna Centlivre (nee Freeman), whose professional life spanned the late seventeenth and early eighteenth centuries, was an example of an actress in male roles as well as a poet and an author of nineteen plays. There are not a lot of verified facts about her life, but according to her biographer, she was found crying at the roadside by a student at Cambridge, smuggled into the college, and disguised as a young man, and she stayed there for some time as a student, her gender undiscovered. A nice story. But more likely, she joined a group of strolling players in Stamford, not far from her hometown of Holbeach in Norfolk, and began her career with them. She supposedly had a "masculine air" and specialized in breeches roles. Unlike some of her contemporaries, however, who donned male attire to titillate the audience, she, like the boy actors of previous generations, aimed to be taken seriously in the part she played. She took the role of Alexander the Great in Nathaniel Lee's tragedy *The Rival Queens, or The Death of Alexander the Great* for the court at Windsor Castle in 1706. Even though she was acting a man, Joseph Centlivre, a cook to Queen Anne, was much attracted to her when he saw her act, and he and Susanna were married the next year. The marriage was a successful one, and the couple lived in Buckingham House where Susanna continued to write.

At the same time as the theater was expanding in Great Britain, the United States too was experiencing a growth in demand for drama. The New England colonies, with their Puritan, Quaker, and Lutheran populations, suppressed "painted vanities" by law and fine, but the more cosmopolitan people of New York and Philadelphia wanted to see entertainment from their homelands. There had been attempts at professional drama in the early 1700s. A first theater was built in 1716 at Williamsburg, Virginia, where performances were given for a season; however, it wasn't until around 1750 that professional theater took off, when Thomas Kean and Walter Murray came from England and performed Shakespeare's *Richard III* and Joseph Addison's *Cato* in Philadelphia, New York, and Williamsburg.

Perhaps the biggest influence on the development of American theater was Lewis Hallam and his wife who brought their company of players from England to Williamsburg in 1752 and traveled on to play in New York and Philadelphia. Finding some opposition to actors, they went to Jamaica where Hallam formed a partnership with David Douglass. When Hallam died, his widow married Douglass, and together in 1758, they formed a new acting company. The company traveled the colonies for some years and are known to have played in Annapolis, Maryland; Williamsburg; Charleston, South Carolina; and Newport and Providence, Rhode Island; as well as the smaller towns of Maryland and Virginia. They put up a temporary theater building wherever they went but also built the Southwark Theatre in Philadelphia in 1766 and the John Street Theatre in New York in 1767. Seen as British and facing opposition during the Revolution, they were forced away from the colonies, and in 1774, they ceased performing when the Continental Congress suspended all public amusements. After the end of the War of Independence in 1783, however, entertainment was in great demand once more. Laws against the theater were repealed, and British and homegrown actors multiplied. Lewis Hallam Jr. reopened his mother and stepfather's theaters and formed the Old American Company that for several years held a touring monopoly. Plays were mostly Shakespeare, Restoration comedies, and satirical farces. The first American play on an American subject written by a Native American was *The Contrast*, written by Royall Tyler, produced at the John Street Theatre in 1787.

The Hallam or Old American Company employed a number of actresses who became famous. Anna West Bignall emigrated from England with her acting family to the United States in 1790 and was engaged with them in the Old American Company until her father founded the Virginia Company. This company toured the southern states of Virginia and the Carolinas. She was the leading lady and one of the star attractions and usually given good reviews by the critics even when a performance was panned. The Hallams formed an acting dynasty. Eliza Hallam, the wife of Lewis Hallam Jr., became a well-known actress in the theater. Nancy Hallam, the niece of Lewis's mother, was part of the American Company from childhood. In 1760, she went to Great Britain to be trained as a singer and returned to the American colonies in 1765 with David Douglass who was visiting England to recruit new actors. She was well known for her Shakespearean roles and for her ability as a singer. Her most famous role was in *Cymbeline* as the cross-dressing Imogen, who dresses as a boy, Fidelio, to seek her exiled husband. Hallam performed this role for the first time in the New Theatre in Annapolis in 1770. And Charlotte Melmoth, having had a stage career in Britain as a young woman playing many of the Shakespearean cross-dressing roles in her youth, emigrated to the United States in 1793 and resumed her interrupted stage career. In her maturity, no longer having the figure to play young men, she became a well-known tragedienne.

At the same time that American theater was growing, one of the biggest influences on theatrical practice was David Garrick. He effected a change in acting styles in Britain and then wherever plays in the English language were performed. In 1737, he arrived in London from Lichfield,[14] accompanied by his friend Samuel Johnson. He became a wine merchant with his brother, but the business failed, most likely due to his interest in amateur theatricals. His play, the satire *Lethe, or Aesop in the Shade* was staged at the Theatre Royal, Drury Lane. He then began to act. Impressed by his portrayal of Richard III and his performances in a number of other roles, Charles Fleetwood engaged Garrick for a season at the Theatre Royal, Drury Lane. He remained with that company for the next five years and purchased a share of the theater, managing it for twenty-nine years. Most important for our story, he promoted more realistic acting that departed from the bombastic style, which had been the norm for many years. Audiences responded well to this change, and other actors adapted their own styles. While the manager of Drury Lane, Garrick also sought to reform audience behavior. He encouraged the audience to pay attention to the action on stage rather than considering the theater a place in which to talk loudly, interrupt the actors, and invade the stage during performances. Such changes meant that all actors had the opportunity to develop their craft, and acting slowly but surely became accepted as a respectable profession.

There were many actresses who became famous in this period, acting often in breeches roles. Kitty Clive began at Drury Lane in the role of the page boy Immenea in *Mithridates, King of Pontus*. Later she joined Garrick's company and played many male characters, including Hamlet. Mrs. (Dorothea) Jordan was an Anglo-Irish actress, courtesan, and the mistress and companion of the future King William IV of the United Kingdom, for twenty years. Audiences enjoyed her performances in breeches roles, and she was well known for her attractive legs. Perhaps the most well-remembered actress from the period is Peg Woffington, who, for a time, was Garrick's mistress. She danced and acted at various Dublin theaters until her early twenties, when her reputation drew a handsome offer from John Rich, the manager of the Covent Garden Theatre, to perform in London. There, she found immediate success in the role of Sylvia in *The Recruiting Officer*, in which Sylvia pretends to be Jack

Wilful. She was equally comfortable playing elegant women of fashion and in breeches roles. One story told of her is that when she was almost caught in bed with Garrick by a visiting jealous lord, the actor fled, rapidly gathering up his clothes. Unfortunately, he forgot his scratch (short) wig. Woffington, ever the actress, was able to convince the noble lord that the wig was for one of her upcoming breeches roles.

She drew particular public attention and praise when, in 1739, she was cast as Sir Harry Wildair in *The Constant Couple, or A Trip to the Jubilee* by George Farquhar, a play that had been in the repertoire since 1700. Actors tended to "own" roles and tried to guard them jealously, and the part of Sir Harry Wildair had been written for Robert Wilks, Farquhar's friend, who had died seven years before. Wilks was said to have well represented the fine gentlemen of his day, and his interpretation of the character was much praised. But now audiences were intrigued to see a woman in the role of the rich, unreliable baronet, one of the five suitors of Lady Lurewell who vie for her affections. It is a comic role but certainly not a typical breeches role. Audiences were expected to accept Woffington as a man, although, of course, they knew her as a fine actress by this time. Mrs. Inchbald,[15] a late seventeenth-century theater critic, wrote praising the portrayal of Sir Harry Wildair by women and compared it favorably with that of Robert Wilks:

No actor, since he [Wilks] quitted the stage, has been wholly successful in the performance of this character; and from Wilks down to the present time, the part has only been supported, with celebrity, by women.

The noted Mrs. Woffington was highly extolled in Sir Harry; and Mrs. Jordan[16] has been no less admired and attractive.

But it must be considered as a disgrace to the memory of men of fashion, of the period in which Wildair was brought to the stage, that he has ever since been justly personated, by no other than the female sex.

By the time the new century dawned, women actors were firmly established on both sides of the Atlantic, playing a whole range of female parts but also, increasingly, trying out their skills in serious male roles. However, few men played women's roles, and usually only as disguise or for comedic effect. One of David Garrick's most famous roles was as Sir John Brute in Vanbrugh's *The Provoked Wife*. Sir John goes off for a drunken night on the town, and to avoid the watch, disguises himself in a set of clothes borrowed from his wife. After his arrest he appears before a magistrate, still dressed in his wife's frock. Garrick was often depicted by artists in this, one of his favorite roles. One painting by Johann Zoffany shows Garrick as Brute with his drinking companions about to be arrested by the watch. But such a cross-dressing role was rare. There were few opportunities, or perhaps little desire, for men to act serious female roles.

In performance, as other aspects of life, fashions are driven by the prevailing cultural, moral, and sexual norms of the day, as well as historical events, particularly wars. Things change. The developing theater and opera; the new genres of pantomime, music hall, and vaudeville; and the availability or not of people of the "usual" gender presented new opportunities for gender experimentation. The next chapter looks at how Shakespeare's famous roles, including Hamlet, Macbeth, and King Lear, have attracted the best of actors since the plays were written, and how they have continued to tempt actors to cross-dress.

4
THE LURE OF SHAKESPEARE

I cannot see Hamlet as a man. The things he says, his impulses, his actions,
entirely indicate to me that he was a woman.

—SARAH BERNHARDT

In 1845, Charlotte Cushman, one of America's most famous rising stars, traveled across the Atlantic. She played Shakespeare's Romeo to appreciative audiences at the Haymarket Theatre, London. Already famous for portraying Shakespeare's women and particularly well known for the role of Lady Macbeth, it was not surprising that she was welcomed by the London theatergoing public. More surprising is that her role was Romeo, an uncommon role for women, and that Juliet was played by her sister, Sarah. Cushman was one of the new brand of independent female actors who disregarded tradition and made their own career decisions, avoiding exploitation, both sexual and financial. Assuming an unfeminine appearance and showing no interest in men, Cushman loved and left many women lovers as she traveled through Europe. She also illustrated how keen actresses were to play the important theatrical roles that had been written for men.

The role of Romeo was an unusual one for a woman to play, but women playing Shakespeare's men was not. Almost as soon as women took to the stage, many felt compelled to try out the big male roles. In the seventeenth century, because professional acting was sufficiently new, it did not carry too much gender baggage. After all, it was just within living memory that boys and young men were considered the norm in playing women; indeed, when women began to play female roles, they were often considered poor replacements for the boys. If audiences could suspend belief for boy actors as women, they could easily do the same for women, and countenance them playing male roles. At first, such cross-dressing was sexualized, with the women costumed to titillate male viewers. But as the century progressed, the changing nature of audiences and of plays saw ambitious actresses keen to expand their repertoires as serious actors by taking on male roles. It has to be said that such casting didn't always come from the women, from an urge to promote their feminist principles. It was more often theater managers who pushed for such casting, still aware that a pair of breeches showed off more leg and bottom than a long skirt. But it did provide opportunities for actresses who felt limited by the roles available to them. Women were increasingly confident about their acting abilities and of their value to the companies that employed them. It was inevitable that the new generation of actresses having played Shakespeare's heroines, few in number compared with the interesting male roles, wanted to show what they could do in the meatier parts. There were female Shylocks, Lears, Romeos, and plentiful Hamlets.

Hamlet, in particular, continues to prove an attractive role for women. As Dominic Dromgoole[1] claims, Hamlet invites open interpretation. Unlike most of Shakespeare's tragic figures, which are more clearly characterized—"Othello the Noble Moor; Lear, the mentally vulnerable tyrant; Anthony, the decaying libertine"[2]—Hamlet's character, that of a young man on the cusp of adulthood and lacking in direction and clarity, gives ample scope for actors to develop the role in a myriad of directions. Dromgoole claims that Hamlet's character is not like what he calls "the masculine boorishness of the Danish court," and his relationship with Ophelia is more a close understanding and a shared feeling than passionate young love. The young prince is ill at ease with what he sees as his own femininity. He is angry that he cannot kill Claudius whom he hates and can only use words to express himself. And although the words and phrases he uses to compare himself with a woman jar with us today, they must have encouraged early actresses to feel that Shakespeare himself would support a more female take on the part.

> *Why what an ass am I! This is most brave,*
> *That I, the son of a dear father murdered,*
> *Prompted to my revenge by heaven and hell,*
> *Must, like a whore, unpack my heart with words,*
> *And fall a-cursing like a very drab,*
> *A scullion!*[3]

Kitty Clive was one of the first female Hamlets. Mrs. Clive, as she was known, specialized in comic parts including breeches roles, so Hamlet must have been an unusual part for her, particularly as she worked for many years alongside David Garrick, one of the most famous Hamlets of his day. Clive was an open supporter of actors' rights and was not afraid to confront theater management. She became one of the highest paid actresses of her time and may have earned more than many male performers, who were traditionally better paid than their female counterparts. Garrick was rather afraid of her. "Whenever he had a difference with Mrs Clive, he was happy to make a drawn battle of it."[4] Perhaps playing Hamlet was a statement of her conviction that she could act as well as him or a challenge to the male domination of the best Shakespearian roles. Whether Samuel Johnson saw her playing Hamlet is unclear, but he rated both her intellect and her comic acting abilities. Long after she retired, Johnson commented to Mrs. Siddons,[5] "What Clive did best, she did better than Garrick: but she could not do half so many things well; she was better romp than any I ever saw in nature."[6]

Kitty Clive did not, it appears, challenge Garrick's claim as the best Hamlet, and her performance has not been described. But in Worcester in 1775, the twenty-year-old Sarah Siddons played the young prince, fighting a duel with her brother, John Kemble. Siddons specialized mostly in strong female roles rather than male. She, like Cushman, became particularly famous for her portrayal of Lady Macbeth, a role she claimed as her own and acted for many years. Her cross-dressing roles were fewer, but she wanted to play male characters on stage not to titillate, but because of the dramatic interest they provided. Her performance as Hamlet was a great success, and she continued to play the role, reprising it in Birmingham and Manchester in 1776, Liverpool in 1778, and Edinburgh and Bristol in 1781. Much later, in 1802, the forty-seven-year-old actress was welcomed in Dublin. But strangely to our modern ears, theatrical audiences in London at the time were more conservative than those in the provinces. London producers would not take the risk. She never played Hamlet in the capital. The first recorded female Hamlet on the London stage was Elizabeth Powell at Drury Lane in 1796, and in 1820, the well-known Julia Glover played him at the Lyceum to critical acclaim. This may have been the performance of Hamlet praised by the famous actor Edmund Kean, who reportedly came behind the scenes at the end of the first act and shook both of Mrs. Glover's hands, exclaiming, "excellent, excellent." Glover, more famous for comedy than tragedy, continued to play Hamlet when touring the provinces. Perhaps this was unwise. In her later years, she became what critics described as "monstrously fat," and on stage, hopefully unintentionally, she drew much laughter from the audience with the line, "Oh! that this too too solid flesh would melt."[7]

As the nineteenth century progressed and American theater developed, the links between the London theater and that on the US East Coast flourished. American actors appeared on the London stage and toured in the United Kingdom, and European actors toured the United States. Some stayed for long periods or moved there permanently. It became increasingly common for women to play male roles, and on both sides of the Atlantic, the roles of Shakespeare's men were those to which many aspired. Sarah Bartley, a British actress, became the first American Hamlet, playing the role at the

Park Theatre in New York in 1820. She had enjoyed limited success in the United Kingdom, but in the two years she spent in the United States, she gained reputation and fortune. Her heart wasn't fully in acting, however, and her performances were infrequent when she returned to England.

Taking on the role of Hamlet was, most likely, a political decision for American Anna Elizabeth Dickinson. She was a radical Republican who campaigned for women's suffrage and for greater rights, both political and social, for women. She was determined that the United States should abolish slavery. Used by the radical Republicans to speak for them, both in the buildup and during the American Civil War, she was a fine orator and could move a crowd by her words. She was a very brave woman who spoke up at a time when women were mostly "seen and not heard," and she earned a standing ovation in 1864 for an impassioned speech on the floor of the United States House of Representatives in front of President Abraham Lincoln. Anna earned her living mostly as an orator, but for a short time, she wrote plays and took on acting roles to supplement her income. She played Hamlet in New York at some point in the 1880s although her performance was unfavorably received. But it is perhaps a tribute to her attitude to what a woman should be able to do that she chose to play such an iconic male Shakespeare role on stage.

Charlotte Cushman, however, was one of the most celebrated American actresses of the mid-nineteenth century. She played a key role in pushing for women's rights and was noted for living a life that she wanted rather than one conventional for the times. Starting her professional life as an opera singer, she turned to acting when her singing voice failed, strained by soprano roles that did not suit her fine contralto. Her career took her touring throughout Europe. She lived for some time in Italy and then moved back to the United States. She had many female lovers. Rather than hindering her popularity, this unusual lifestyle helped her establish relationships with many artists, writers, and politicians whom she met on her travels. Although most famous for her Lady Macbeth, she took cross-dressing male parts, including Romeo, and in 1861, she played Hamlet at the Washington Theater.

But the best known of the early cross-dressers playing Shakespeare was undoubtedly Sarah Bernhardt, "the Divine Sarah." The famous actress and theater manager played several male roles in the course of her career. These she liked to perform because she thought them to be more intellectual than those of women. Her Hamlet was one of the key roles in her long and illustrious career.

Bernhardt's personal life was varied to say the least; she worked as a courtesan in her early years, and she had affairs with the rich and titled as well as many of her leading men. She is even thought to have had an affair with the Prince of Wales, the future Edward VII, who frequently attended her London and Paris performances. Perhaps her intimate knowledge of many men was the reason why her travesti performances were seen to be particularly authentic. She was an expressive actress with a wide emotional range who was capable of great subtlety in her interpretations. She was said to have a commanding stage presence, a unique voice, and a purity of diction that was highly praised. Her movement was flamboyant, and she used a great deal of gestures and physical action.

In 1899 at the age of fifty-five, she performed as Hamlet in Paris in a French prose adaptation of the play in twelve scenes. Later in the same year, she appeared as Hamlet at the Samuel Pepys Theatre in London. Traveling on to Stratford-upon-Avon, she gave one matinee performance at the Shakespeare Memorial Theatre on June 29.

Another actress, Elizabeth Robins, published a full account of Bernhardt's performance.[8] "Madame Bernhardt's assumption of masculinity is so cleverly carried out that one loses sight of Hamlet in one's admiration for the *tour de force* of the actress. . . . She gives us . . . a spirited boy; doing it with an impetuosity, a youthfulness, almost childish." In giving advice to the players, she was "a precocious young gentleman, who . . . thoroughly enjoys laying down the law to plodding professionals." And in the play scene, "with something a little reminiscent of an urchin swarming over an orchard wall, [Hamlet] crawls up to the throne, till his eyes, not sombre and horror-stricken, but keen and glittering, are on a level with the King's. When he has surprised the guilty terror there, this Hamlet actually bursts out into peal on peal of laughter. His clever trick has succeeded, his *Schadenfreude* overflows."

Bernhardt's Hamlet was a sensation. Wherever she appeared, theaters were sold out, and her portrayal of the prince was remembered by many as a high point in her acting career. Her performance, however, did have its critics. Crossing gender boundaries was uncomfortable to some, and one early London reviewer complained, "A woman is positively no more capable of beating out the music of Hamlet than is a man of expressing the plaintive and half-accomplished surrender of Ophelia."[9] Refreshingly for its time, another critic's piece was more concerned with her portrayal of the role than her gender. After the Stratford performance, the *Birmingham Gazette* published a review, which included the phrase "too short a time the philosopher and too much the man of wrath and vengeance. . . . Mme Bernhardt . . . puts his passion in the foreground, and every monologue becomes a diatribe."[10]

Le duel d'Hamlet, a 1900 French film adaptation of an excerpt from Hamlet, is believed to have been the earliest film adaptation of the play. The film shows a still-lithe Bernhardt to be a fine fencer with a natural grace and looking good in doublet and hose. Clement Maurice, the director, made a phonograph recording so that the film could be accompanied by sound. Unfortunately, the sound of the clashing wooden prop swords was not loud and realistic enough, so Maurice had a stage hand bang pieces of metal together in sync with the sword fight. The short film was presented to the public at the 1900 Paris Universal Exposition as part of Paul Decauville's program, Phono-Cinéma-Théâtre, which included similarly short films of many other famous French theater stars of the day. Bernhardt was said to dislike her appearance in this short film clip. It didn't put her off filming, however, and she continued to act on screen well into the 1920s, with some of her roles being male ones. In the weeks before her death in 1923, she was preparing to make another motion picture in her own home. She told journalists, "They're paying me ten thousand francs a day. . . . These are American rates, and I don't have to cross the Atlantic! At those rates, I'm ready to appear in any films they make."[11] Unfortunately, she died just before the filming began.

Up to this point, all the female actors playing Shakespeare's men were cross-dressing—they were impersonating men and wanted the audience to suspend belief and accept the changed gender. Even Bernhardt, who professed to believe that she could not see Hamlet as a man but only as a woman, played the role conventionally as male. But there is a Danish legend from the twelfth century that tells the story of a girl Hamlet who is brought up as a boy by her royal parents to secure her claim to the throne. This theme was developed in the book *The Mystery of Hamlet*, written in 1881. The author, Edward P. Vining, argues that Shakespeare's text indicates that he might have "dallied" with the idea of a female Hamlet. Vining gives various examples to support his theory.

HAMLET'S NATURE ESSENTIALLY FEMININE. Hamlet's Impulsiveness His Love for Mockery His Disgust with Revelry His Pretty oaths His rear of Breaking into Tears His Admiration for Manly Virtues and Detestation of Feminine Weaknesses His Eulogy of man His Panegyrics of his Father His Treatment of his Mother and Ophelia Comparison with the Interviews between Viola and Olivia and between Rosalind and Phebe May not Shakespeare have at last entertained the Thought that Hamlet might be a Woman? This was not his Original Conception of the Character Shakespeare may never have fully yielded to the Fancy but certainly dallied with it. And his love for Horatio and jealousy of Ophelia.[12]

Whether Vining was right or not about how Shakespeare went about writing Hamlet, the theory of Hamlet as a woman was used as the basis for a 1920 film by a Danish woman, Asta Nielson, who directed and took the leading role. This production changes the gender of the character completely. Released in the sexually liberated Weimar Germany in 1921, it is based on the old legend. Hamlet is played as a cross-dressing girl who is brought up as a boy by Gertrude and Claudius and who is in love with Horatio.

Since the eighteenth and into the early part of the twentieth century, women had played male Shakespearian characters. Apparently, there was little opposition to such cross-dressing. In World War I, an all-women troupe produced Shakespearian plays and pageants in a hut in Bloomsbury for soldiers on leave. Actresses played all the parts, women and men, and the famous Ellen Terry played the cross-dressing Portia there. But after the 1920s, just at the point when women in both the United Kingdom and the United States had won the vote, and one would expect more experimentation with gender in the theater, there were far fewer women playing male Shakespearian roles. The reason for this change is debatable and probably complex. It could be that once women actors felt that suffrage was achieved, they did not have to advertise their defiance of convention by playing male roles. Possibly, between wars and after World War II, it would be considered unpatriotic to take a role that could be played by one of our "heroic boys" who had served in the forces. Professor Tony Howard[13] believes that the increasing use of male critics with what he termed "bourgeois values" banished women from such roles. Such cross-dressing roles, perfectly normal up to that point, were considered improper. Producers need plays to succeed and be financially viable. Risking such criticism would be dangerous. Whatever the reasons for the reduction in Shakespearian cross-dressing, it would be almost three-quarters of a century before, once again, the theater began seriously to experiment with such roles.

There are few intermittent examples of women taking male roles in Shakespeare during that period, however. Frances de la Tour played Hamlet in a promenade production at the Half Moon Theatre, London, in 1979. "She is tough, abrasive, virile and impassioned," wrote the *Guardian*'s Michael Billington of a production full of "bruising intimacy."[14] De la Tour's Hamlet was an interpretation of perceived male behavior rather than a feminine take on the character. Ruth Mitchell played Hamlet in the Roaring Girls' version of *Hamlet* at the Warehouse Theatre in Croydon in 1992. Theater critic Ian Shuttleworth, writing in *City Limits*, did not think that cross-dressing in that production, by women interpreting male behavior, gave any new insights: "On paper it looks terrific," he wrote, "*Hamlet* through the filter of Moll Cutpurse, the cross-dressing roisterer of the period—setting up a dialectic about gender and roles. The reality is shockingly deficient: a three-minute prologue followed by a three-hour-plus version of *Hamlet*, virtually uncut and stultifyingly unadventurous. Yes, the actors are all female. Yes, some of them play male parts in breeches and others in skirts (with no discernible basis for the differentiation). Big deal."[15]

Female actors continue to covet the major male roles in Shakespeare whether in all-female or mixed-gender productions, and when successful, their interpretations can add to our understanding of the complexity of such characters. One actor, Jessika D. Williams, was so keen to play Othello that she has risked her professional future to take the part. In the midst of the coronavirus epidemic in 2020, needing work when there was little work in the profession, she joined the American Shakespeare Center in rural Virginia, a theater that decided to ignore Actors Equity, which for safety reasons barred its members from live performances. Time will tell whether her future will be affected by leaving her union, but Williams was adamant that it is the right time to play Othello, both as a woman and as a black woman.

> *I was doing a lot of research into the men who have played this before me,*
> *and something that came up a lot was, how do you play this beautiful person*
> *and not fall into the trap of perpetuating the idea that Black people are over-*
> *emotional, monstrous, barbarous creatures? As a woman, I feel like I was*
> *able to get around the fear of that, because it didn't have to do with being*
> *a man, it just had to do with being a human being. . . . We've seen female*
> *Hamlets, female Richard IIs, we recently saw a female Lear—and I think*
> *that's important that women can tackle these epic roles.*[16]

Whether successful or not as a performance, and whatever the reader's opinion about going against union guidelines, the lure of Shakespeare's strong
role obviously overrode the criticism Williams received from within the profession.

But what about men playing women in Shakespeare? So far, you must be
thinking, it has all been about women playing men. Was there not an equivalent queue of men desperate to play Lady Macbeth or Ophelia? Well, no!
There wasn't. The really good women's parts in Shakespeare are few compared
with the male roles, so why would actors insist on playing women? There
was male-to-female cross-dressing in the nineteenth and twentieth centuries,
and plenty of it. The music halls, vaudeville, pantomime, television, and film
abound with performers who assume characters of another gender; however,
any real movement toward men in female Shakespearian roles had to wait
until the turn of the century.

At the end of the 1990s and in the first decade of the twenty-first century,
directors began seriously to challenge established notions of gender in casting Shakespeare's plays. There were many experiments in such casting—some
successful and others not—and critics were often divided. Driven by the
notion of equality, and in an attempt to take a fresh view of the complexities
of Shakespeare's characters, women took more of the big Shakespearian roles.

In some productions, women cross-dressed in male attire and were directed to act the part conventionally as male. In March 1997, Charles Spencer, theater critic for the *Telegraph*, rather grudgingly praised Kathryn Hunter's performance as King Lear at the Leicester Haymarket Theatre. The review began this way: "Kathryn Hunter's performance in the title role of King Lear puts one in mind of Dr Johnson. 'A woman's preaching,' he told Boswell, 'is like a dog's walking on his hind legs. It is not done well; but you are surprised to find it done at all.'" Continuing, he describes her costume as one that indicated she was male, and concludes that her gender did not affect her portrayal of Lear:

> *Her Lear has long white hair, a tiny goatee beard and wears a black three-piece suit several sizes too large. For an actress not yet forty, Hunter gives a remarkable impression of a strong spirit trapped inside a frail, shrunken body, while her voice, deep, guttural and resonant, is often highly expressive, at least at low volume. Indeed after a few minutes, Hunter's sex ceases to be an issue. I found her casting far less distracting than Fiona Shaw's overpraised performance in the more "feminine" role of Richard II.*[17]

But Fiona Shaw's portrayal of Richard II was defended by others, including Paul Taylor of the *Independent*. He did not consider that it had been overpraised by critics. He commented,

> *It's odd, for example, that some critics have assumed that the production is aiming to be gender-blind when the slightly unearthly, ambiguous figure Shaw cuts—in her portrayal of the monarch as an anguishedly insecure, clowningly exhibitionist man-child—mirrors more than subliminally the psychological confusions caused by the identity crisis of a King's dual nature: the anointed, mystique-ridden role having to be filled by the all-too-fallible human being.*[18]

There was—and still is—some debate about cross-gender casting in Shakespeare. In September 2007, Michael Billington, the long-standing theater critic for the *Guardian*, sounded a note of caution. He wrote a piece called "What I Like about Cross-Dressing." In it he examines what he calls gender-switching in the theater, not only in Shakespeare but also across all types of productions. He comments that the practice has been a vital part of theatrical tradition but that "the current fashion for turning male classical roles over to women and vice versa—can have very mixed results." While he argued for more gender-switching and praised Frances de la Tour for her Hamlet, Kathryn Hunter's Lear, and Mark Rylance's Cleopatra, he thought there were practical limits. Agreeing that the great tragic roles in Shakespeare are universal property, he had doubts when there was a gender switch in the "socially specific field of comedy." As an example, he cites the actor Marjorie Yates playing Sir Toby Belch in *Twelfth Night*. The character is a specific type, he argues: "the upper-class parasite who battens on everyone and drowns his self-hatred in drink."[19] The actor had to be padded and don a wig and a beard to play the part. Another critic agreed, saying that Yates playing Sir Toby, and indeed other actors in that play impersonating other genders by cross-dressing, reminded him of the travesti acts in Victorian music halls. What was the point, Billington concluded, in merely replicating the opposite gender? While cross-dressing is part of theatrical tradition, its real use should be to offer illumination of the role rather than impersonation.

Maxine Peake's interpretation of the role of Hamlet at the Royal Exchange in Manchester in 2014 certainly did this. Although Hamlet is the male Shakespeare role most favored by women actors, this was the first female Hamlet on a major stage in the United Kingdom since that of Frances de la Tour thirty-five years previously. Peake's performance was highly praised by critics for its freshness and originality:

She is a stripling prince, almost pre-sexual, who glides, without swagger and without girlishness. . . . Peake's delicate ferocity, her particular mixture of concentration and lightness, ensure that you want to follow her whenever she appears. Anger is her keynote. Her voice is reedy with indignation. . . . She is precise rather than cloudy, cutting rather than meditative. She is a damn good fencer.[20]

In 2015, the Manchester Royal Exchange production of Hamlet was made into a film. I found Peake fascinating, so new and different in the role. Peter Bradshaw, the *Guardian*'s film critic, described the film as fast, fluent, and revelatory. He was at pains to argue that casting a woman in the role is not a gimmick and that even he, presumably as someone familiar with Shakespeare, had learned something new from the portrayal:

Her casting isn't a gimmick. Peake looks like a stowaway, or a French resistance fighter in disguise: her femaleness gives a new edge of differentness and alienation and anger. . . . This is a truculent and lairy Hamlet; Peake really lets rip with Hamlet's bipolar delirium. . . . Interestingly, Maxine Peake's delivery of the "To be or not to be" speech (while covered in blood) brought home a great truth to me: it is not simply an abstract discourse, but an agonised self-harming rant, triggered specifically by his grotesque accidental homicide of Ophelia's foolish parent.[21]

It has been suggested that having Shakespeare for four hundred years as the national dramatist makes it harder in Britain to move away from the highly masculine approaches of the past. Changing gender roles in Shakespeare plays seems to incite comment and be controversial. Other countries are much more flexible about the Bard and are perhaps more able to look at his plays differently. All-female productions of Shakespeare are much more frequent in the United States than in Britain, although there are some fine examples in both countries. In 2003, the Globe Theatre in London mounted an all-female version of *Richard III*, directed by Barry Kyle. It was very well received, and Kathryn Hunter's triumphant central performance was particularly praised.

In 2012, the Donmar Warehouse produced an all-female version of *Julius Caesar* directed by Phyllida Lloyd with Harriet Walter as Brutus and Cush Jumbo as Caesar. Michael Billington of the *Guardian* awarded the play four stars. He wrote,

> *I don't think we should get carried away and start arguing that single-sex Shakespeare is the only way forward. But, like Mark Antony, Phyllida Lloyd is a "shrewd contriver"; and her all-female production of* Julius Caesar *is witty, liberating and inventive, and taps into the anti-authoritarian instinct that runs through the play.*[22]

On the contrary, Charles Spencer of the *Telegraph*, obviously no supporter of all-female casts, gave it two stars:

> *Before seeing this women-only* Julius Caesar *I vowed that I wouldn't resort to Dr Johnson's notorious line in which he compared a woman's preaching to a "dog's walking on his hind legs. It is not done well, but you are surprised to find it done at all." And in fact some of the acting is excellent, with the great Harriet Walter, sporting an exceptionally nifty haircut, in particularly strong and persuasive form as an often anguished and deeply sincere Brutus. She is well matched by Jenny Jules who splendidly captures both the intemperance and the emotional neediness of Cassius.*
>
> *Watching this pair at their best, you genuinely forget their gender and simply admire their acting, and the truth of their response to Shakespeare's richly drawn characters.*
>
> *But Frances Barber is little more than a ranting, leering, pantomime villain as Julius Caesar, and it is a great relief when she gets her quietus,*

which in this production involves a bottle of bleach being forced down her throat. By the time the conspirators have pulled on bright red Marigold gloves to signify their bloodstained hands, and Mark Antony's great rabble-rousing speech over Caesar's corpse, has been squandered by crass, attention-seeking staging, one begins to feel that it's not just Caesar who has been murdered but the play itself.[23]

Ouch!

But perhaps it is to be expected that such varied reactions are engendered in critics, especially male ones who still seem to be in the majority in the major papers. And perhaps when all the parts are chosen to be of the same gender, it is absolutely essential that each actor is chosen who can best portray the character. Weak cross-gender casting in any of the parts comes under close scrutiny. All-male Shakespeare productions are perhaps, understandably, less controversial and usually well received. The plays are cast how they would have been four hundred years ago, with young men playing the female parts, although their characters are thoroughly modern. Propeller is a touring company that presents Shakespeare's plays in the United Kingdom and around the world. The casts are exclusively male actors. And in 2016, the Shakespeare Theatre Company in Washington, DC, staged director Ed Sylvanus Iskandar's interpretation of Shakespeare's *The Taming of the Shrew* with an all-male cast. He says he serendipitously cast three Asian actors in leading roles; Maulik Pancholy, known for his roles in *Weeds* and *30 Rock*, played Katherine. And in the same year, the Festival Players Theatre Company toured what was described as "a dynamic, all-male production of Shakespeare's famous tragedy *Hamlet*" to outside venues throughout Europe.[24]

All-male casting has also been used in the main Shakespeare theaters, too. Mark Rylance won a Tony (his third) for portraying Olivia on Broadway in Shakespeare's Globe Theatre's all-male take on *Twelfth Night* in 2013 (the original production debuted at the Globe in 2002). Eddie Redmayne played Viola in London while Samuel Barnett took on the role at the Belasco Theater Broadway. In an interview with Ben Brantley, the *New York Times* theater critic,[25] Rylance explained the meticulous preparation he undertook to play the role of Olivia. Building up a dossier of useful information, he studied historical pictures, visited English stately homes, and saw the great Kabuki actor Tamasaburo twice in Tokyo. Before going on stage, he would listen to a recording of actress Judi Dench performing an Alan Bennett monologue to help him find the right timbre for Olivia's voice. Clothes also helped. Olivia is an Elizabethan aristocrat in mourning, and costume designer Jenny Tiramani did meticulous research to create the silk velvet gown that such a character would have worn. And Rylance wore the dress over a corset. "It was incredibly tight, so I wouldn't be able to run very far; I would be breathless."[26]

Rylance's performance in the cross-dressing role was hailed as magnificent. Ben Brantley describes his reaction to Rylance's performance. "I have met her [*sic*] three times, once at the Globe in London in 2002, and then twice when she came to the Belasco Theater on Broadway and on each occasion she left me in a state of contented tears. She is, hands down, my favorite of all the Shakespeare performances I've had the chance to review. As incarnated in that production, the reserved but emotionally ripe Olivia seemed to be woven out of starlight—when she walked it was as if she never touched the ground—and yet she was profoundly, fallibly human, too."[27] This was a performance of an actor playing a role to perfection. The issue of gender was irrelevant.

But not everyone sees all-male productions as harmless. There has been some general disquiet and specific protests about all-male Shakespeare on a number of counts: that it denies work to women and also emphasizes our history of sexism and inequality. Critics also say that claims for authenticity are groundless. Shakespeare's women were originally played by boys, not men.

Mark Rylance's middle-aged Olivia in *Twelfth Night* is no more authentic than casting a woman in the role.

In the second decade of the twenty-first century, we are seeing gender-blind casting becoming the norm in the production of Shakespeare's plays, certainly in the main companies, just as it is in other areas of performance. And the term *cross-dressing* is increasingly redundant. The costuming of many plays is gender neutral with modern unisex jeans and T-shirts or military uniforms commonly used. There are more women directors, both of theaters and of individual plays. Michelle Terry, appointed in April 2018 as artistic director at Shakespeare's Globe, says she is committed to a fifty-fifty gender split in casting. Her 2019 and 2020 seasons included an all-female *Richard II* and a winter production of *Richard III*, with the title role played by Sophie Russell. The actor wore the ubiquitous unisex jeans and T-shirt at the start but, later, a smart white suit. The Globe's *Henry IV*, the three parts edited into a single play, had Jonathan Broadbent in the leading role. The *London Theatre Review*, however, reported, "The casting at times is gender-blind—Queen Margaret is tenderly taken by Steffan Donnelly, while Leaphia Darko makes credible work of Salisbury, Northumberland and Rutland."[28]

Many reviewers still comment on the fact that a Shakespeare play contains gender-blind casting before going on to appraise the acting. But it is becoming less frequent. As the decade progresses, we should expect less emphasis on the gender, color, physical ability, or indeed the age of players, and more concentration on what actors bring to their roles.

In 2016, Glenda Jackson, at almost eighty years of age, returned to the stage after a twenty-three-year absence; she took on the title role in William Shakespeare's *King Lear* at the Old Vic Theatre in London. Praise was heaped (by most critics) upon her portrayal of the role, and she was nominated for Best Actress at the Olivier Awards.

[S]he is tremendous in the role. In an uncanny way, she transcends gender. What you see, in Deborah Warner's striking modern-dress production, is an unflinching, non-linear portrait of the volatility of old age. Jackson, like all the best Lears, shifts in a moment between madness and sanity, anger and tenderness, vocal force and physical frailty.[29]

GJ is tremendous as King Lear. No ifs, no buts. . . . Barely have you had time to register her—in black top and trousers with flowing silken red shirt— than this Lear is giving away the kingdom, weighing her daughters' love. When I say "her," the trick is that Jackson is allowed to be herself (there's no male impersonation) but the lines haven't been modified to alter Lear's masculinity; this is a Glenda-bended, not a gender-bended production.[30]

Lear is a remarkable act of stamina, memory and emotional reserves for any actor. It becomes, in Jackson's initially ferocious and ultimately desperately vulnerable presence, a tour de force. As she stumbles about the heath, her bony legs exposed, you know everything of Lear's age and rage and what these events have cost him.[31]

At the age of eighty, after a quarter of a century away from theatre. . . . Here she is making her first return to the stage in a gender-blind assault on the most daunting role for senior actors in the Shakespearian repertoire.[32]

She reprised the role three years later at the Cort Theatre in New York. While the rather muddled production was not a hit with most critics, Glenda Jackson certainly was.

Yet there, amid the chaos, is Ms. Jackson, like a sharp and gleaming scythe slashing through an overgrown field. Lear may be one of world literature's most disturbingly lost souls. But Ms. Jackson hews to his tortured path with such insight that we register every twisting contour in a dispossessed mon-arch's road into madness and redemption.[33]

Perhaps that review in the *New York Times* sums up what the result of gen-der-blind casting in Shakespeare should be: a fine performance of a fine role.

5
WITCHES, BITCHES, AND BRITCHES

OCTAVIAN: *Nein, nein, nein, nein! I trink' kein Wein.*
Nein, nein, nein, nein, i bleib' net da.

—RICHARD STRAUSS, *DER ROSENKAVALIER*[1]

The curtains open on Richard Strauss's opera *Der Rosenkavalier*. Marie Therese, the aristocratic Marschallin, is in bed with her very young lover, Count Octavian Rofrano. The young man sings ecstatically of his overwhelming love while the Marschallin, much more aware of the way in which the passions of youth can change, gently responds. Octavian is sung by a mezzo-soprano, and the part can be a triumph for the right singer. She has to convey Octavian's youthful masculinity, his zest for life, and his amorous but jealous nature. She also needs to show how both his relationships, with the girlish, pretty Sophie and the mature Marschallin, compete for his youthful affections. The role is a breeches or travesti role for mezzo-sopranos, who often, rather ruefully, refer to themselves as being best known for singing witches, bitches, and britches.

Octavian, who is a young woman playing a seventeen-year-old boy, has also to act a comic part. As did Mozart's librettist when writing the role of Cherubino in his late eighteenth-century *The Marriage of Figaro*, Strauss's librettist Hugo von Hofmannsthal plays with the erotic possibilities of a young woman playing a boy disguised as a girl. After the loving vocal exchanges in the bedroom, loud voices are heard outside. The Marschallin, believing that her husband has returned early from a hunting trip, has Octavian hide. He subsequently emerges in a skirt and bonnet as the maid "Mariandel," a simple country girl who attracts the amorous attention of the lecherous visitor

Baron Ochs. Back in his own clothes, Count Octavian is chosen to bear the rose that will begin Ochs's courtship of the young Sophie. Meeting the young girl, Octavian falls in love and, wanting to prevent her marriage to Ochs, prepares a charade that will expose Ochs as both lecherous and as a bigamist. In a comic episode, the Baron attempts to seduce Mariandel at a cozy dinner at a table for two. He encourages "her" to drink more and more wine, which she refuses. "Nein, nein, nein, nein! I trink' kein Wein." "Nein, nein, nein, nein, i bleib' net da." With the gauche coquetry of a supposedly country girl, she tipsily sings an aria about the passage of time, a parody of the Marschallin's reflections on the same in act 1. After some heavy Austrian "prank" humor, the police arrive. Mariandel retires behind a screen with the Police Inspector, supposedly to make a statement, and when Ochs sees articles of women's clothing coming into view, he realizes he has been fooled. Any young mezzo-soprano playing Octavian has to act both an aristocratic adolescent and a boy pretending to be a simple country girl, a serious and intense lover, and a comedy pastiche. *Der Rosenkavalier* was a tremendous hit. There were excursion trains laid on from all over Germany expressly to take people to see it. And Strauss's breeches role of Octavian was so successful in 1911 that, a year later, he insisted on writing the ardent male composer in *Ariadne of Naxos* for a mezzo-soprano. Not quite such a key part as Octavian, but the composer does get to sing the attractive aria "Sein wir wieder gut!" (Let's be friends again).

The use of cross-gender casting goes back to the beginnings of opera. The term o*pera* is short for the Italian *opera in musica*, a dramatic work set to music in which the music is integral. The words of the play, in the form of arias, ensembles, or choruses are sung to the accompaniment of instruments. There may also be dialogue (recitative), which can be accompanied or not. Opera as we know it today was developed by Claudio Monteverdi (1567–1643). Influenced by earlier operas by Florentine composers, he introduced two new approaches, the portrayal of real or humanized rather than myth-ical characters and the use of arias to tell their stories. His opera *La Favola d'Orfeo*, now more often named *L'Orfeo*, was produced in 1607 and was the first accompanied by a full (for that time) orchestra. Georg Friedrich Han-del (1685–1759), who devoted much of his creative life to writing operas, composed operas in Germany and then, meeting Italian composers in Berlin, and later Arcangelo Corelli and the father and son Alessandro and Dome-nico Corelli in Florence, he began to compose in the Italian style. Many operas followed and were staged in Florence (*Rodrigo*), Venice (*Agrippina*), and Hanover where he was employed by the Elector of Hanover. On a visit to London in 1710, he composed *Rinaldo*, an Italian-style opera seria, with a large orchestra and flamboyant staging, achieving instant success.

Before 1700, solos were often given to tenors, and in the very early operas, including Monteverdi's *Orfeo*, the leading roles in opera were also written for them. But castrati were also in use at this time and with such voices began the creation of cross-dressing roles. Although Orfeo himself was originally a tenor or high baritone, the part of Euridice was a cross-dressing role sung by a castrato. As the eighteenth century progressed, the tenor voice was not as popular as those in the higher range, and the lead was usually a high-voiced male. Having a castrato in a cast certainly helped any new opera to be a success.

Castrati singers were at their height of popularity in opera seria at the end of the 1700s, but by this time they were becoming scarce. Having a child castrated before puberty, often performed by the child's mother, was an attempt to secure a continued singing role in church choirs. The practice was outlawed by Pope Benedict XIV in the mid-1700s, calling it "an unnatural crime the victims of which are young boys, often through the complicity of their parents." Obviously castrating boy singers could not in any way guar-antee that their boyish treble developed into a fine singing voice, and many castrati led hard lives estranged from normal relationships. But outside of Italy, in countries where castration for such purposes was never practiced, castrati became objects of fascination. Their singing abilities were much praised, and those who were successful earned astronomical fees and often attracted the social and sexual favors of both men and women; however, there were double standards among their public. Although feted and admired for their skills they also suffered ridicule for their "incompleteness," and the singers often made excuses for their condition by claiming they had suffered an accident in childhood. A bite from a wild boar or a kick from a horse were typical reasons given for their condition.

It is sometimes thought that women singers merely replaced castrati in major opera seria roles when the fashions changed, and that replacement is the origin of some of the most well-known breeches roles. To some extent, this is true. The public did, and still do, want to hear the operas in which the original male parts were scored for castrati. The list of castrati roles now performed by women is long. They are mature, heroic roles, often involved in fighting for love or country. For this reason, the quality of the voice is important. It needs to be powerful, so female singers have the challenge of singing music that was not composed for their type of voice. One of the advantages of using castrati was the enormous breath control, which developed over long, strenuous hours of study. Long phrases, coloratura passages, and strength of voice were characteristics of a man's voice in the castrato condition. Yet castrati became scarce, and different choices had to be made. Countertenors, although their voices have strength, do not sound like castrati. Female voices can match their pitch but without the strength. So, staging some of these old operas requires a choice. If directors want the male roles played by men, they use countertenors or tenors; if they want to maintain the voice type, they choose cross-dressing.

However, not all mezzo-sopranos in male roles in eighteenth-century operas are merely substitutes. While many of the leading castrati parts were subsequently taken over by countertenors or by female voices, composers often wrote heroic male parts with vocal options, for either castrati, sopranos, or contraltos. Handel's *Radamisto*, first performed at the Kings Theatre London on April 27, 1720, had Margherita Durastanti, a soprano, as Radamisto, a male part that Handel scored alternatively for a soprano or an alto castrato voice. In a revised version on December 28 of the same year, the famous castrato Francesco Bernardi, stage name Senesino, took the title role, and Margherita played his wife Zenobia. Another male role in *Radamisto*, Tigrane, Prince of Pontus, was scored for either soprano or castrato and was played by a castrato at the first performances of both versions.

And then there was Mozart!

Wolfgang Amadeus Mozart's operas comprise twenty-two musical dramas in a variety of genres, and most of his mature works remain staples in all the world's opera houses. He too wrote for castrati. Idamantes in his early opera *Idomeneo* (January 1781) was originally scored for a soprano castrato or later a tenor. In modern performances of the work, the role can be sung by a tenor, but as a mezzo-soprano, it is equally successful. Sesto in Mozart's late opera *La clemenza di Tito* (which premiered in September 1791) was originally for the castrati voice but is now sung by a mezzo-soprano or a countertenor. Both these operas retain a reasonably high profile in the list of often performed pieces.

But perhaps his best-loved and intentionally breeches roles appear in his lighter operas. In the mid-1780s, Mozart and his most empathetic librettist Lorenzo di Ponte, wrote the opera-buffa *The Marriage of Figaro*, which premiered at the Burgtheater in Vienna on May 1, 1786. The role of Cherubino, the count's page, is a breeches role and sung by a soprano. Performed at its best, especially if the singer looks like the boy he is meant to be, the part is one of the most comic but also touching adolescent roles. It requires the singer to go through all the strong feelings of a boy growing up and trying to cope with his burgeoning sexuality. He has to be passionate and totally sincere in his love for any woman, but especially the countess, to appear truly embarrassed when teased by Susanna and Figaro, and also to seem genuinely scared of his master the count. He needs to wriggle and move like an adolescent boy who can't keep still, one who probably keeps the eighteenth-century equivalent of girlie magazines under his mattress.

> CHERUBINO: I no longer know what I am or what I'm doing,
> Now I'm burning, now I'm made of ice.
> Every woman makes me change colour, every woman makes me tremble. . . .
> I speak of love when I'm awake,
> I speak of it in my dreams. . . .
> And if I've none to hear me,
> I speak of it to myself.[2]

Figaro, the older man, teases him when the count attempts to get rid of him by sending him to be a soldier. Cherubino is devastated at being sent away.

> FIGARO: No more, you amorous butterfly,
> Will you go fluttering round by night and day,
> Disturbing the peace of every maid,
> You pocket Narcissus, you Adonis of love,[3]

Many fine singers have taken the role of Cherubino, but for me one of the most authentic portrayals was by Rinat Shaham in the Royal Opera House, London, production of 2006. Slight and boyish at that time, she conveys such adolescent male angst that it is difficult to believe she is a woman in her twenties. I can watch it over and over again. Young singers often cut their operatic teeth on such roles. Later, when their vocal ranges settle into their mature range, some to soprano voices, others to the lower mezzo-soprano, they move on to sing major roles. Now a fine mezzo-soprano, Rinat Shaham has acquired a reputation for her performances as a sensuous Carmen, a role she has sung in many of the world's opera houses.

Mozart was probably the first to recognize the erotic potential of the trouser role; previous casting of women as men had been predominantly in heroic roles in opera seria. He also added extra sexual comedy to the role of Cherubino by having Susanna and the countess dress the boy in women's clothes to hide him from the wrath of the count. Aspects of this role and that of Octavian in *Der Rosenkavalier* reflect Shakespeare's similar "double" cross-dressing roles such as Viola in *Twelfth Night* and Rosalind in *As You Like It* where boy actors in female roles were then asked to change into their "real" gender roles as disguise. Mozart used cross-dressing to develop the comedy in his *Cosi fan tutte* (1790) when Despina, the maid of Dorabella and Fiordiligi, dresses first as a doctor and then a notary to confuse the sisters.

The decision to compose a breeches role for an opera is taken at the com-position stage; although where the composer gives a choice of high voices, it will be a decision for the director. It is entirely due to the vocal range required by the piece. The operatic concept of the trouser or breeches role assumes that the character is male and that the audience accepts him as such even though they know that the actor is not. But where a character takes on male clothing for temporary disguise, this is not considered in opera as a breeches role. In contrast, a breeches role in non-musical plays is seen quite differently. In that case, the decision to use a female in a role written as male is taken at the production stage and for various reasons. In Restoration comedies, some such roles were played by women to draw attention to their physical attractions, the close-fitting breeches being thought erotic. However, serious characters, such as Shakespeare's Hamlet have often been played as breeches roles, the female actor fully accepted as the character she portrays. And unlike in opera, a breeches role in a dramatic play is usually one where a woman is pretending to be a man, usually temporarily, for disguise. Portia, dressing as a lawyer in *The Merchant of Venice*, would be typical of such a role.

In the early nineteenth century, mezzo-sopranos or sopranos increasingly took on lead heroic roles, rather than comedic ones, notably in Italian operas written by Gioachino Rossini and Vincenzo Bellini. Rossini, after a series of very successful comic operas, including *The Barber of Seville*, *La Cenerentola* (Cinderella), *Il Turco in Italia* and *The Italian Girl in Algiers*, began to write more serious works.

Tancredi is an opera seria or "heroic" opera in two acts by composer Gioachino Rossini and librettist Gaetano Rossi. Its first appearance was at the Teatro la Fenice in Venice on February 6, 1813. Set at a time of war between the Byzantine empire and the Saracens, the opera tells the story of the soldier Tancredi. He and his family have been stripped of their estates and inheritances, and he himself has been an exile since his youth. The opera begins with his return to Syracuse and goes on to examine the complications of his relationship with the supposedly unfaithful Amenaide. Originally having a happy ending with the lovers reunited, it was revised with an alternative ending, the Ferrara version, where the hero is fatally wounded and dies in Amenaide's arms.

The different endings were chosen in different productions. After initial enthusiasm for the work, it went out of favor; there was a performance in Bologna in 1833, and then it was not staged again for almost 120 years. The Ferrara ending was rediscovered in the mid-1970s and is the version most often used when the opera is performed now. The lead male role of Tancredi is played by a mezzo-soprano or contralto as a breeches role. His squire Roggiero is often a cross-dressing role, too, although it can be sung by a tenor. Disembarking from his ship to pledge his help to the city in defending it against the invaders, Tancredi sings the magnificent aria "Oh patria! dolce, e ingrate patria" (O my country, dear, thankless native land). The tune became a favorite of the Venetian gondoliers and was heard all along the canals of Venice until displaced as an earworm by *Donna e Mobile*, from Rigoletto in 1851.

Marilyn Horne, the wonderful American mezzo-soprano, had expressed interest in performing in the Ferrara version of *Tancredi* if it ever came to light. When it did reappear, she took on the title role at the Houston Grand Opera on October 13, 1977, and quickly became strongly associated with the role. She insisted on the tragic Ferrara ending, saying that she did not find the happy one convincing. Thanks to Horne's championing of the opera, it was very popular during the late part of the twentieth century.

It can help visually if the woman who takes the role of Tancredi has the figure to look convincing as an active fit young soldier, able to win the heart of Amenaide. Horne never really looked the part of Tancredi. Not all mezzo-sopranos playing the role do. But for those who love opera, it is the voice that matters. If there is a choice between a wonderful voice that is totally right for the singing role and a convincing figure, the voice wins out every time. Although opera audiences may prefer their singers to look the part rather than not, and costume armor often helps in heroic roles, they accept the plump middle-aged tenor playing the young lover, the mature soprano singing the songs of a lovelorn teenager, or the well-covered singer as a tubercular seamstress. They also accept a shapely, mature woman pretending to be the heroic male. I last saw *Tancredi* in a new staging of the opera in 2009 at the Teatro Regio di Torino. Daniela Barcelona sang the title role, and when Tancredi died on his shield at the end of the opera, there was no doubt among the audience that a heroic soldier had met his end.

Rossini's *Semiramide* is another opera seria that contains a great breeches role, Arsace. Like *Tancredi*, the opera was very popular in the early years after its composition but was almost unheard by the end of the 1800s. From the

1930s, it had intermittent performances, but it is estimated that between 1962 and 1990, seventy opera houses staged the work. The Met revived it in 1990 with Marilyn Horne as Arsace, the male lead although not the title role. In November 2017, the Royal Opera House, London, mounted its first production of the opera since the 1890s, with Joyce DiDonato in the title role and Daniela Barcellona, well known for playing travesti roles, as Arsace. Rossini originally created the role of Arsace to be sung by a contralto, the lowest range of the female voice. True contraltos are rare in opera today, however, but some mezzo-sopranos can use that lower range. The role of Arsace needs a powerful voice, and the best travestis of today can convince audiences that they are the long-lost sons and innamoratos of the queen, Semiramide. Of particular resonance, too, is Arsace's relationship with his rival for Princess Azema's affections, Assur, sung by a bass. Arsace comments on the difference between the feelings of a young and an older man from the arrogance of youth, "You have no idea what love is," the younger man tells the older (Aria/duet: "D'un tenero amor" / "That fierce heart of yours is not capable of tender love." It is unlikely that a singer young enough to really look like they could be the child of the lead actress can play Arsace. Indeed, when Horne played the role in the 1990s, she was old enough to be the mother of June Anderson, her Seriramide. But it doesn't matter. Joyce DiDonato and Daniela Barcellona are exactly the same age, and both sing in the mezzo-soprano range, but the different timbres of their voices are right for the parts they fill. We hear those splendid voices and accept their characters as who they are meant to be.

Rossini's near contemporaries Gaetano Donizetti (1797–1848) and Bellini (1801–1835) also wrote breeches roles, although most were sidekicks rather than heroes. Smeton in Donizetti's *Anna Bolena* (1830) is scored for a contralto as is Orsini in his *Lucretia Borgia*, first performed in 1833 in Milan. In the same year as *Anna Bolena*, Bellini's *I Capuleti e I Montecchi* was premiered in Venice with the twenty-four-year-old Giuditta Grisi in the breeches role of Romeo, perhaps one of the first roles where a mezzo-soprano was cast in a lead role as a young ardent lover rather than a predominantly military man.

In the nineteenth century, there was an explosion of operatic travesti roles written, particularly in France, for young, or at least youthful acting mezzo-sopranos and sopranos. With exceptions, particularly the boy Jemmy in *William Tell* (Rossini, Paris, 1829), which is a small but strong role, they are not usually given key roles but those of pages or lovesick adolescents. They were known for singing the beautiful arias that punctuated the performances. And such roles were often inserted into operas even if the story line did not warrant their inclusion. Ascanio, Cellini's apprentice in Berlioz's *Benvenuto Cellini* (premiered 1838) sings the aria "Mais qu'ai-je donc" (But what do I have). Siébel, a young lover, played by soprano or mezzo in Charles Gounod's *Faust*, has two individual arias, including the always enthusiastically received "Faites-tu mes aveux":

> Confess to her for me,
> Give her my wishes,
> Flowers who bloomed at her side,
> Tell her she is lovely.[4]

And it was Gounod, too, who wrote the lovely "Que fais-tu, blanche tour-terelle?" (What do you do, white dove?) for the invented role of Stephano, Romeo's page. In act 3 of the opera, he sings the aria to taunt the Capulets that their "white dove," Juliette, will marry a "pigeon," Romeo. Perhaps a more substantial role, although not one noted for arias, is the mezzo role of Nicklausse in Jacques Offenbach's *Tales of Hoffmann*, premiered in 1881. As the friend of Hoffmann, Nicklausse, although sometimes exasperated at Hoff-mann's behavior, protects him from others who could harm him. The scenes are played against an imaginary performance of *Don Giovanni*, Hoffmann being in love with the prima donna Stella, who is performing in the Italian opera. The role of Nicklausse can be seen as a parallel to that of Leporello, the servant of Don Giovanni. Although French opera composers tended to use breeches roles for minor parts, there were also some who wrote heroic male roles in comic operas. Prince Charming in Jules Massenet's *Cendrillon* is played by a woman in male clothes, very like the convention in pantomime. Massenet originally wrote the part for a "Falcon"[5] soprano, or *"soprano de sentiment,"* a rare voice type between the dramatic soprano and the mezzo-soprano, but when performed now, a lyric mezzo-soprano such as Alice Coote sings the role.

These roles and others are all breeches roles written by French composers to show off the high voices of women. But this didn't happen only in France. Giuseppe Verdi's *Un ballo in maschera* (The Masked Ball) received its premiere performance at the Teatro Apollo in Rome in 1859, and although it has a history of being beset by political censorship because of its setting and story line[6] and going through a number of major changes, it has become a staple of the repertoire and is now performed frequently. Although Verdi reputedly did not like trouser roles, he wrote the part of Oscar, Riccardo's young page, to be sung by a soprano. The singer has two arias, three duets, and thirteen ensembles in the opera. His aria in defense of Ulrica the fortune-teller, "Volta la Terrea," allows a lyric-coloratura soprano to show off her skills, and it is a well-loved highlight of the opera.

Unlike the French roles and Verdi's *Oscar*, the trouser roles in late nineteenth-century and early twentieth-century German opera are mainly those of children—limited although strong roles. Engelbert Humperdinck's *Hansel and Gretel* (1893) has one of the title roles, the boy Hansel, played by a mezzo. The schoolboy in Alban Berg's *Lulu* (premiered 1937) is also sung by a mezzo-soprano who in addition plays a theatrical dresser and a valet, as Berg requested. A child, too, figures in an opera by Maurice Ravel. In the early part of the twentieth century, the French composer wrote a strange opera, *L'enfant et les sortilèges*, which was first performed in Monte Carlo in 1925. It has a cast of humans, animals, plants, household furniture, and goods, played by singers across the vocal range, many with double or treble roles. The rude boy who is at first punished by all the objects and nonhuman characters and then forgiven is played by a mezzo-soprano.

Composers from other countries, too, have used cross-dressing roles in their operas. Leoš Janáček's bleak opera *From the House of the Dead*, which premiered in 1930, two years after the composer's death in Brno (former Czechoslovakia), has such a role. It has no main leads and instead tells the different stories of prisoners incarcerated in a Siberian prison. All the characters are male but just one; Aljeja, a young Tartar, is played by a mezzo-soprano. Ideally it requires both a good voice and acting skills to represent the pitiful situation of the young boy. He sees hope when he is taught to read by the aristocratic political prisoner Goryančikov. But while the nobleman is eventually freed, the child faces a bleak future of continuing imprisonment.

So, there are many genuine breeches roles in opera. But there are also other cross-dressing roles, those that require the female singer to disguise herself as a man for at least part of the story. Such roles are rare, but there are a few. In Handel's *Alcina*, which has had a revival in recent years, Bradamante disguises herself as her own brother to rescue her betrothed, Ruggiero, from a variety of strange and difficult situations caused by the sorceress Alcina. She spends most of the opera in armor pretending to be a man. Another disguise role more often seen is that of Gilda in Verdi's *Rigoletto*. To remove her from Florence and the clutches of the immoral Duke whom she loves, her father Rigoletto orders her to dress as a young man to protect herself as she travels. She listens at the door of the assassin Sparafucile, the man her father has paid to kill the Duke. Overhearing him agree with his sister, who has fallen for the Duke, to kill the next person who knocks at the door instead, she sacrifices herself to save her lover. So not a very good outcome for the disguise, then. But Gilda never really masquerades as a man. She is merely mistaken for one.

A much stronger cross-dressing disguise role is in Ludwig van Beethoven's only opera, *Fidelio*. Premiered in Vienna in 1805, it was shortened and then changed; the final version, which is most often seen today, had its first performance at the Kärntnertortheater in Vienna on May 23, 1814. By convention, only this version is called *Fidelio*; the first two go under the name of *Leonora*. In this final, most performed version, the heroine, Leonora, feels that her missing husband Florestan is still alive and remains in the notorious state prison of Seville, Spain. The governor of the prison had seized him two years previously in revenge when the young nobleman exposed his wrongdoing. Florestan is kept in chains in the prison's most secret dungeon. Already when the opera begins Leonora is masquerading as a man as the assistant to the chief jailer, whose daughter has fallen in love with "him" and is planning a married life. The mezzo-soprano in the main role is in ordinary workman's clothes throughout the opera; there is no heroic armor to hide behind, and we never see her in women's clothes. She must exhibit male characteristics—the walk and the physical strength of a young man (carrying heavy chains)—and an appearance that, although the viewers are fully aware that she is a woman, must be sufficiently credible for an audience to believe that the jailer's daughter loves "him." There are some excellent Leonoras, but also unconvincing ones that visually, usually because of their womanly figures, are unable to look the part. But we can shut our eyes and enjoy the singing.

But the men? Don't they get the chance to cross-dress in opera? Very, very rarely. And usually only as disguise. In *The Comte Ory*, Rossini's comic and very funny opera set at the time of the Crusades, both the lead tenor and the men of the chorus disguise themselves as a group of female pilgrims or nuns needing shelter from the storm. The Comte, as Sister Colette, plans to gain access to the castle and to seduce the Countess. The plan starts to work, as the hospitable Countess, seeing the group of peculiar looking women led by "Sister Colette," thinks that she should be particularly charitable and takes pity on them. She is somewhat taken aback by the unusual behavior of her chief guest. The sleeve-note from a Glyndebourne recording sums up how the character Ory is best played to release the true humor. "The mother superior comes to express her gratitude which she does in an unexpectedly pressing manner, which smacks more of the codpiece than the convent."[7] The group of nuns presents a most unconvincing rabble. One of the Comte's men, Rimbaud, finds the key to the cellar, and the group gets increasingly drunk. Eventually the Comte is revealed as a man and escapes. Done well, the comedy is a delight.

Perhaps less well known than other examples of cross-dressing in opera, the baroque opera *Les Indes gallantes* by Jean Philippe Rameau (premiered 1735) has disguise roles. The third entrée, "Les Fleurs," has one of the male characters, Prince Tacmas, dress (originally) as a merchant woman, so that he can access the harem and test Zaire's feeling for him. Fatima, the slave of his favorite, Ali, dresses as a man. All four parts in the piece were originally sung in high registers: Tacmas by a haute-contre, an unusually high tenor, and the others by sopranos. But in recent performances, the male parts have been sung in lower registers, and thus the cross-dressing appears as true drag. A revolutionary new production by the Paris Opera in 2019, which challenges the underlying racial stereotyping and colonialism of the plot, has Krump street dance at center stage. In this version of "Les Fleurs," one male character, a tenor, is in drag disguised as a brothel worker while the female cross-dresser is androgynous.

It might be expected that if women sopranos and mezzo-sopranos can successfully take male roles in opera, that some female roles might be played by high-voiced men, the countertenors. Perhaps the difference in physical characteristics is the reason that most composers have not gone down this route. In opera, while a woman's physical form can often be accepted as male for operatic purposes, the reverse does not seem to be true. Countertenors almost exclusively play male roles or nonhumans. But in the main, when men dress as women, as in *Le Comte Ory*, they are seen as comic characters. For instance, since the first performance of Henry Purcell's *Dido and Aeneas* (1869), the witches have at times been sung for comic effect by falsetto countertenors, as in the recording of René Jacobs's Age of Enlightenment[8] version with Dominique Visse and Stephen Wallace playing the parts. Of course, as this is a recording and not a staged performance, the witches are not appearing in women's clothes. Nevertheless, Elizabeth Holland[9] argues that Nahum Tate, the librettist of the opera meant the witches to be more malevolent than comic, and thus they are usually mezzo-sopranos. She argues that had the composer and librettist wanted comic witches, they would have used the old tradition of countertenors in drag rather than designate them as mezzo-sopranos. They would have written the parts in a range for such voices. In the same opera, there are other examples of possible cross-dressing. The Sorceress can be sung as a mezzo, a contralto, a countertenor, or even a bass, and the gender of the role can be retermed as a sorcerer. And in 1989, a version of the opera adapted to modern dance premiered at the Théâtre Varia in Brussels with choreographer Mark Morris dancing both the female roles of Dido, the Queen of Carthage, and the Sorceress. This version has been performed many times and was filmed in 1995. Each character is portrayed by a dancer on stage and also by a singer offstage or in the orchestra pit.

A true travesti singing role for a countertenor exists in *Phaedra*, a concert opera by Hans Werner Henze, which was first performed at the Berlin State Opera in 2007. The Goddess Artemis, who brings the fatally wounded Hippolytus back to life, is a countertenor role. Though it is a travesti role, however, it cannot be said to be cross-dressing. Unless the director of the piece requires it, the singer does not have to dress up on stage for this concert opera. But despite a significant growth of interest in the countertenor voice since the twentieth century, there are few newer roles for that voice register that involve cross-dressing.

John Lunn's modern chamber opera *The Maids* was premiered by the Royal Opera of Stockholm in 1994. Based on a play by Jean Genet, *Les Bonnes*, it outlines the sad lives of two maids, Claire and Solange. Powerless in their lives, they take it in turns to play Madame, their employer, replacing their drab uniforms with Madame's finery. It ends tragically as Solange drinks the poison intended for Madame. Genet intended his play to be cast with young men playing women; however, Genet's wishes were not met in early productions of the play nor of the opera. In Stockholm, three women sang the main roles: Anna Eklund-Tarantino (soprano) was Claire, Eva Pilat (mezzo-soprano) played Solange, and Gunilla Söderström (mezzo) was Madame. However, later productions of both play and opera have been gender fluid. In a 1998 English version of the opera at the Lyric Hammersmith, the maids of the title were sung by brothers. Although Christopher Robson (Claire) is a countertenor, Nigel Robson who played Solange has the lower voice of a tenor. Both cross-dressed for their roles.

And what about true travesti roles for men singing female roles in the much lower voice registers? There aren't many as yet. But in the same way that theatrical directors have explored the possibilities of cross-gender or gender-blind casting, some directors of opera have done the same. Famous actors have taken to the stage with great success to play Lady Bracknell in Oscar Wilde's play *The Importance of Being Earnest*, notably Brian Bedford in Stratford, Ontario, in 2009 (he received a Tony nomination for the role in 2011); Stephen Fry at the Theatre Royal Drury Lane in 2014; and David Suchet at the Vaudeville Theatre in 2015. These of course were speaking roles. But in 2013, at the Opera national de Lorraine bass Alan Ewing sang the cross-dressed role of Lady Bracknell in the first fully staged performance of Gerald

Barry's opera based on the play. Concert versions of the opera had taken place in 2011 and 2012. Barry cut a great deal of the play script, although he retained the famous line "A handbag!" and emphasized the references to food, particularly Lady Bracknell's cucumber sandwiches. Smashed plates and marching boots form part of the score. Although the actor Stephen Fry, himself a Lady Bracknell on stage, commented that making an opera setting of Wilde's play was like "taking a machete to a soufflé," critical reception of the opera has been generally very positive. The *Los Angeles Times* wrote of the staged premiere, "The world now has something rare: a new genuinely comic opera and maybe the most inventive."[10]

In the current canon of opera, there are far more opportunities for women to cross-dress than for men. Unlike some other genres of the performing arts, the voice type and the balance of voices are of key importance in any production. As long as our development as human sexual beings affects the type of voice we have, tenors, countertenors, baritones, and basses will continue to sing the great majority of the male roles, certainly in traditional operas. But there are exceptions. Lucia Lucas is an American transgender baritone. In March 2018, she made history as the first female (transgender) baritone by singing the title role in *Don Giovanni* with the Tulsa Opera. The following year she played Public Opinion in *Orpheus in the Underworld* at the London Coliseum. Although the role is often played by a mezzo-soprano, she sang it as a baritone. Director Emma Rice's highly reworked story line did not suit all critics, but much of the singing was praised. The *Stage's* opera reviewer wrote, "Lucia Lucas fields a sterling baritone as Public Opinion—here an affable London cabbie with a somewhat improbable accent."[11] And Norwegian mezzo-soprano Adrian Angelico transitioned in 2016 but did not take testosterone because it would affect his voice. He specializes in trouser roles, male roles requiring a soprano or falsetto voice, but he also accepts female mezzo-soprano roles, which he plays in drag.

Things are obviously changing, even in much loved pieces that are staples of the operatic world. In seventy years, there have been six productions and 347 performances of Mozart's *The Marriage of Figaro* at the Royal Opera House, Covent Garden, London. But on June 29, 2019, there was a new experience for the audience. Cherubino, the desperately loved-up adolescent page boy, was played by a man. The role is almost always sung by a mezzo-soprano or soprano passing themselves off as a man, and Korean American countertenor Kangmin Justin Kim made Covent Garden history when he played Cherubino in a revival of the opera by David McVicar. Sir John Eliot Gardner who conducted had argued for Kim to play the part. He said that the current debates over gender politics gave the casting an interesting topicality. "I think this is a rather intriguing turning point," he said.[12]

Composers, librettists, and opera directors are imaginative and innovative. It is likely that in the interests of production freshness, gender equality, and the move toward more gender-neutral casting, they, like their counterparts in all other genres of the performing arts, will continue to experiment. They will try out different voices in old parts and create new roles for the great opera singers of the future.

6

LEAPING THE DIVIDE— CROSS-DRESSING IN DANCE

Then there are the fearless multiple revolutions to pirouettes, 32 fouettés, more turns, more jumps—sometimes finishing having done the original choreography straight but adding double tours en l'air. Wowza!

—DEAN SPEER, DANCER AND JOURNALIST[1]

As though flying, muscular male dancers in feathered britches with bared chests and black face markings leap from the wings. Hissing aggressively, these swans protect their patch against the interloper prince. The audience is taken aback; any vocal sound from dancers is a rarity in ballet. When Matthew Bourne's ballet *Swan Lake* burst on to the stage at Sadler's Well in 1995, it changed forever the way we viewed the story and, in particular, the swans. Bourne shifted the focus of Tchaikovsky's well-loved ballet, a staple of any ballet company, away from the swan queen, Ondine, to the prince. Although the theme of doomed, forbidden love is at the heart of both the traditional story and of Bourne's, in his version it is the Prince who is in mental distress and seeks love. And unlike the original, where the mortal is unfaithful to the nymph, in Bourne's ballet it is the Swan who betrays the mortal Prince with the Stranger and causes his death. The emphasis of the ballet is changed too by having a man in the role of lead swan. Repressed gay love and desire are much in evidence, especially in the sensual pas de deux between the Prince and the Swan in act 2. Bourne said that it made complete sense to him to have men as swans as the strength and enormous wingspan suggested a male musculature to him. Anyone who has seen swans protecting their young would agree with him. Wings out, neck fully stretched and hissing, they are powerful and frightening. In no way do they bring to mind the traditional presentation of swans in the classical version of *Swan Lake*: a corps de ballet of slim ballerinas in white tutus. Of course, Matthew Bourne's swans are not cross-dressing. Even though the roles are usually played by women, there is nothing about his swans that suggest they are female. And strictly speaking the term *cross-dressing* is usually applied to humans choosing to represent another gender, and not to creatures. But this shift toward using men in traditional women's roles in classical ballet was a surprise in 1995. And it illustrated how few true cross-dressing roles there are in traditional dance pieces.

Like opera roles, but unlike many in the theater, the physiological differences between those born with male or female sexuality affect how dancers can be cast. In opera, composers have to decide how they want the voice to sound. If the voice best thought to suit the opera and be appreciated by the audience is one in a high vocal range, then a countertenor, mezzo, or soprano will be cast, whatever the gender of the character. In dance, too, there are physiological factors to consider. If the role requires the dancer to lift, then a dancer with strong musculature is needed. If the part is that of someone who has to be lifted, then a female is the norm, although pieces with male pas de deux are possible and increasingly familiar.

Most of the few cross-dressing roles in traditional ballet, like most gender-swap roles in other performance genres, are those of comic characters. *En travestie*, the term used for cross-dressing in ballet, is most usually associated with burlesque and parody and mostly with male dancers dressing as women. If asked to name the best known of such comedy roles, most ballet fans I suspect would cite the Widow Simone in Frederick Ashton's version of *La fille mal gardé* (1959). The role is traditionally played by a man in an outfit bordering on the pantomime dame. The clog dance, in which the Widow dances with the girls celebrating the harvest, is a comic highlight of the show.

Travesti roles are key to modern versions of *Cinderella*. There were ballet versions of the story before the Bolshoi's production of *Cinderella*, but that 1945 production is seen as the first of note. However, it is Frederick Ashton's version that has two fine comedic travesti roles. Other choreographers often use a male dancer in the role of the wicked stepmother, but Ashton dispensed with the stepmother altogether and featured the two ugly sisters in travesti. In true British pantomime tradition, they are grotesquely made up and wear outrageous clothes, in sharp contrast to the ragged servant Cinderella who is transformed into the beautifully dressed princess for the ball. The parts of the sisters were danced originally by Robert Helpmann and Ashton himself. And as if two "pantomime dames" aren't enough, other versions of the ballet, for instance, that by Les Grands Ballets Canadiens de Montreal in 2003, have three cross-dressing roles: the wicked stepmother as well as the two sisters. Although David Bintley had danced an ugly sister in Ashton's version of *Cinderella*, his idea of the sisters was quite different when he himself choreographed the ballet. His *Cinderella* for the Birmingham Royal Ballet returned to the original idea of the sisters being ugly on the inside, rather than on the outside. It is interesting to see the sisters not as the stereotyped pantomime grotesques often seen in both the theater and ballet versions of the story. Rather they are real young women relating to a sister they despise and to each other's differing personalities, alternately at odds with each other and supportive siblings. Bintley gives female dancers the choreographed steps to play the sisters as very funny comedy roles. The wicked stepmother is an elegant imperious "baddie," danced by a female dancer.

Unlike the comedy roles in *Cinderella*, the role of Old Madge, the witch in August Bournonville's *La Sylphide* (premiered in 1836) is a serious role. Based on the original libretto, with music by Herman Severin Løvenskiold, this version of the story has been danced in its original form by the Royal Danish Ballet ever since its creation. The story centers on a young Scot, James

Ruben, who is about to be married but is attracted to a nymph, a forest spirit, who dances around him as he sleeps and kisses him before disappearing. Old Madge, an old witch who is warming herself by the kitchen fire, is a feared, strange character. Effie (James's bride to be) and her bridesmaids ask her to tell their fortunes, and she gleefully says that James loves someone else and will never marry Effie. James throws the witch out of the house. Old Madge retreats to the forest where a *Macbeth*-style scene shows the witch and her companions dancing satanically around a cauldron. The witch's predictions come to pass as Effie accepts the proposal of the faithful Gum and the Sylph dies in the arms of James. In other versions of *La Sylphide*, Madge is a part danced by either a male or female dancer depending on the choice of the director, and it can be a wonderful cross-dressing part for a male dancer. Swathed in voluminous drapes and a cloak and her face made up as a caricature witch, she holds the attention of the audience from the moment she appears. In more recent productions—for the English National Ballet and Boston Ballet, for instance—the role is danced in a more nuanced way by a female dancer who tries to communicate her character as more than just an evil presence. And in the Scottish Ballet's version of Matthew Bourne's *Highland Fling*, Bournonville's witch Old Madge becomes a female role, a drug-dealing tarot reader who pushes James toward the Sylph, away from the much more wholesome Effie.

Fairy tales, which show how the good triumph over the wicked, often provide the potential for caricature parts. Carabosse, the evil fairy in *The Sleeping Beauty* (1890) can be danced by a male dancer. This part, too, is not comedic, and it is interesting to note that most Carabosses in modern productions of the ballet are female dancers who play the role as a commanding, frightening figure. But the first Carabosse was a man, Enrico Cecchetti, a famous Italian dancer and coach. Born in a dressing room of the Tordinona Theatre, Rome, in 1850, to parents who were also dancers, he joined the ballet at the Marinsky Theatre in St. Petersburg in 1887 as a principal dancer. Through his teaching at the Russian Ballet School, he developed many young dancers, including Anna Pavlova who exemplified the impeccable Russian Cecchetti technique. Particularly, he worked tirelessly to change the nature of Russian ballet, especially by expanding the male technique, and by championing the creation of more male roles to counteract the many that had been relegated to servants who merely partnered a ballerina.

Traditionally, male dancers do not dance on points whereas ballerinas do. Consequently, if the choreographer requires the dancers to dance on points, the role is usually danced by female dancers. Points are part of the classical training of female dancers, but not usually male. Specially designed shoes stiffened with glue allow the dancers to balance their entire body weight on a small flat surface. There is no reason why men cannot dance on points. They just need larger shoes. And some modern choreographers have put male characters *sur les pointes* to comic effect, for example, Bottom in Frederick Ashton's *Midsummer Night's Dream* (although his is not a cross-dressing role). Yet one dance company, now firmly in the mainstream of dance entertainment, has turned the idea that "points are for the girls" on its head.

Les Ballets Trockadero de Monte Carlo has a whole troupe of dancers able to play both male and female roles equally, and many can dance *en pointe*. The Trocks, as they are affectionately known, are an all-male drag ballet troupe that parodies romantic and classical ballets but still takes the art of dance seriously. Founded in 1974 by three dancers who had belonged to the Trockadero Gloxinia Ballet Company, which performed in an experimental club in Manhattan, they soon started to be noticed by critics. A favorable review in the *New Yorker* led to their discovery by a wider audience, and since the mid-1970s, the Trocks have toured the world with great success. All the members of the troupe are technically accomplished dancers. They perform excerpts from classical ballet with a comic twist; the Dying Swan from *Swan*

Lake in which the dancer's feathered costume molts, scattering feathers all over the stage, is a particular treat to watch. They also perform other ballets; some are well known and others are pieces that have been created for them. Many of the dancers take on both male and female roles and adopt comic long Russian-sounding names for each persona. Robert Carter, who joined the troupe as long ago as 1995, is Olga Supphozova when *en pointe* and Yuri Smirnov as a male dancer. Philip Martin-Nielson is Nadia Doumiafeyva and also Kravlji Snepek; and Roberto Vega, who joined in 2017, is both Ludmila Beaulemova and Mikhail Mypansarov.

Although the Trocks poke fun at ballet's seriousness with mobile face expressions and intentional faux pas, they never criticize the art form itself. Jack Furlong, who joined in 2014, explained that the Trocks sought to strike the balance.[2] He remembered that the first time they danced excerpts from *Napoli*, a ballet created by Bournonville for the Royal Danish Ballet in 1842, they were coached by Karina Elver from the Danish company. The dancers needed to adopt an authentic Danish style that emphasizes lowered arm movements and effortless-looking footwork. They also had to avoid the mobile facial expressions they used in other pieces. Serious concentration was required. The group is amusing to watch. They are all experienced dancers who respect the tradition they come from. Writer Dean Speer, himself a dancer, and an authoritative commentator on ballet, has great respect for them.

> If you want to see some really good dancing, go and see *The Trocks*, comedy and all. Even with the spoofery, the dancing remained superb and was often spot-on, both in terms of technique and style. Perhaps without realizing it they've created something quite extraordinary—not just well-trained male dancers doing both male and female parts of ballets but when the males do the female parts, they inject such a level of strength and degree of attack and control that may be well out of the reach of the female set.

Speer goes on to describe the technique of one of the dancers in the romantic ballet *Paquita* (Opera de Paris, 1846):

> *Nina Enimenimynimova (Long Zou) was letter-perfect in "her" Paquita lead ballet variation. I know how hard (and fun) Paquita can be. . . . Superb technique, finish and line. And then for the coda's requisite 32 fou-ettes, she began with 4 turns from fourth position and then, up to number 16, alternated with doubles and then singles through 32. The only hee-hee being that she "high-fived" one of the corps members as she ran off stage.*[3]

The Trocks may not be for the classical ballet purists but they are dancers who take their art seriously. Tory Dobrin, the artistic director and one-time Trock feels that the troupe have established their street cred with the traditionalists, "and for those who don't know much about ballet, we're a good introduction. Still, we're a niche—all-male comedy ballet—and we intend to keep going as long as we can."[4]

A very different dance style than classical ballet—and with no reliance on points or lifts—is the dance style developed by American Martha Graham, often termed the Mother of Modern Dance. Born in 1894 and living for practically the whole of the twentieth century, she was both a dancer and choreographer. The Graham technique reshaped American dance and is still taught worldwide. Graham proved to be a major agent of change; her influence on dance in the twentieth century was immense and has been compared with that of Pablo Picasso on the visual arts, Igor Stravinsky on music, and Frank Lloyd Wright on architecture. Graham wanted to make dance an art form that reflected the rawness of the human experience and not just a form of entertainment. Stripping away the more decorative movements of ballet, she concentrated more on the foundational aspects of movement. Her style emphasized the weightiness and groundedness of the human body in direct opposition to classical ballet techniques, which typically try to create an illusion of weightlessness.

Martha Graham's dancing has been well described and documented, and the woman herself was a recognizable character; however, it is almost impossible to know exactly how Martha Graham moved on stage. She resisted the recording of her dances, claiming that live performances should only exist on stage as they are experienced in the moment. Perhaps, then, it is even more surprising that Richard Move, a present-day choreographer, should choose to cross-dress and impersonate Martha so successfully in his stage performances. Dressed in Graham's iconic loose costumes, he talks to the audience about Martha Graham and dances short, reconstructed versions of her epic ballets. Selby Schwartz describes the impact of his performance:[5]

> *Martha Graham is instantly recognizable: the high dark bun piled up on her head, the severity with which she holds her shoulders, and that throaty, semi-divine voice pronouncing its truths. . . . Only Martha Graham could reign upon the stage like this.*
>
> *However, Martha Graham hasn't performed since 1969—she died in 1991. The figure onstage is 6'4", a good 16 inches taller that Martha Graham ever was. And when the famous purple-gray costume of Lamentation stretches over her body, you see that this dancer, this self-proclaimed realist, is not the woman she says she is. She is more Martha than Martha. She may be a dancer and a realist, but she is also a man.*

Dance critic Deborah Jowett describes Move's work as "not so much a travesty as a sincere imitation based on considerable knowledge and research. . . . And comical." A flavor of this comedy is Move speaking directly to the audience about a critic reviewing one of her (Martha Graham's) performances. "When I premiered the dance Lamentation. . . . A prominent critic wrote that I looked like I was about to give birth. . . . To a CUBE!"[6]

Move and others in a small group of contemporary performers use drag in the context of dance to explore the nature of performing itself, says Schwartz. They dream up an identity for the body that stretches its physical and visible limits. Move says that drag can be the most welcoming kind of thing for people like him "where real identity politics manifest in brutal ways." Martha Graham is not his only cross-dressing role but is probably the most admired. Commenting on one of his performances, *Cave of the Heart*, one of Graham's signature pieces that is based on *Medea*, Move reminds us that "people have forgotten that this comes from ancient theatre."[7]

Audiences in classical Greek theater would have expected Medea to be a man in drag; Martha's idea of performing Medea herself would have been shocking then, whereas Richard Move's interpretation would have been perfectly "straight." Watching Move portray Martha Graham in his version of "*Martha—the 1963 Interview*," when she was interviewed by Walter Terry,[8] reviewer Catherine Bravo marveled at the impersonation, "I would have easily presumed Graham's distinct style of speaking to be incapable of being mimicked and impersonated. Her intricate explanations, her rhythmic, poetic choice of words, and her capacity for seemingly going off on tangents are unique and true to her."[9]

Move's performance, which is definitely meant to be funny, is also realistic. In the same way as Les Ballets de Trockadero performances, it represents the type of cross-dressing that is somewhere between "straight" drag in dance, where roles are cast to another gender, and the obviously parodic. In the Paris Opera Ballet in the early nineteenth century, for instance, male patrons insisted that male roles be danced by women who wore fitting costumes and would show off their legs in tights. Old Madge, too, when portrayed by a man, is a "straight" cross-dressing role. The audience is expected to suspend belief. And it is worth noting that actor Lisa Kron, who cross-dressed to play Walter Terry to Richard Move's Graham in their staged version of the 1963 interview gave an excellent straight portrayal. Male dancers as the Ugly Sisters in *Cinderella* are parodic cross-dressing roles. We are expected to be amused at men dressing up as women and are in no way confused. Richard Move and other dancers like him use cross-dressing in the medium of dance to explore the body and its capabilities. They use the inherent strengths of male sexuality while using comedy to point up assumed gender differences.

Since the emergence of modern dance in the early twentieth century and into more recent times, the need to emphasize gender in dance has slowly declined. The change from classical dance is sometimes considered to have emerged as a rejection of, or rebellion against, classical ballet, although his-torians have suggested many other factors, including industrialization and the loosening of social constraints, which led to an interest in more physical fitness. All through the twentieth century, choreographers and dance teachers developed a range of styles that have fused and changed. Modern dance has evolved with each subsequent generation of participating artists. Artistic con-tent, too, has morphed and shifted from one choreographer to another. Of course, dancing continues to be a wide-ranging medium. Audiences continue to enjoy *The Nutcracker,* but Tango, break-dancing, hip-hop, and salsa are just some of the types of dancing that can be seen not only in their "pure" form but also as influences on contemporary dance. Many pieces in modern dance do not tell a conventional story based on myths, fables, or folk stories, as tra-ditional ballet often did; they attempt instead to convey to the audience the feelings of the dancer. According to Treva Bedinghaus, a dancer and writer interested in all aspects of dance, "Modern dancers use dancing to express their innermost emotions, often to get closer to their inner-selves. Before attempting to choreograph a routine, the modern dancer decides which emo-tions to try to convey to the audience. Many modern dancers choose a sub-ject near and dear to their hearts, such as a lost love or a personal failure. The dancer will choose music that relates to the story they wish to tell, or choose to use no music at all, and then choose a costume to reflect their chosen emotions."[10] Cross-dressing can be less relevant as dancers—of whatever gender—use their bodies to express whatever the choreographer intends. Of course, choreographers are aware of the differences between male and female physicality when creating their pieces, and this usually dictates who dances the parts, but some roles do allow a choice to be made between a male or female dancer.

Anne Teresa De Keersmaeker's three works set to scores by Béla Bartók, Beethoven, and Arnold Schoenberg are all constructed around the relationship of movement to music. Although created in the 1980s and 1990s, they were first performed at the Palais Garnier in 2016. The first work, *Bartok's Quatuor No. 4*, a joyful, fun piece, is all female. Four dancers synchronize their movements, jumping and clicking their heels, in places rather reminiscent of clog-dancing. Otherwise dressed all in black, they bend and jump to show their white-knickered bottoms to the audience. The second piece, *Verklarte Nacht* (Transfigured Night), danced to music by Schoenberg with six female and four male dancers, tells the romantic story (originally a poem by Richard Dehmel) of a woman walking through a dark forest on a moonlit night with her new lover and explaining to him that she is expecting the child of another man. The lover happily and forgivingly accepts the situation. As you would expect from their subjects, De Keersmaeker's first two pieces are very gender specific; however, in the Palais Garnier's production of the third of the trio, the all-male piece set to the music of Beethoven's *Dei Grosse Fuge* was not, this time, all-male. One woman, Alice Renavand, joined the seven men in their eighteen minutes of moving, pounding acrobatic steps with the dancers leaping high and then banging down to roll on the floor. Cross-dressing in the same dark suit and white crumpled shirt as the men, she was a full participant in all the dance. Apart from being obviously much smaller and slimmer than her colleagues, there was nothing that separated her from them. I admired the whole performance. But such cross-dressing can still be contentious or at least puzzling to some critics. Reviewer Patricia Boccadoro could not see the point of including her in the dance: "The resulting work was excellently danced by seven men, and by one woman, but why Alice Renavand was present, dressed as a man, was hard to understand."[11] And perhaps that comment gets to the heart of cross-dressing in dance. Were we expected to see Alice Renavand as a man and not notice her different stature? Was she masquerading as a man by cross-dressing? If so, the work would remain an all-male piece, differentiated from the two previous works in the set, the first definitely all-female, and the second strongly heterosexual. Or was she just a good dancer with the skills to dance the work well? If gender wasn't the issue, then the suit and shirt she wore could be seen merely as the costume that all the dancers wore for the dance and not cross-dressing to impersonate a man. If the dancers had been dressed in gender-neutral jeans and T-shirts, would it have been seen differently?

Cross-dressing in dance is not common. It is used for comedy in some classical works, and some choreographers choose to use male dancers to portray women, usually in old or character parts. There is little evidence of women dancing roles usually danced by men, except in all-female dance groups. The days of female dancers donning tights to titillate the men flocking to the Paris Opera in the mid-1800s are, thankfully, behind us. The Trockaderos and other groups like them, challenge gender stereotypes and show how male physicality can add a different dimension to roles usually danced by "ballerinas." They happily mix quality performance with comedy. And the type of dancing pioneered by Martha Graham is imitated faithfully by Richard Move.

It is unlikely, however, that the traditions of classical dance with clear roles for male and female dancers will change any time soon. But perhaps there is a slow move by modern choreographers and directors to look at traditional works in a new light. Matthew Bourne's *Swan Lake* changed the emphasis in the ballet from heterosexual love to homosexual, thereby changing the way in which traditional roles were danced. And particularly in works that are more abstract rather than representational, there are moves toward gender-blind casting. Perhaps in the future, the fact that Alice Renavand danced the same dance steps alongside seven male dancers will not be worthy of comment—except to admire the dancing.

7

MUSIC HALL AND VAUDEVILLE

My heart is fairly melting at the thought of Julian Eltinge;

His versa, Vesta Tilley, too.

Our language is so dexterous, let us call them ambi-sexterous;

Why hasn't this occurred before to you?

—DOROTHY PARKER[1]

The orchestra strikes up. There is an expectant flutter of sound throughout the audience. A pause. This artiste likes to raise expectations. The orchestra starts up again. This time, a young man in an immaculate seaside dandy outfit strolls in from the wings. He stands in the center of the stage and observes the audience quizzically through a monocle; the perfect picture of a young man about town out for a stroll in the seaside sun. There is a ripple of whispered conversation from the auditorium. Isn't there a rather curvy shape to the waist? Aren't the hips unusually rounded? The young man begins to tell the audience about Bertie, the young clerk from a London office who for one week of the year comes down to Brighton and masquerades as a "swell."

Burlington Bertie's the latest young jay

He rents a small flat somewhere Kensington way

He spends the good oof that his pater has made

Along with the Brandy and Soda Brigade.[2]

This is no young man; this is Vesta Tilley, famous for more than thirty years in both Britain and the United States, particularly for impersonating a man on stage. Perhaps unique among other male impersonators, she was able both to parody and mock the state of maleness in roles ranging from the comedic to the patriotic to the sentimental, from small boy to soldier, from young men behaving badly to pantomime Principal Boy. Both men and women loved her.

Although one of the most successful female music hall stars ever, she was not alone in choosing to impersonate the opposite sex. The late part of the nineteenth and the early twentieth centuries saw the heyday of both male and female impersonators, mostly found on the stages of the British music hall and American vaudeville theaters and later in the variety theaters and Follies. Unlike the travesti roles and disguises of legitimate theater and opera, such impersonators were acts; they performed on stage in routines that emphasized their cross-dressing. Audiences were in collusion with the performers and expected to be amazed, admiring or sometimes amused at the way in which biological males and females represented another gender. Although on both sides of the Atlantic, it was both culturally and sometimes legally unaccept-able for women to don trousers or for men to wear frocks in public, stage acts showing such subversion were highly popular. By the turn of the twentieth century, British music hall and vaudeville had a similar range of such acts. Indeed, many famous stars from Europe, and particularly Britain, traveled freely to perform on American vaudeville circuits. Famous American per-formers crossed the Atlantic in the other direction to be welcomed in London and on tours of the provinces.

The reasons that individual performers chose to be impersonators were complex and different, as were the outcomes for performers and their audi-ences. But although such choices were to some extent dependent on personal circumstances and the cultural context at the time, the different ways in which music hall and vaudeville developed also strongly affected the type of acts that were appreciated by audiences. Music hall and vaudeville had different roots, and this too determined the origin of both male and female impersonator acts and their success. Additionally, the music hall and vaudeville in turn affected how society regarded gender. It is probably true to say that the seeds of female emancipation and of a more open gay culture were partly sown in music hall and vaudeville even though both needed years of nurture in other aspects of life before they flourished.

The origins of British music hall are firmly rooted in the working class. With the Industrial Revolution, people flooded into the towns and cities to work, and after a hard day's work in factories, warehouses, and markets, they wanted entertainment. The "penny gaffs" sprang up, often just basic spaces in the back rooms or basements of public houses. They were rough. Entrance was just one penny, and any entertainment was really just an opportunity for the landlord to sell more drink. Clowning, dancing, singing, and plays were popular, and the plays often featured gory murders or mangled Shakespeare. Soon slightly more salubrious venues, drinking establishments for men, began to provide musical clubs on a Saturday night to accompany the food and drink. As these became more popular, landlords attached a room to their taverns so that they could provide entertainment two or three times a week. Supper rooms, slightly more refined, but only slightly, and aimed at the middle classes, opened from the 1830s. Such venues were hard places in which to perform. The audience, all male, would talk all the time, and if they didn't like an act, they would throw anything to hand—bottles, shoes, and even dead cats. They wanted raunchy and preferably obscene acts. Performers came from the same working classes as most of their clientele, and a few women singers and comedians took up the opportunity to earn alongside men. But, in this early part of the century, the audiences were still men, and most women in the room who weren't on the stage were likely to be prostitutes.

The explosion of demand for entertainment by the 1850s led to changes in the way that acts were presented and to the building of glamorous purpose-built theaters. The introduction of gaslight meant safer streets and the opportunity to light stages and auditoriums to show off performances. In 1849, Charles Morton and Frederick Stanley, his brother-in-law, purchased the Canterbury Arms, in Lambeth, south London, and Morton decided to offer music, singing, and sketches on Saturdays in the back room. Soon, Morton added a Thursday evening program to accommodate the crowds, and he decided to admit women, giving the venue wider appeal than the old-time song and supper rooms, which were male preserves. This format was so successful that he was eventually able to build the much larger New Canterbury Music Hall accommodating 1,500, which opened in 1856. This hall was lavishly decorated with fine ceilings, chandeliers, and a carpet, providing a taste of luxury for those who would never be able to afford it themselves. The number of music halls grew in London; more opened in towns throughout Britain. Until the 1880s, they were patronized by the working classes, tradesmen, clerks, and the occasional upper-class "johnny" looking for a frisson of excitement by roughing it with the lower classes. Many acts developed particularly topical songs that reflected what was happening in the world outside. They kept the audience aware of workers' rights, political intrigues, and domestic situations. Morton encouraged women to come to the shows by having special ladies' nights when women could accompany men. Which women they could bring was not specified, however, and wives were often left at home. Prostitutes brazenly walked up and down the aisles touting for custom, and the halls quickly acquired a reputation for vulgarity.

During the next twenty years, many more halls opened, and by 1875, there were 375 halls in Greater London alone as well as those throughout the country. As entertainment became more important, eating and drinking were separated from the performance areas, and the theaters became what we would expect of a large theater today, with rows of fixed seating and a proscenium arch to the stage. The new halls offered more entertainment that appealed to women and families, and many more women appeared on stage, although they still came predominantly from the working class. Acts of all kinds, some extremely eccentric, developed to meet the expanding need for entertainment.

In 1879, Charles Dickens Jr. wrote in his *Dictionary of London*:

Ballet, gymnastics, and so-called comic-singing form the staple of the bill of fare, but nothing comes foreign to the music-hall proprietor. Performing animals, winners of walking matches, successful scullers, shipwrecked sailors, swimmers of the channel, conjurers, ventriloquists, tight-rope dancers, campanologists, clog-dancers, sword-swallowers, velocipedists, champion skaters, imitators, marionettes, decanter equilibrists, champion shots, "living models of marble gems," "statue marvels," fire princes, "mysterious youths," spiral bicycle ascensionists." Flying children, empresses of the air, kings of the wire, "vital sparks," "Mexican boneless wonders," white-eyed musical Kaffirs, strong-jawed ladies, cannon-ball performers, illuminated fountains, and that remarkable musical eccentricity the orchestre militaire, all have had their turn on the music-hall stage.[3]

A decanter equilibrist? A mysterious youth? It's difficult to see the attraction. Successful performers were in demand by many halls and chased across town each night as they jumped into cabs to make it to the next hall in time for their slot on stage. No wonder many such artistes died young. By the end of the century, music halls were offering twice-nightly programs, where acts were contracted for a period of weeks rather than by slot, and they no longer had to risk health and digestion by the nightly scramble.

The rise in awareness of political and other events, often alluded to in the songs and sketches of music halls, coincided of course with the rise in political unrest across the Channel. The French reacted strongly to unacceptable authoritarian control at the same time as France was becoming rapidly urbanized. According to Fern Riddell,[4] to allay the fears of similar uprisings by the working class of Britain, the intellectual elites and middle classes in Britain slowly effected a change in song topics. Managers of music halls who were beginning to seek this more profitable clientele rejected the songs that critiqued political and social inequalities. Such songs were replaced by the mildly lewd, inuendo-loaded ones of the "'Ere, 'e's got an awful big carrot in 'is barraaa (wink, nudge nudge)" variety. The music halls altered from a true expression of the working classes to a middle-class stereotype of working-class character. Large numbers of men from the middle class began, albeit surreptitiously, to attend the halls from the 1870s onward, but it took until the turn of the century before many women were seen in the audiences.

As the century drew toward its end, the halls segued into palaces of variety that women were keen to attend; the halls were cleaned up and became increasingly respectable. This happened not through any planned strategy but due to cultural and legal changes and the individual preferences of hall managers. The United Kingdom's Theatres Act of 1843 (enforced until 1968) allowed local authorities to grant licenses for popular entertainments, such as those that took place in saloons and pubs. Those entertainments developed into music hall, and this accounts for London County Council's jurisdiction over their premises. Not all the rules that music halls had to follow were imposed primarily for moral reasons. For example, sketch length was a contentious issue. The spoken drama was prohibited at music halls because the legitimate theater was its home, and lengthy sketches could only be seen as drama. In 1912, Lord Chamberlain solved the problem by insisting that for every sketch, there must be six other variety turns on the bill. Music hall was attacked on moral grounds, too. In 1894, Mrs. Ormiston Chant[5] and her colleagues, who were scornfully labeled "prudes on the prowl" by *Daily Telegraph* reporter Clement Scott, began to attack music halls as temptations to vice. The Empire Theatre of Varieties in Leicester Square, for example, had a spacious promenade at the back of the dress circle, which became a focus of

Greek actor's masks, male and female.
Can Stock Photo Inc

Roman bronze from 1st century BC/AD in the
form of an actor's mask, eyes inlaid with silver.
Courtesy The New Art Gallery Walsall

Edward Kynaston, one of the last and most famous
of Restoration boy actors. PD (old art) / Wikimedia
Commons

Nell Gwynne, one of the first actresses on the
English stage and the long-time mistress of King
Charles II. Arianammayy / Wikimedia Commons

Bernhardt as Hamlet with Marthe Mellot
as Ophelia at Adelphi Theatre London.
Front sheet of *The Graphic*, June 17 1899.

Martha Fuchs as the young Octavian
in the opera *Der Rosenkavalier*,
1937. Bundesarchiv / Wikimedia
Commons

Anna Harvey as Cherubino and David Ireland as Figaro in Mozart's *Le Nozze di Figaro* Welsh National Opera, 2016. Richard Hubert Smith photographer

Dancers of Les Ballets Trockadero de Monte Carlo in the Grand Pas from *Paquita*, Cologne, 2003. dpa / Alamy Stock Photo

Vesta Tilley, the best known female impersonator of the British music hall and American vaudeville stages. Her career lasted from 1869 to 1920. Courtesy British Music Hall Society collection

Douglas Byng, female impersonator. Billed as "Bawdy but 'British.'" Courtesy British Music Hall Society collection

Bert Errol, the most successful female impersonator in British Music Hall. Courtesy British Music Hall Society collection

Julian Eltinge in *Cousin Lucy*, New York, 1915.
Pictures Now / Alamy Stock Photo

Gladys Alberta Bently, male impersonator
famous for her top hat, tails and suggestive
songs. Archive PL / Alamy Stock Photo

WW2 concert party performed by British prisoners in Prisoner of War camp, Poland, 1940-1945. Imperial War Museum

Arthur Lucan in costume as Old Mother Riley, a garrulous Irish washerwoman. RGR Collection / Alamy Stock Photo

Vesta Tilley as principal boy in pantomime. PD-US / Wikimedia Commons

Pantomime Dame Sam Rathbone as Dame Dolly in *Dick Whittington*, Garrick Theatre, Lichfield. Christmas 2018. Pamela Raith Photography

Dame Edna Everage (Barry Humphries) with her trademark "wisteria hue" hair and cat glasses ("face furniture"), London 2013. WENN / Alamy Stock Photo

Brendan O'Carroll as Mrs Brown at the National Television Awards, London 2015, with presenter Dermot O'Leary. Ian West / Alamy Stock Photo

RuPaul, surrounded by famous drag queens, opening DragConUK at Olympia, London 2020. SIMON DAWSON / Alamy Stock Photo

Tony Curtis and Jack Lemmon in *Some Like it Hot*, 1959. Screen Prod / Alamy Stock Photo

Quentin Crisp as the old Queen Elizabeth I and Tilda Swinton as Orlando in the film *Orlando*, 1992. RGR Collection / Alamy Stock Photo

moral anxiety about prostitutes associating with young men of the town. A group of such, including a young Winston Churchill, a future prime minister, tore down a screen that had been erected to conceal such goings-on from view and deposited it in pieces outside the theater.

The Theatres Act devolved much of the responsibility of deciding what should or should not be censored to the individual managers and owners. With an eye to the chance of encouraging the more prosperous middle classes and women to variety performances, some managers, including Morton, insisted on no alcohol, prostitutes, or innuendo on his stages. But innuendo there was, and it was a key part of Victorian and Edwardian enjoyment. Marie Lloyd performed on the music hall stage from the mid-1880s and was known for turning what would appear to be innocuous songs into dirty ones by her use of winks, nudges, and knowing smiles. When accused of any sort of obscenity by anyone who would seek to censor her performances, she would sing the song straight. Baffled critics had to accept that the words were not in any way a danger to public morals. A typical example was the following:

> She arrived at Euston by the midnight train.
> But when she got to the wicket,
> there was someone wanted to punch her ticket.
> The guards and the porters came round her by the score.
> And she told them all that she'd never had
> her ticket punched before.[6]

Delivered straight, who could possibly say it was obscene!

There is little evidence that women appearing dressed as men on stage were considered to transgress standards of decency; male impersonators quickly established their acts as an art form. The separation between what was acceptable on stage and what a woman could wear on the street was clear and well understood. There seems to have been no suggestion that lesbianism, which was still underground and almost ignored at the time, was indicated by such cross-dressing for performance. Female homosexuality was never explicitly targeted by any legislation in the United Kingdom. Discussed for the first time in 1921 with the view to introducing discriminatory legislation, it was rejected by both the House of Commons and House of Lords due to fears that it would draw attention to lesbianism and encourage women to explore it. It was also assumed that very few of the female population practiced lesbianism. So, too, the United States never legislated against female homosexuality as such, although as lesbian subcultures became established toward the 1920s, there were some raids by police who could close down locations for "obscenity."

Certainly there were some male impersonators who were lesbians, but many were not. Whether performers were gay or straight offstage, they were very popular with men and with women in their audiences. Although there were some advocates for more practical women's wear in the late 1800s, especially for the new sport of bicycling, it was still thought culturally inappropriate—and in some countries, illegal—for women to wear trousers. In the United States, Mary Edwards Walker, the abolitionist and Civil War surgeon who had worn bloomers while working at a military hospital, openly wore men's trousers. She was arrested several times between 1866 and 1913, for wearing male attire. Even in Britain in 1912, and although male impersonators had been around for a half century, it was still considered daring to show a woman dressed as a man to royalty. The press reported that at the first Royal Command performance of 1912, when Vesta Tilley performed "The Piccadilly Johnny with the Little Glass Eye," Queen Mary and her ladies lowered their eyes during the act, shocked at the sight of a woman in trousers.

Whatever the cultural norms in the "real" world, there were numerous successful male impersonators on stage in British music hall and American vaudeville. Many copied the *lions comiques*, the male music hall singers who parodied upper-class toffs. They appeared on stage in evening dress singing of the delights of idleness, womanizing, and drinking. Annie Hindle,[7] one of the first male impersonators, enjoyed wearing men's clothes at an early age and began performing on the British musical stage at the age of six. She emigrated to the United States in 1868 and was a great success. Her low voice and ability to look like a man were so convincing that reviewers commented that she could be mistaken for one. Other well-known male impersonation acts also were of this "realistic" type. The frisson in the audience came from marveling at how accurately the women portrayed men; how they could change costumes, voice, and gestures to become upper-class "johnnies" or working-class men. Ella Wesner, a music hall expat from Britain, at one time a dresser for Annie Hindle, became one of the most convincing male impersonators. Never marrying, she caused a scandal by eloping to Paris with the notorious Helen Josephine "Josie" Mansfield, who had been the mistress of both robber baron Jim Fisk and Edward S. Stokes, Fisk's murderer. The relationship didn't work out, and returning to America, Wesner resumed her career in vaudeville and began her most successful period in what became known as the "Golden Age" in the 1880s. Her songs celebrated the "sporting" life, her comic skits included one of a drunkard getting shaved, and her famous monologues gave advice to men on how to court and satisfy women.

Although some male impersonators tried hard to be mistaken for men on stage, and some succeeded, most of the well-known male impersonators were at pains to emphasize their femininity offstage, and many were married. Ella Shields, born in Maryland in 1879, became a vaudeville performer, singing and dancing with her sisters. In 1904, a talent scout persuaded her to move to London where she sang in the music halls as "the Southern Nightingale." The story goes that in 1910, she was at a party with members of other show business acts, and they were performing to amuse themselves. As one of a male duo was ill, she donned trousers to fill in for him. Her male impersonation act was born. In 1915, her husband William Hargreaves wrote, "Burlington Bertie from Bow," a comic ditty about a penniless Londoner who affects the manners of a well-heeled gentleman. It was a parody of an earlier song, "Burlington Bertie," made famous by Vesta Tilley, and arguably even more successful.

> I'm Burlington Bertie, I rise at ten thirty
> And saunter along like a toff
> I walk down the strand with my gloves on my hand
> Then I walk down again with them off
> I'm all airs and graces, correct easy paces
> So long without food I forgot where my face is
> I'm Bert, Bert, I haven't a shirt
> My people are well off you know
> Nearly everyone knows me from Smith to Lord Rosebury
> I'm Burlington Bertie from Bow.

The most famous male impersonator went a step further. Vesta Tilley never sought merely to copy men. She dressed mostly as an androgynous young man and sang in her naturally high voice. Her act of songs and monologues often parodied and poked fun at men from all levels of society and walks of life, from men in high society, successful or fallen, to soldiers in World War I or middle-class social climbers. Vesta Tilley thought carefully about how men might feel and act in certain situations, her words and gestures reflecting her conclusions. Despite the gentle mockery, both men and women on both sides of the Atlantic warmed to her; men even instructed their tailors to copy her outfits, and women wrote her love letters. Adolescent young women in particular worshipped her; some wanted to lie at her feet or live with her. Perhaps her perceived sexual ambivalence appealed to girls on the threshold of womanhood, between "crushes" on older girls or teachers and the attractions of boys and young men.

Like many of the male impersonators during World War I, Tilley spent part of her act dressed as a soldier. She earned the nickname of "Britain's best recruiting sergeant" thanks to her speeches at recruiting rallies and patriotic songs such as "It's a Fine Time for a Soldier" and "The Army of Today's Alright," which were sung by armies on the march and appeared on recruitment posters. In one week alone, while performing in Hackney, she managed to encourage the enlisting of a whole battalion, known as the "Vesta Tilley Platoon." The chorus of "The Army of Today's Alright" suggests that whoever joins the army adds a great deal to its success, and Tilley was keen to support that view.

> So it's all right now, there's no need to worry any more
> I saw the army wasn't strong
> Everything was wrong till the day I came along
> Then the band played, and they all hoorayed
> The guns fired a salvo of delight
> I joined the army yesterday so the army of today's all right.
> Yes, it's right.[8]

Some songs were insightful rather than comic. She took seriously and verbalized for her audience the fears and suffering of those going to fight in World War I and unable to explain their fears to their families in "Six Days Leave." She celebrated the wounded soldier, the ordinary Tommy, in the song "A Bit of a Blighty One," which she performed at hospitals for the wounded. Although the lyrics were risky in that they suggested that an injured soldier might be grateful that he is hospitalized in "Blighty" (home in Britain) and no longer a "hero" in the trenches, Sara Maitland, in her biography of Tilley, reflects that "it was because of her delicate burlesque that the rather hideous hospital blue, the red tie and khaki cap became a fit habit for heroes."[9]

> I'm having a cootchie time but nothing to speak of.
> I'm treated like a long-lost son.
> When I think about my dugout
> Where I dare not poke me mug out,
> Oh, I'm glad I've got this bit of a blighty one.[10]

Just before and then after the war, Vesta Tilley began to sing songs that gently satirized the social pretensions of the suburban lower middle classes who attended the halls: the clerks and shopkeepers, the skilled artisans and supervisors, rather than soldiers or "toffs." The many songs of this type accurately pinpointed the aspirations and behavior of such men, but with underlying sympathy and understanding. After all, she was one of them. Born into a music hall family and on the stage since the age of four, she married Walter De Frece in 1890, and together they rose in fame and fortune. Walter became an impresario and later the Member of Parliament representing Blackpool. In 1920, the year after her husband was knighted, Vesta Tilley retired from the stage and spent the rest of her life as the very feminine and elegant Lady De Frece. Tilley was one of the many male impersonators loved by audiences on both sides of the Atlantic.

But what about men impersonating women? Drag was a staple of Anglo-American comedy throughout the development of variety entertainment that became vaudeville, from the pantomime dame to the "wench" of American minstrelsy (white men playing black women). Any skilled comic in the halls or in vaudeville had to play many characters, usually including a plausibly hilarious female. Most of the British comedians who included "dames" in their acts of this type also played them in pantomime at Christmas; Dan Leno and George Robey are two of the best known. The characters portrayed by such comedians were well-known types who would be personally familiar to their lower-middle-class audiences. Mrs Kelly, a gossipy neighbor, was one of Dan Leno's memorable creations. Most of these comedy women were "dame" types, dressed as homely middle-aged or older women. American Bert Savoy, however, was not a dame character and, in the early years of the twentieth century, was perhaps the first well-known drag artiste of a type we would recognize today as drag queens. Born Everett McKenzie in Boston in 1876, by his teens he was trouping throughout the United States, in medicine shows, honky-tonks, stock companies, and carnivals (he was jailed at least once for cross-dressing). Bert was later teamed with straight man Jay Brennan as the Society Jesters, doing a highly successful two-act in vaudeville. In their act, the dapper Brennan chatted with the flashy, trashy Savoy (whose character was not named), mostly about the doings of her even trashier friend Margy. A 1919 New York newspaper recounted a typical Savoy joke:

> Savoy told [the audience] of a preacher who was "raking Margy over the coals" for jazzing-up her piano playing during Sunday Church services. The preacher tearfully asked her if she had ever heard of The Ten Commandments. "Margy" replied, "Don't know it, preacher . . . But if you'll hum a bit of it for me, I think I can pick out the tune."[11]

It is said that Mae West picked up her hand-on-hip swaying walk from Savoy and her "Come up and see me sometime" line from his tag line, "You *mussst* come over." "Wearing a bright red wig and the latest in Paris frocks, Savoy camped and minced and limp-wristed his way into drag history."[12]

Billed as "Bawdy but British," Douglas Byng, too, was an openly gay performer. Famous for his female impersonations, he appeared in revues and, in the late 1920s, his own night club, where he first performed the camp drag songs for which he is best remembered. His material was said to be a mixture of sophistication, schoolboy humor, and sexual double entendre but never crude. His famous numbers included "Milly the Messy Old Mermaid," "The Lass Who Leaned against the Tower of Pisa," and "Sex Appeal Sarah."

> I'm a middle-aged vamp on the movies
> I was born in the south strange to say.
> But not old Barcelona no, nearer to Brixton
> While Mother was out for the day.
> Way back home in Los Angeles West,
> I dance in a comb and a Milanese vest. . . .
> I'm chic Sal, I'm a wow of a gal,
> Though I own I'm a bit underdressed.
> But as I'm a bit passé, and can't be too classy,
> I shimmy my chassis and hope for the best.
> I'm Sex Appeal Sarah.[13]

But the period 1910 to 1930 also saw something different: young males impersonating real, glamorous young women. There were many American acts of this type; Julian Eltinge was probably the most famous but was certainly not a rarity. Karyl Norman, famous for his gowns that his mother sewed; Tom Martelle, "the boy with the pretty gowns"; Francis Renault, the "Parisian fashion plate"; and Ross Hamilton from Canada were all famous on the American vaudeville circuit of the 1920s and 1930s. Eltinge, however, was specially so. If Savoy was popular because of his flamboyance and bawdy act, audiences loved Eltinge for how he accentuated a soft feminine allure in his characters. He was never vulgar. Having first appeared in drag at the age of ten, he made his debut in musical comedy on Broadway in 1904. Dressed beautifully, his goal was to be both elegant and convincing. Both men and women found him fascinating.

He appeared in vaudeville, toured Europe and the United States, appeared in a series of musical comedies written to showcase his talents as an impersonator, and returned to vaudeville in 1918, topping the bills. He was known for appearing consecutively on stage as different types of women. At one time you might see him as a Gibson girl, the personification of American beauty around 1910, one with a curvy figure, upswept hair, and a long skirt; another time he would appear as a young girl in a pretty party frock. His Japanese dresser, Shima, laced him into corsets to achieve a female shape. Spending two hours on makeup and dressing, he used a whole array of makeup, nail varnish, and numerous wigs. He even shaved his arms and fingers to achieve the illusion of smooth skin. To distance himself from the gay subculture or any suggestion of "perversion," he went in for macho behavior and made sure that stories that circulated about him, whether true or not, referred to his involvement in boxing, fist fights, and drinking. Always dressing as a man offstage, he insisted that his act was an illusion, a skilled depiction of women, and something he did for a living. His act was always classy and in good taste.

But, surprisingly, despite the many male impersonators on the halls, there are few examples of British men impersonating beautiful women on stage. Only one, Bert Errol, could be said to be the British counterpart to Julian Eltinge. From 1909, Errol became the most successful female impersonator in British music hall. He started performing as a concert singer in his hometown of Birmingham, but by the time of his first appearance at the London Pavilion in 1909, his act had evolved into a series of impersonations of popular female singers, as well as characters of his own devising. As he became more successful, his act became more comedy based, and his routines featured lightning-fast costume changes. As well as his success on the variety stages in Britain, he also made frequent appearances on the big-time vaudeville circuits in the United States. Despite his definitely masculine features, photographs reveal a very stylish and fashionable figure, and he enjoyed a long and successful career. When he got older and was no longer able to create the illusion of youth, like many other music hall stars, he worked as a pantomime dame. Bert Errol was a rarity as a British female impersonator of beautiful young women.

Why was there so much difference between the number of male to female cross-dressing acts that originated in Britain's music halls and American vaudeville? The answer lies partly in how each type of entertainment developed. The difference in attitudes toward homosexuality at the time in the two countries also played a part, as did the way in which women began to see themselves. Female impersonation supported the move toward what Laurence Senelick[14] describes as the "masculinised femininity" of the American woman.

Although vaudeville originated in France as the name for a mixed show of a comedy interspersed with songs and ballet, it became very popular in the United States and Canada from about 1880 until 1930. But it had changed radically from its beginnings. Variety had been a staple of entertainment right back to the time when Americans first had time to enjoy their leisure, and almost always, such entertainment was linked with the sale of alcohol. But by no means did all Americans want such fun. From the 1620s, Puritans began colonizing the Plymouth, Massachusetts Bay, Rhode Island, and Connecticut areas, and Puritanical ideals formed the basis of culture there for more than three hundred years. Punishable crimes included "lascivious dancing to wanton ditties," celebration of Christmas, stage plays, and other theatrical amusements, as well as the more expected misdemeanors—adultery, fornication, and idolatry.

But the United States was not colonized by Pilgrims alone; many cities were founded on commerce, and by the mid-eighteenth century, Boston, Williamsburg, New York, and Philadelphia had grown sufficiently affluent to support an entertainment industry. Early eighteenth-century theaters closed down because of the American Revolution, and it was not until 1798 that New York's first professional theater, the Park, opened its doors. Performances there would be, as in England at the time, Shakespeare plays or a Restoration sex comedy, but there would also be variety acts before, during, and after the plays. A cross-section of the population—from the president to dockworkers—formed audiences, and as in saloons at the time, people would shout, join in the action, and throw things at each other and at the players. As New York boomed with vast numbers of immigrants, the number of theaters expanded apace. They catered to the working class who wanted a "rip-roaring good time." Any program of entertainment, even one based on drama, was variety. Dancers, singers, banjo players, gymnasts, jugglers, and comedians—in fact, any act likely to entertain the clientele—would offer a break from the serious acting. S. D. Trav comments that during her first US tour in 1880, "Sarah Bernhardt was discomfited to find acts of her *Camille* broken up by can-can dancers and a xylophone player."[15]

The United States is a big country, so it is not surprising that vaudeville developed not in a straight developmental line from one source but, instead, from many. From rough saloons where entertainment was an afterthought to the real business of drinking, through the gamut of traveling freak and medicine shows, burlesque, circuses, "museums," and that peculiarly American genre, minstrelsy, theatrical entrepreneurs realized that a stream of changing and entertaining acts would bring in the punters. Two of these genres were related institutions that would play a key role in the development of vaudeville—namely, museums and circuses. Already by 1800, museums—which were often collections of "unbelievable oddities" (e.g., a five-headed cow, natural history specimens, wax figures, and historical artifacts) supplemented by lectures, scientific demonstrations, and magic-lantern shows—attracted the public.

In 1941, Phineas Taylor Barnum, well before he became a circus proprietor, acquired a run-down museum and turned it into Barnum's American Museum. It was genuinely educational and retained some of the oddities and trickeries to be gaped at such as the pin-headed man and the Fee-jee mermaid, a hoax creature with the body of a monkey and the tail of a fish. Barnum was the archetypal publicist, using whatever advertising methods available to tell people what he was offering. To sell more tickets, he added magic, ventriloquism, jugglers, and magic lantern shows. He gradually transformed his lecture room into a respectable theater, and perhaps this was his greatest contribution to the evolution of variety into vaudeville. A convert to temperance, but also aware of what would sell tickets, he wanted to change the view of theater from a "den of evil" to palaces of clean entertainment for the burgeoning respectable middle class. He attracted families, and his approach helped win the approval of the moral crusaders of New York City. He started the nation's first theatrical matinees to encourage people to bring their children to shows. People who feared the night crime rife in downtown areas liked matinees, too, and felt safe in daylight. In 1870, Barnum established "P. T. Barnum's Grand Traveling Museum, Menagerie, Caravan & Hippodrome" in Delavan, Wisconsin, with William Cameron Coup; it was a traveling circus, menagerie, and museum of "freaks."

There is no real evidence that such rough early variety shows emphasized cross-dressing of any kind, although it is likely that female impersonators featured as traveling performers to logging camps and other places where women, except for prostitutes, were rarely seen. And in such all-male situations, some men would wear labels to designate themselves as temporary dance partners. In his book, *Days without End*, Sebastian Barry writes about a traveling drag act that toured American mining towns just before the Civil War. The book shows an imaginary but well-researched aspect of entertainment in the remote new townships. Male impersonation also formed a small part of some early acts. Lotta Crabtree, the daughter of an unsuccessful gold prospector, toured mining camps and rough settlements as a dancer. She was spotted by an agent who booked her into San Francisco melodeons where among other acts she did male impersonations. Later she became a legitimate stage actress in New York.

But it was minstrelsy that provided the strongest element of cross-dressing that was key to later vaudeville drag acts. In minstrelsy, black and white immigrant traditions were intermixed. Irish jigs and reels were performed alongside African shuffles and breakdowns. The original African stringed instrument, popular on plantations and that later became the "banjo," became popular on the American stage along with the tambourine and the bones (animal bones clicked together like castanets). "Blacking-up"—white men pretending to be black—causes outrage now but cannot be denied as part of the history of American performance culture. And not only in the United States. As late as 1978, *The Black and White Minstrel Show* was popular on BBC television. Because of its use of blackface, black antiracist groups in the United Kingdom rightly condemned the show and accused it of racism and ethnic stereotyping.

> *Minstrelsy's cultural legacy makes the form extremely problematic for the vaudeville fan. On the one hand, its racial depictions are uniformly heinous. At its very best, it is merely patronising. But, on the other hand, minstrelsy's songs, sketches and monologues laid the foundation for the character of American show business for all time.*[16]

Part of this foundation was the development of the comedy team, and this is where female impersonators could be found. The centerpiece of a mid-1800s minstrel show was a variety program with drag acts, including a female impersonator known as the "wench." Female characters in minstrelsy ranged from the sexually provocative to the laughable. These roles were almost always played by white men in drag, even though outside minstrelsy at the time there were few female impersonators and there were many actresses on the theater stage. The matronly *Mammy* or the *old auntie* was lovable to both blacks and whites. Her main role was to be the devoted mother figure in scenarios about the perfect plantation family. Another stock character was the *funny old gal*, a slapstick role played by a large man in motley clothing and large, flapping shoes. The humor in this role was the desire that male characters showed for a woman whom the audience would perceive as unattractive. In contrast, the *wench, yaller gal,* or *prima donna* was a mulatto who combined the light skin and facial features of a white woman with the perceived sexual promiscuity and exoticism of a black woman. This role emerged as the most important specialist role in the minstrel troupe after the Civil War period. She was beautiful and flirtatious, and the male characters pursued her, although she was often capricious and elusive. Men in the audience could be titillated while women could admire the illusion and high fashion. The role was most strongly associated with the song "Miss Lucy Long," sung by a male character. The female impersonator was often given that name in the sketch.

> Oh! I just come afore you,
> To sing a little song;
> I plays it on de Banjo,
> And dey calls it Lucy Long.[17]

Most famously, George Christy, Francis Leon, and Barney Williams, performing as blackface minstrels, made the prima donna a fixture of their acts. Actress and journalist Olive Logan commented that some actors were well fitted by nature for the role, having well-defined soprano voices, plump shoulders, beardless faces, and tiny hands and feet. Many of these actors were teenaged boys. For the first time, women began to admire and aim to copy the style and dress of female impersonators, and one which personified independence and choice. Women's emulation of variety's drag artistes was to reach its peak with Julian Eltinge more than fifty years later.

Minstrelsy was just one of the strands of variety that came together, in a zeitgeist moment, in the 1880s. Many men claimed to have had the idea first. As S. D. Trav puts it,

[V]audeville was like the hub of a wheel and its creators like spokes converging from different directions. From saloons came Tony Pastor, Henry Clay Miner, Koster and Bial, Alexander Pantages, and John Considine; from dime museums B. F. Keith, Edward Franklin Albee and Sylvester Poli; from variety theaters Hyde and Behman, and F. F. Proctor; from legit theatre Percy Williams; from opera the Hammersteins. Significantly, Pastor, Keith, Albee and Proctor had all worked for circuses.[18]

All of these businessmen, many of their names now forgotten, realized the potential for making what had been seen as sordid into family entertainment (as circuses were). All were threads woven together into the tapestry of vaudeville. Their efforts were supported by liberal theologians who were preaching compromise, that wholesome pleasures—rather than base, sinful ones—were good for people. Churches, too, began to support what they saw as noncorrupting entertainment. The Latter-day Saints, better known as the Mormons, also believed that wholesome entertainment was an important part of human and spiritual development, and their communities enjoyed plays, musical performances, dances, and lectures. The Mormons obviously did not think female impersonation was at all sinful. From 1885 to 1900, Brigham Morris Young, one of the sons of Brigham Young (the founder of the Latter-day Saints), began publicly performing as a cross-dressing singer. Under the pseudonym Madam Pattirini, he took the stage at north and central Utah venues. Because he produced a convincing falsetto, many in the audience did not realize that Pattirini was Young. This new cultural climate suited the development of a sanitized version of variety: vaudeville.

Tony Pastor, an entrepreneur with a long history in many types of entertainment, is credited with the start of true vaudeville, although he did not use
the word. Pastor had been successfully expanding the variety aspects of his
productions, as afterpieces to plays and comedies, for some time. In 1881,
after a failed attempt to stage a parody of *The Pirates of Penzance*, titled *The
Pie Rats of Pen Yen*, at his new location, the Tammany Hall theater on Union
Square, New York, he decided to offer straight, clean variety. He attracted
women by staging a Friday ladies' night and offered prizes to his female
patrons, including dress patterns and sacks of potatoes. When he upped his
offers to silk dresses and sewing machines, women flocked to his shows. The
name *vaudeville* was possibly contributed by B. F. Keith, the originator of a
huge empire, refined and managed by Edward Franklin Albee, which spread
across the continent. His theaters were squeaky clean; performers could be
canceled immediately if they swore or even said such things as "slob" or "Holy
gee." He is credited, not knowingly, for creating the term *blue* for rude, inappropriate language. If his performers did or said something the Keith management disapproved of, they would be sent suggestions for improvement in
a blue envelope.

By the turn of the twentieth century, vaudeville circuits stretched across
the United States. Acts were self-contained and were plugged in like car parts
to their rigid timetables. Unlike music hall, which retained its reputation for
rude comic innuendo, vaudeville was thought to be wholesome and suitable
for the whole family. This wholesomeness is reflected in the way that drag
performers impersonating young, beautiful females were accepted and considered as role models for women.

Beauty culture was booming in the United States in the early twentieth
century. Thanks to advancements in the cosmetics industry and increased
marketing, American women took an increasing interest in their appearance. The physical fitness of a clean-cut, attractive American girl was to be

emulated. Average women were able to go to beauty parlors, wear makeup in public, and read magazines containing tips on how to look good; these were the same women who were likely to attend variety theaters in the first two decades of the new century. But even if there was a real interest in beauty products and how to use them, *The Julian Eltinge Magazine and Beauty Hints* produced for the first time in 1913 seems strange. Responding to an assertion by English novelist Marie Corelli that British women were the prettiest in the world, the magazine pointed out that American women could easily compete, albeit with Julian Eltinge cold cream and powder. Photographs of Eltinge looking like a young woman were interspersed with he-man photographs. He encouraged women to learn to box. The magazine also contained the performer's endorsements of footwear and cosmetics, reportedly used by him. Perhaps important to the acceptance of such suggestions by women, Eltinge explained how much hard work was involved in achieving his beauty, not only the application of the cosmetics he used but also the tight-laced corsetry. If a large man could achieve feminine grace by such effort, perhaps all women could. It was a time of change. Women were seeking an identity that would allow them to be women but more like a man. They began to seek an identity that would allow them to step away from a total emphasis on hearth and home and move toward personal individuality, to education, and to a career. Most of the women who read the magazine, however, would not necessarily have been tempted by their more adventurous "sisters" who wished to adopt a more androgynous sporty appearance.

> Eltinge's gender intermediacy qualified him to serve as a middleman between traditional standards of curried comeliness and the newer ideal of masculinised femininity. The genteel woman of ripe charms whom he impersonated was licensed by his status as a biological male to engage in adventures and to show off an ostentatious wardrobe without provoking complaints that such behaviour was respectively unladylike and unwomanly.[19]

The few drag artistes in Britain at the time who impersonated glamorous women, most notably Bert Errol, did not tempt women to dress or look like them. Errol was admired for his skill to transform himself into copies of famous stars and singers, but he was not seen as a role model. This is perhaps because the British class system meant that the middle-class women attending variety shows were encouraged in their magazines to be homemakers and cooks. Style magazines were still for the better off, with British *Vogue* beginning as late as 1926. True female emancipation was some way off; the average woman had no encouragement to adopt manly traits.

But perhaps another strong reason for the lack of female impersonators in turn-of-the-century Britain compared with the United States, apart from in coarse comedy, was due to attitudes toward homosexuality. Although Eltinge, for example, was at pains to prove his masculinity offstage by his macho behavior, as were others, who advertised their married state, other drag artistes such as Bert Savoy were not. Drag in vaudeville was not really performed or perceived as "gay" until Savoy appeared on stage. His was one of the first acts to be associated in the minds of the audience as overtly homosexual in theme. Audiences loved it. And he was equally "camp" offstage. In the United Kingdom, however, it was different. The period of music halls and palaces of variety, from the mid-1800s to the 1930s, contained changes to the laws on male homosexuality. Only in 1861, with the passing of the Offences against the Person Act, was the death penalty for sodomy changed to ten years imprisonment, and in 1885, any male homosexual act became illegal, even in private. An affectionate letter between two men could result in a prosecution, and the legislation became known as the "Blackmailer's Charter." Male homosexuality was brought strongly to the public's attention by the trial in 1895 of Oscar Wilde, one of the most successful playwrights of late Victorian London. At the height of his fame and success, he had the Marquess of Queensbury prosecuted for libel. The marquess was the father of Wilde's lover

Lord Alfred Douglas and had left a calling card for Wilde with "For Oscar Wilde, posing sodomite" on it. Various letters between Wilde and young men as well as the likelihood of male prostitutes giving evidence against him caused Wilde to drop the case, but it was too late. Tried for sodomy and gross indecency, he was eventually sentenced to two years hard labor, from 1895 to 1897. Many friends, fearing their own prosecutions, left for France. The public interest was enormous and mostly condemnatory. It was no wonder, then, that male impersonators were wary of being accused of homosexuality, although cross-dressing was never really an issue in homosexuality trials. Most performers in Britain stuck to representing women as comic, usually middle aged or old, figures. The nearest impersonator the United Kingdom had to Eltinge was Bert Errol, and he was careful to include his wife in his act.

As the twentieth century progressed, there was little difference between music hall and vaudeville acts. Theaters offered variety, and some were named palaces of variety. The best acts moved between the United States and the United Kingdom, and vice versa, and toured the world. But in the 1930s as the Great Depression was felt in both countries, the demand for staged variety entertainment waned. Dance halls, radio, and films offered alternatives to variety. The type of male and female impersonators beloved by both music hall and vaudeville audiences were no longer in demand. There were notable exceptions. Hetty King and Ella Shields strutted their stuff as male impersonators in variety into the 1950s, and this chapter could not end without mentioning others who, before their time, gave the public a flavor of what was to come around fifty years later.

Bert Savoy was quite different than the Julian Eltinge type of female impersonator. Over-the-top in the 1920s, his act was a true forerunner of the drag queen performances that went mainstream around the 1980s. In burlesquing the current styles of the time with huge jewelry items from his ankles to his bright red wig, and with large flashy and colorful garters, he was never pretending to copy a real woman of the time, or to be a beauty. He challenged gender stereotyping, and who knows where his act would have taken him if he hadn't died untimely, being struck by lightning on a beach on Long Island in 1923. A male impersonator, Gladys Alberta Bentley, was an early equivalent of Savoy. One of the most famous entertainers in the United States for a period in the late 1920s and early 1930s, she was a black, lesbian, cross-dressing performer. She did not in any way try to copy what men of the time would look like; she was herself. Top of the bill at Harlem's Ubangi Club, she was backed up by a chorus line of drag queens. She dressed in men's clothes (including a signature tuxedo and top hat), played piano, and sang her own risqué versions of popular songs of the day in a deep, growling voice while flirting with women in the audience. Squeaky clean vaudeville it was not. She too was before her time. As federal laws changed, Bentley had to carry special permits to allow her to perform in men's clothing. She was frequently harassed for dressing as a man and, at one point, claimed to have become a woman again and to have married. But she probably would have supported and admired the drag kings who strut their stuff on stages now without risk of prosecution.

The end of music hall, vaudeville, and early variety brought to a close the careers of most cross-dressing artistes. But as demand for theater, film, and television boomed in the twentieth century, a new generation of performers keen to show off their gender-swapping skills claimed the limelight.

But that's for another chapter.

8
WAR IS A DRAG

Meet the gang, 'cos the boys are here,
The boys to entertain you.
B, O, B, O, Y, S—Boys to entertain you.

—*It Ain't Half Hot Mum*[1]

When, in August 1945, the Seventh Infantry Division, US Army, was sent to Korea on occupation duties, the soldiers soon realized that there was very little to do. No real work, no entertainment. They were bored.

Korea was seen as a side show by the US planners, and although the USO (United Service Organization) shows were toured to the American troops in Japan, American servicemen in Korea had to provide their own fun. GI Dan Ruff and Private First Class Don Lavoie decided to produce a traveling burlesque show for the troops. Dan, a DJ in the army, had done drama in high school. Don Lavoie, a hairdresser by profession, had been a vaudeville performer on the side, as drag act Tony Starr. The two men set about recruiting suitable performers and crew. Those who had acted or played instruments as amateurs or at school were particularly useful. All the soldiers who were prepared to join the show received a letter from division command ordering their release from other duties. The show, *Bits of Burlesque*, was a great success and traveled throughout South Korea for six months until the official USO shows started to arrive there.

One of the GIs performing in the *Bits of Burlesque* show remembers that he and his colleagues were dressed in short skirts with coconut-stuffed bra tops. They did chorus dances in combat boots making for a hilarious act.

The drag acts were accompanied by vocalists, accordion and harmonica players, and comedy skits. But not all men dressed as women were comic. The undoubted star of the show was Tony Starr with his striptease act, and rumors spread among many of the GIs in the audiences that he actually was female. In January 1946, the US military newspaper *Stars and Stripes* named him the new nominee for the "pin-up queen of Korea." On one base the "girls" were invited to the officers' mess, to the great discomfiture of their hosts when they turned up in uniform. Tony Ruff said later that there was "nothing gay" about *Bits of Burlesque*, but it was likely, he said, that Don Lavoie or Tony Starr was.

Cross-dressing in amateur military groups goes back much further than perhaps readers would expect. For three years in the 1780s, Admiral Horatio Nelson was in command of the ship *Boreas* in the West Indies, then being notoriously unhealthy islands. He was known to pay particular attention to the health and welfare of his crew. He established a mess for the officers. On August 3, 1784, to start it off, he ordered to be sent from St. John's by the sloop *Fury*, a hogshead of port and one of the best white wines, twelve dozen porters in bottles, fifty pounds loaf sugar, a firkin of butter, two baskets of salt, and two pounds black pepper. During the time his ship was in the West Indies, not a man died, which was unparalleled in such a climate. When possible, he kept the ship busy moving about the sea, exercising the crew, but in the hurricane months he had to remain at anchor in the English harbor in Antigua. Here the men enjoyed music, dancing, and singlestick (a game using cudgels to train sailors to fight). He also encouraged the officers to put on plays. All these activities helped to occupy their time and keep up the spirits of the ship's company. The plays included *The Orphan, King Henry IV, Lethe, The Lying Valet, King Lear, The Fair Penitent*, and *The Tragedy of Jane Shore*. There is little doubt from this list that some of the officers would have had to act the female roles.

Men dressed as women has been a feature of life as a soldier, sailor, or airman, or as a prisoner of war (POW), in many conflicts and well into the postwar period after World War II. Groups of servicemen preparing for action, on occupation or peacekeeping duties, or interned in camps as prisoners need to keep active. Dressing up and putting on a show has often relieved the boredom and the tension. In recent and current conflicts, however, those on military service have access to the same contacts and amusements as civilians. Soldiers in Iraq and Afghanistan, for instance, have social media and mobile phone contacts by which they access home, receive photographs, read, and see films. But those of previous generations, in the absence or infrequency of official entertainment, had to make it themselves.

There has been much debate about the reasons for such a great deal of female impersonation within closed military communities. There is the argument, perhaps most acceptable to the official military at the time, that it was good fun; men dressed as women made for much hilarity. The many postcards showing men in drag, which were sent by soldiers to their families in World War I, suggest that cross-dressing was considered, at least by the senders, as a bit of a lark. However, there have been many different possible explanations put forward as to why there was so much female impersonation in wartime. Lisa Z. Sigel[2] suggests that female impersonation became a coping strategy in the harsh and difficult times of World War I, a way of rejecting the boundaries of regimentation and boredom at best or brutality, violence, and horror at worst. Other writers emphasize that, in the absence of glamour and femininity, men in drag reminded servicemen of their wives, sweethearts, and mothers. More recently it has been accepted that some of the performers had a desire to be in drag, which they could not usually express in a military context. And for some of those watching, there was a homoerotic frisson when admiring "women" who were known to have male genitalia—in colluding with the pretense. For some gay servicemen, without any urge to admire women on stage or to emulate them, the ability to belong to a small theatrical community within a military unit was a powerful reason to join in the shows. For a period of time, they were able to distance themselves from the normal "macho" culture of military life. And for some men, the opportunity to dress as women without danger of being dismissed was a great attraction. "The visible gays were mostly drag performers in concert teams. Regarded with considerable affection, their camp humour helped lift the men's spirits."[3]

There were, however, heterosexual men who dressed as women to entertain but were determined not to be taken for gay. In his admirable book *Fighting Proud*,[4] about gay soldiers, Stephen Bourne refers to an interview in 1991, given by soldier Tommy Keele, then age 98, who had been a lance corporal on the western front in the Great War of 1914–1918. In 1917, he joined a concert party called the Ace of Spades and, taking the name "Dot" Keele, took female parts in theaters behind the lines. "People didn't always know I was a man dressed as a woman. I was wearing a very low-cut evening dress." He remembered occasional disgust but also the adoration of many of his soldier fans who asked him for signed photos, which brought him a nice little income. But being heterosexual and dressing almost permanently as a woman had its dangers, he recalled. One night while sharing a comfortable bed with a sergeant who he had taken pity on because he was so exhausted from trench warfare, he found the man on top of him. After punches and threats, the sergeant threatening court-martial, and Tommy reminding the sergeant that buggery carried the death penalty, presumably the affair was forgotten. Tommy said that he felt a bit sorry for the sergeant afterward. There were no real girls around for the man; however, he (Tommy) was not going to be a substitute.

Until 1982 there was no official ban on homosexuals serving in the US military, although sodomy was considered a crime. During World War II, the Korean War, and the Vietnam War, homosexuality was defined as a mental defect; homosexuals, therefore, were barred from serving on medical grounds. When the need for more personnel increased in times of combat, however, the screening criteria were reduced, and many gay men and women served honorably in these conflicts. In 1982, the Department of Defense put into writing that "homosexuality was incompatible with military service," and thousands of men and women were discharged. But in the 1980s, there was increased pressure by advocates of gay and lesbian civil rights for the military to reverse their stance. In 1993, the US military adopted the "Don't Ask, Don't Tell" policy. In 2010, this policy was repealed, and since then homosexuals have been free to serve in the armed forces openly.

In the United Kingdom, homosexuality only became legal in 1967, but with stipulations that any acts could only be consensual, in private, and between those twenty-one or older. But during World War II and right up until 1999, there was an official ban on lesbians and gays serving in the forces. Homosexuality was grounds for dismissal. As usual, however, rules are ignored when there is a crisis. People were put in the forces without question when they were needed to fight the Nazis, and there was no homophobic uproar, as there was later, about how gays might undermine military discipline and effectiveness. In both world wars, the war in Korea, and in other insurgencies, gay UK servicemen had to be wary of others knowing their sexual orientation, although many men quietly outed themselves to their comrades and were integrated into their units. Peter Tatchell tells the story of Private Dudley Cave,[5] who served as a soldier in the Royal Army Ordnance Corps as a driver and fought in the Far East. He was captured and did back-breaking work on the Thai-Burma railway, work that killed many of his comrades, before his hospitalization and eventual repatriation. "All the gays and straights worked together as a team." He said, "We had to because our lives may have depended on it." He noted that there was never any disciplinary action taken against gay men in his unit, even one who was known to offer his services to both gay and straight men in the nearby mangrove swamps. "You could say he did a lot to maintain the unit's morale," commented Cave. Yet many service personnel had to be careful of homophobia, which might mean them being reported to military authorities and facing dismissal and harsh imprisonment. What comes through clearly, however, in the many accounts of gay soldiers, airmen, and sailors who served in the wars of the twentieth century is that, despite the dangers of being outed and court-martialed, they were often fully integrated into their unit and managed to avoid trouble.

Just good fun? Glamour in the harsh conditions of war? Something to keep men creatively busy? To take their minds off what might be coming? Reminders of femininity? Longing for mothers and girlfriends? The chance to be more openly gay? All the many suggestions as to why there was so much theatrical cross-dressing on military bases and in prisoner of war camps are most likely true. Whatever the reactions to female impersonation by audiences, it became a key part of both official wartime shows and unofficial theatricals in the military, and wherever large groups of men were stationed. And reasons for enjoying looking at cross-dressers were probably as many and as varied as the men who performed and watched the shows.

For much of World War I, from 1914 to 1918, the sixty-five million men who served in the armed services and the eight million POWs were largely segregated from women. While there were female nurses, drivers, messengers, and some civilians, most servicemen lived in all-male communities. Conditions were harsh. Violence and horror on the front, mud, rats, dead bodies, and trench living, which we all have seen in photos and films from that time, were only replaced by boredom and restrictions behind the lines. Entertainment helped raise morale. At the beginning of the war, the task of entertaining the troops was undertaken by professional and amateur performers who offered their services freely under the sponsorship of the YMCA (Young Men's Christian Association), the Salvation Army, and the Red Cross.

But as the war dragged on, the responsibility for entertaining the British and Canadian troops in France diverged, and concert parties from both nations toured widely. Such concerts—often consisting of songs, drama, and music—were popular, but as the soldiers on the front line experienced the horrors of war, they wanted less serious amusements to take their minds off the conflict. They wanted comedy and girls, no matter if the latter were men in women's clothes.

Many divisions on or near the front line were quick to make their own entertainment and created concert parties that put on shows, many including drag acts of some kind. The Canadians in France set up a "Dramatic School" under the general control of the YMCA, which trained concert parties and stored, altered, and constructed costumes and sets.[6] But even before the school, divisions had organized their own concert parties. The best remembered because of their continuation after the war are the Rouge et Noir of the First Division and the Dumbells of the Third. Using servicemen as performers became the norm in these troupes, and, relieved from other duties, they toured widely—although it was always possible that they might be recalled to their units for active service at the front at any time. But the visit of such well-organized and semiprofessional groups of performers to the troops behind the lines, certainly in the earlier days of the Great War, could only be spread thinly, and units often made their own fun. Sometimes the concert parties became organized and semipermanent; others came and went, put together for one or two shows.

The names given to the groups most often reflected where the servicemen hailed from: the Tykes was the concert party of the Forty-Eighth (West Riding) Division of the British army; the Leeds Pals came from the Fifteenth West Yorkshires; and the Balmorals were from the Fifty-First Highland Division. The names of others acknowledged their military birth, such as the Shrapnels of ANZAC (Australian and New Zealand Army Corps) and the Whizz-Bangs of the Forty-Sixth Division. Others took on generic concert party names such as Follies or Fancies, and many names belonged to more than one party. My favorite name, for its grim humor, was that of a field ambulance unit in Salonika called the Splints.

According to Laurence Senelick,

> By the time the United States entered the war [in 1917], the provision of theatrical units had become a matter of military logistics. Orlin Mallory Williams, a YMCA costumier, was stationed in Paris to provide costumes and wigs (many of the garments were contributed by professionals in the States). There was a corps of seamstresses to renovate and enlarge the costumes to fit the bodies of males who tended to tread on their chiffon. Supplying gowns for AEF chorus girls, often from Lucille, Paquin and Worth, became a major enterprise; in March: in March 1919, 36,118 men were costumed for 4,000 productions, divided between 134 units in 281 different theatres. But by this time the war was over and, and those trained to perform to fellow soldiers now, like the Dumbells, presented their shows to civilian audiences.[7]

In 1919, an all-soldier musical farce, *Let's Beat It*, was presented at the Century Theatre in Philadelphia, and the Splinters, a troupe of British ex-soldiers, toured their shows around Britain well into the 1930s.

J. G. Fuller[8] analyzed soldiers' journals from the time, many of them containing impressions about the shows they had seen. The female impersonators did not make caricatures of their roles but played them as realistically as they could. And although Fuller is skeptical of how glamorous such impersonations could be, he quotes one man as claiming, "judging from the way (the men) sat and goggled at the drag on stage it was obvious that they were indulging in delightful fantasies that brought to them substantial memories of the girls they left behind them in London, Manchester, Glasgow, wherever." In his opinion, the fact that until 1917 some troops would have encountered ordinary peasant women working hard on farms, in cafés, and bars did not make such female impersonators less popular. It was glamour— not the lack of women—that mattered. Femininity was the key to the success of such impersonators. Costumes including frocks and lingerie were carefully chosen and procured when on leave or sent out from home.

Twenty years later, at the start of World War II, the armed services, remembering the experiences of World War I, realized that entertaining their (mostly) men was essential to maintaining morale, and set up official organizations for the purpose. The USO and ENSA (Entertainments National Service Association) provided entertainment for the US and British military personnel, respectively. The USO was known for its live performances, or "Camp Shows," which began in October 1941. By the end of that year, there were 186 military theaters registered in the United States. In November of that year, the shows began touring overseas, and by mid-1942, in thirty units of six members each, they had visited the Americas, the United Kingdom, and Australia. The provision of such entertainment grew apace, and during 1942, there were seventy units with a total of around one thousand members. Famous Hollywood performers were keen to show their patriotism, accepting the low pay of $10 per day. Their less-famous colleagues were paid $100 a week. In 1944, Camp Shows traveled in small units of five performers or less to entertain troops in Normandy. This was just a month after Operation Overlord, the Allied operation that launched the successful invasion of German-occupied Western Europe.

The British ENSA shows, a mix of famous, talented, and frankly amateur performers toured bases, camps, and ships and did a sterling job. Despite the acronym ENSA becoming Every Night Something Awful, the troops looked forward to their visits. Even if the result of an off-key singer or amateur band was amusement at the expense of the performers, the shows nevertheless relieved the monotony of life on military bases or lightened the tension in war zones. The Canadians, too, entertained their troops. The *Army Show*, a musical revue for the Canadian army, opened in Toronto in 1942, then toured the country and eventually split into five units to be sent overseas. Divided even further into smaller groups, they entertained troops throughout England, and in 1944, after the Allied invasion of Western Europe, they performed on the front line. There were some women as part of these troupes, and whatever their talents, the female singers, dancers, and instrumentalists—sometimes the first women the men had seen in months—helped inject a bit of glamour into camp life. They reminded the men, and it was always men, of their wives and current or potential girlfriends.

The Kiwi Concert Party, officially the Second New Zealand Expeditionary Force Entertainment Unit, (2NZEF), performed for all Allied troops, as near to the front line as possible. They were different than the other official wartime concert parties in that they were also a self-contained military unit. Half their rehearsal time was spent in combat training. The all-male troupe created revues in the vaudeville style, a mixture of drama, comedy, novelty items, and music, with men cross-dressing when female characters were needed. Photographs of the concert party show male performers looking very glamorous in women's clothes. In early May 1941, the concert party was sent to Crete where they performed for four days while under enemy bombardment. Pushed back, they had to leave all their costumes, instruments, and equipment behind, and five of their members were captured by the Germans. After Crete, the group reequipped and performed five times a day on the front lines in the Middle East and North Africa. Two other Kiwi concert parties were formed, one in 1943 to tour the Pacific, and the other in 1944 to tour Italy.

There was, therefore, a real effort to entertain the Allied troops. Big stars, professional and amateur musicians, singers, and actors, as well as many serving servicemen and women, gave their time at very low cost. The official shows were, however, spread thinly, and for most of the time in military camps in the twentieth century, the troops had to make their own entertainment. And in the absence of women in these communities, cross-dressing was the only way in which women could be represented in the revues, plays, and concerts that were staged. Many drag artists appeared in the official shows, but there were imposed limits as to how they could portray women; the theatrical subunits, however, could tailor unofficial entertainment to the tastes of their colleagues. Uncomfortable as some of the acts might seem to contemporary audiences, many were of a comedic type familiar to the men. Richard Buckle, an officer in the army, dressed as a pubescent girl and sang an obscene song, "My Little Pussy," which obviously hinted at pedophilic desire. And yet it was very favorably received and was seen in the same way as were Donald McGill's bawdy seaside postcards or the double entendre songs of the music hall, or, well after the war, the humor of the *Carry On* films. In some units, there was a demand for straight plays, and here too men played women. In an article by Emma Vickers and Emma Jackson,[9] there is an account of a review of the camp's production of Keble Howard's *Lord Babs* suggesting that the performances of the male cast were parodies of real women: "Charles McDowell's buxom Bible-quoting, whiskey gulping Nurse Rounce was very effective." "John Bradbrook 'played a feminine part— [the] Countess of Sawbridge. A blue-blooded old bitch, always thrusting her ever-ready-to-be-shocked modesty in front like a whitlow.'" The performances were enjoyed and appreciated for the evocation, albeit exaggerated, of some of the women back home. A reviewer of a soldier's production of A. A. Milne's *The Boy Comes Home*, a popular play in the 1920s and 1930s, spoke of the authenticity of the female characters, all played by men.

Perhaps one of the most surprising aspects of cross-dressing in wartime is the emphasis on femininity. Some photos of concert party acts, both amateur and official, do show the cross-dressers replicating a pantomime dame style or the burlesque. But many others show the servicemen attempting to convey the appearance of real women, sometimes very successfully. Depending on the available materials, the men often look mildly comical with emphasis on busts, occasionally padded and motherly, and with long hair; however, in many photographs they appear extremely glamorous and "real." These were men moving away from the then-recognized concept of "drag": from mimicry, where there is an implicit understanding by the audience that the person on stage is a man, to mimesis where the attempt is to make the difference between the "her' and the genetic woman as slight as possible. Dr. Clare Makepeace[10] quotes different diary entries from soldiers in the audience watching female impersonators. While one POW writes that the "women" who appeared in the shows were "most laughable, honestly" and another that "all the female parts have to be played by men, and therefore have to be comic parts," far more commented on how realistic they seemed. As in the Great War, some performers went to great lengths to be overtly sexual. Many were gay and used performance as a way of exploring their sexuality and gender and sometimes extended performance to life offstage, which perhaps made some of their fellow servicemen feel uncomfortable. Charles Pether, a postman and a female impersonator in the Royal Air Force, was aware that, because he looked androgynous and acted in an effeminate way, his best way of fitting in with his unit was to join the concert party.[11] He delivered bawdy songs with as much Hollywood glamour as possible. His costumes were homemade out of parachute silk and mosquito netting, and to replicate shoes he cut the tops of his plimsolls and had them silvered. Strutting on to the stage he sang "I'm the Naughtiest Girl in the Forces."

I'm the naughtiest girl in the forces
The fellows declare I'm a lad,

The things that I show to our youngest M.O.

I wouldn't ever show to my dad.[12]

Many of his listeners believed him and followed him back to his quarters after performances, queueing up for his favors. He said that he assessed the success of his performance on the length of the queue. Dennis Prattley, a naval rating, spent most of his naval career in drag. He saw his role to be a sexual surrogate for many heterosexual colleagues who frequently informed him that he reminded them of their "girl back home." Of course, by no means all female impersonators were gay. Many men performing in drag left their female personas on stage, and many of their comrades were glad that they did.

Whatever the type of entertainment the unit members preferred—bawdy, burlesque, straight drama, or glamour—the shows had to be created and organized. In some camps, there were those who had been in the business prewar and in others total amateurs, so productions could be as well organized as the official touring shows or totally ad hoc. Daniel Patrick Carroll, later to become Danny La Rue, the highly successful female impersonator, pantomime dame, and actor, served in the British navy during World War II. In his autobiography,[13] he recalled his time on HMS *Alania* en route to Singapore just after the war ended. One of the ship's officers had had theatrical experience and got permission to start a concert party troupe on board. It was done properly. Auditions were held, and Danny, who had a good speaking voice and had acted in amateur plays before the war, won a place. But he hadn't any real urge to perform at that time, he said; it just seemed a good way of getting off duties. Some of the other troupe members had "dabbled a bit in the profession. There were a few old-stagers aboard." They put on two or three shows a week, from old-time music hall to revues. Danny's first part was a send-up of Leon Gordon's *White Cargo*, about tea planters in love with a native girl, played by Danny. He remembers being very brown from the sun, having almost black hair, and wearing just a sheet as a costume "nicked from the officers' quarters." It was the cheapest costume he ever had. Much later Danny La Rue would be famous for the expensive and extravagant costumes he wore in his acts. Although he was very convincing as a woman, he claimed that he never wanted to be taken seriously. "It's all a glorious joke," he said.[14] And indeed, when he was a famous drag act, he always ended his shows by changing back into his normal male clothing. When the *Alania* arrived in Singapore, the troupe became the concert party in residence and were asked to perform for the army and Royal Air Force personnel. Well organized, and using homemade props, scenery, and costumes like most such concert parties, their shows were great fun and gave pleasure to both performers and audiences.

Different from Danny's experience, there were many bases and camps where there was no one with any claim to show business experience and few resources. But the urge to entertain and to be entertained as well as the need to see women, however ersatz, resulted in a host of shows, most including female impersonation. On shore leave, Dennis Prattley met up with another gay sailor who wore makeup and had named himself Bette after the Hollywood star Bette Davis. He told Dennis that he couldn't do without his makeup and that as there was no law against it, he wore it on board. Dennis was introduced to two more gay sailors who took the names Rita Hayworth and Katharine Hepburn. The others christened him Ann Sheridan, another star of the time, and he became Sherry in the concert party that they put together. Although the shows were initially amateur, their success meant that he spent most of the rest of his navy career in drag, and he and his pals believed that they could make careers as entertainers—if they could leave the navy. Hoping to be discharged by the navy as undesirable, the concert party members insisted they were homosexual; however, the navy wanted them, and they served right up until the end of the war.[15]

It was not just servicemen from Allied countries that dressed up in drag. Martin Dammann, an artist, assembled a series of amateur photographs of Nazi soldiers cross-dressing in private groups of friends at the front and while POWs in Allied camps. There are scenes of young soldiers dressing up and clowning around, with soldiers posing in elegant frocks as well as photos of female impersonators in front of an audience.[16] One photograph shows a soldier in a bra stuffed to create an illusion of breasts and wearing makeup on his lips, eyes, and cheeks. Another shows five young soldiers as a dance troupe in skirts made of blankets and towels. Such behavior is not at all exotic but may be seen as confirmation of the normality of the situation and not the contrary. In the absence of women, men seek to create their illusion. But perhaps one of the most surprising aspects of wartime performances is how popular men dressing as women was for POWs, particularly in German POW and internment camps for just some, comparatively fortunate, British officers.

The treatment of prisoners of war in World War II differed greatly. There were roughly one thousand prisoner-of-war camps in Germany during World War II, called *Offlags* for officers and *Stalags* for noncommissioned servicemen. Germany was a signatory at the Third Geneva Convention, which established the provisions relating to the treatment of prisoners of war. These conventions were not always followed, but on the whole, the Germans behaved fairly toward British and Commonwealth prisoners. But conditions were tough, and rations were inadequate. The majority of prisoners, but not officers, were put to work at heavy laboring in mines, fields, shipyards, and factories on a diet of about six hundred calories a day. Despite stories about breakouts from POW camps, some of which were successful, most prisoners were too weak to attempt to escape. Unfortunately, the Germans did not treat the Allied Jewish servicemen and suspected communists in the same way; they were usually shot out of hand. Russian prisoners ended up in different sections of the German POW camps than the British and Commonwealth prisoners, and because the Germans considered them to be racially inferior, they were starved and treated brutally. In 1945, as the tide turned in the war and Soviet ground forces approached some POW camps in Germany, many already weakened Western Allied POWs were forced to march long distances toward central Germany by their captors, often in extreme winter weather conditions. They suffered greatly, and many died.

Prisoners of the Japanese found themselves in camps in Japan, Taiwan, Singapore, and other Japanese-occupied countries. Prisoner-of-war camps in Japan housed both captured military personnel as well as civilians who had been in the East before the outbreak of war. The terms of the Geneva Convention were ignored by the Japanese who made up rules and inflicted punishments at the whim of the camp commandant. More than 140,000 white prisoners were interned in Japanese POW camps. Of these, one in three died from starvation, overwork, punishments, or diseases for which there were no medicines to treat. Of course, the Allies too took many prisoners of war. Prisoners in the POW camps in England, mostly Germans, were reasonably well fed, but food for ordinary Russians at the time was scarce so men imprisoned by the Russian army suffered greatly.

According to Sigel,[17] where you were interned made a difference to how you experienced a POW camp, but of importance too was the class of military to which you belonged. Unlike servicemen who were still at war and lower ranks doing hard work in other POW camps, some captive British officers had little to do and faced months, and more likely years, of incarceration. Officer camps in Germany and Holland and other theaters of war, including the western and Salonika fronts, had bathing facilities and access to chapels. The men were also allowed to receive packages from home courtesy of the Red Cross. They had the time and energy to indulge in amateur theatricals to alleviate boredom. Some felt humiliated about being taken prisoner, and such activity helped take their minds off the fact they were no longer able to influence the outcome of the conflict in any way.

A major feature of the camp theatricals was the amount of cross-dressing. The fact that the prisoners were so keen on watching female impersonators is not surprising; thousands of men were miles from home, surrounded by hundreds of men with no possibility of female comfort. From the work of Dr. Clare Makepeace,[18] who examined the log books, diaries, and letters of British POWs in World War II, it appears that dressing as a woman to perform was popular in officers' camps and that performers were admired by their fellow prisoners who were attracted to them. This was not unusual in itself and was replicated in many military concert parties in both world wars; however, what was unusual, and somewhat disconcerting, was that chosen performers rehearsed six hours daily and were taught elocution and acting skills including how to walk with small steps and sit gracefully like a woman. Cast members had to grow their hair long and have their limbs shaved of hair and their eyebrows plucked. They used greasepaint, cosmetics, and nail varnish. Clothes and sets were equally elaborate. To support the performers, dresses were replicated from pictures in magazines, and material from Red Cross parcels sent to POWs, as well as stolen sheets and mosquito netting, was used to create the drag costumes. Realistic wigs were created "strand by strand" from parcel binding. One man spent a month hand-stitching a dress, and another spent days making a pair of shoes. A huge amount of time and effort went into the productions. The guards in the camps where Dr. Makepeace's contributors were imprisoned were supportive of the shows. Keeping the prisoners busy must have helped discipline and made for a more peaceful life for the guards—and provided them entertainment, too. They often took photographs of the show or gave cameras to the POWs to do so, and they often sat in the front row to enjoy performances. In one camp, where officer-guard relations were particularly good, the guards borrowed clothing from the local opera company for the camp's production of *Puss in Boots*.

When wars end and the surviving men go home to their womenfolk, to mothers, wives and girlfriends, it might be expected that they have no further need to admire female impersonators. But this was not so after both world wars. All-male shows continued to be popular for many years on both sides of the Atlantic. Despite many different Canadian military concert parties performing in France during World War I, the name of the Dumbells resonated most strongly among released Canadian troops. Impresario Merton Plunkett had taken performers and material from many of the different troupes and blended them together to create the touring Canadian show. The Dumbells when in France had been the Third Division Concert Party, but at home in Canada they became the Canadian Army Concert Party. "Veterans in the audience were not seeing the Dumbells on stage, but their own concert party in memory. For those who had spent the war years at home, however, it brought a sample of what had sustained the forces in the field in a variety of forms. For them, the Dumbells came to mean the concert party."[19] And the popular all-male revue Les Rouges et Noir with its origins in World War I France toured the British provincial theaters right up to the beginning of World War II; they even had a season in London's West End at the Queen's Theatre.

The upsurge in the number of very popular all-male revues after World War II mirrored that success. Some shows, like Ralph Reader's *Gang Show*, had existed in wartime, but others such as *Pacific Showboat, Forces Showboat*, and *Soldiers in Skirts*, although billed as family entertainment, flooded the market with female impersonators. They played many of the top theaters as well as minor ones, capitalizing on the audience's appetite for ex-servicemen in drag. *Soldiers in Skirts* was the longest running of all the contemporary all-male shows, starting at the close of the war in 1945 and touring until 1952. The shows were well rehearsed and well presented with a mix of music, dancing, and humor, as well as glamour, courtesy of female impersonators. This could be an impersonation, a comedy act, or a chorus line of long-limbed young men. Former navy serviceman Danny La Rue, who was to become one of the most successful drag performers of the twentieth century, joined *Forces Showboat* in 1949. In his autobiography, he recalled his days with all-male concert parties in the years just after the war.

Back in civilian life after the navy, he was working once again as a window dresser. He had moved from his hometown of Exeter to London, excited at the chance for a new life. He would have loved to make a life in entertainment after his success performing in wartime concert parties, but as this seemed unlikely, he had to settle with acting in the local amateur dramatic group. But one day in London he met an old colleague from the navy who was in the capital for an audition for *Forces Showboat*, an all-male revue about to go on the road. Danny was able to lend him some material to make a costume and then helped him get into his stage outfit and makeup. Unfortunately, his friend Tony didn't get into the show but persuaded Danny to try for it himself. Borrowing Tony's wig and arranging the same material into the semblance of a dress, he went back to the audition room, and the rest is history. He started his long professional career as a chorus "girl" in the show.

Perhaps the success of such all-male revues that followed both wars did help remind ex-servicemen of the comradeship of the past and provide a link to such experiences for those who hadn't served. Certainly, these must have been two of the reasons why the shows became popular for former servicemen and why many ex-soldiers, who had performed in concert parties, wanted to join them. But the popularity of all-male shows, particularly those with ex-servicemen in drag, was due to more than nostalgia for wartime friendships or interest in what the men had been doing while resting from warfare.

Some men who had served in the forces and had discovered or built on their skills as performers in wartime concert parties used the all-male shows to launch or relaunch their showbiz careers. The young Harry Secombe, a former lance bombardier in the North African campaign, Sicily, and Italy who had developed his own comedy routines to entertain the troops, was in *Forces Showboat*, along with Danny. Already making a name for himself as a comic, he joined the show as a specialty act. His comedy routines (supplemented at times with song) were seen throughout the country as the show toured. After the tour, his career blossomed: on radio, on television, in musicals, and as a member of the Goons.[20] He was to become one of Britain's best-loved performers. Bartlett and Ross, perhaps not names familiar to current audiences, were the best-known duo of female impersonators in Great Britain in the years after World War II. Already establishing themselves before the war as professional drag artists, as ex-servicemen they became a highly successful act and toured with *Forces Showboat*. They became one of the best-known pairs of "ugly sisters" in pantomime. Pianist Trevor Stanford, later to be famous as Russ Conway, appeared in Arthur Lane's ambitious forces revue *Tokyo Express* (1946). This show with lavish scenery and costumes—and sketches by Noel Coward—toured Europe, Canada, and the Pacific for the services, and after the war, the show became a popular attraction in variety theaters. Careers in show business suddenly opened up for many men who, prewar, had not hoped or even thought of making it in the profession.

The war had allowed many gay men to take to the stage, to belong to all-male nonjudgmental groups in concert parties, and for some, to develop skills as female impersonators. They had often simulated chorus lines, singing, and dancing in unit shows. The all-male revues after the war gave opportunities to extend these activities into their civilian life with safety. It was still illegal for same-sex people to engage in sexual acts, but dressing as a woman was not; however, dressing as such in public meant harassment or ridicule, and men dressing as women had a hard time of it. But being a member of an all-male concert party meant considerable freedom to cross-dress more openly. Danny

La Rue, although he enjoyed touring with the shows and thought it a valuable and rewarding apprenticeship, was uncomfortable with some of the behavior of his fellow cast members.

> Some of the behaviour of my colleagues in the chorus line was outrageous. It was far too high camp for me. I was surrounded by boys who would literally have preferred to be women . . . they lived in women's clothes for much of the time and they desperately wanted other people to accept them as women. . . . On train journeys . . . they would sit in the carriages in sequin dresses doing their wigs.[21]

Danny, who was very likely gay and lived with his partner Jack Hanson for forty years but never "came out," never wanted to be taken for a woman. He only donned a frock and wig for comedic purposes; he revealed himself as masculine at the end of his acts and always wore "male" clothes offstage. Although he disapproved of his colleagues' high-camp behavior, the opportunities to behave as they felt, a continuation of their wartime performances, must have helped these men live less covertly until the LGBT (lesbian, gay, bisexual, transgender) laws changed. As the memories of war faded, the chorus line employed fewer ex-servicemen and replaced them with professional performers. Tastes in entertainment changed as a new decade began and the enthusiasm of audiences for all-male shows waned. The men who had sustained the shows moved on to other roles in the profession, many very successfully, or faded into obscurity.

Twenty or more years later, viewers of the BBC were reminded of the past war, when men were separated from women and made their own entertainment by forming concert parties. This reminder came in the form of *It Ain't Half Hot Mum*, a hugely popular BBC comedy that ran from 1974 to 1981 in eight seasons and fifty-six episodes. It is set during World War II (in the period just after the German surrender when the Allies were trying to finish the war by defeating Japan in Asia). The members of a concert party are stationed at the fictional Royal Artillery Depot in Deolali, India, where soldiers were based before being sent to fight at the front lines. Later in the series the action moved to Burma (now Myanmar). Its two creators—who had already had a great success with the BBC's *Dad's Army*, about a fictional World War II unit of the Home Guards—now used their own wartime experiences; Jimmy Perry had been a member of a concert party in India while David Croft had been an entertainments officer in Poona. Although the action covers much more than the staged shows, the program does convey, albeit in a much lighter tone than would have been the reality at the time, the oppressive heat and the potential dangers. It is very uncomfortable now to watch the caricatured master-servant relationships portrayed between the civilian Indians in the camp and the soldiers, particularly the officers. And it would be unacceptable now to have a white male actor (Michael Bates) "blacking up" to play the Indian bearer Rangi Rama. Some of the language was criticized as homophobic and racist. Uncomfortable as it is to watch the episodes now, there is no doubt that it was authentic in reflecting some wartime attitudes. In 2003, Jimmy Perry commented to a reporter from the *Guardian*, "People complain that the language was homophobic, and it was, but it was exactly how people spoke. And I should know—I was in a Royal Artillery concert party that travelled around India."[22]

Although not a major theme, the program also showed, in a microcosm, the differing reactions of both officers and enlisted men to cross-dressing and to what is seen as effeminate behavior. "Gloria" Beaumont is the soldier portrayed as effeminate and as a man who cannot handle the violence, heat, and mosquitoes of army life in India very well. Portrayed as a transvestite and not homosexual, he considers himself an artiste, and as he much prefers the show business to the soldierly part of his role, he thus incurs the wrath of the sergeant major, Tudor Bryn "Shut Up" Williams. Ginger Rogers is his favorite film star, and he dresses up as her during the concert party shows. His sexuality is left obscure, as at one point he is engaged to a nurse although we never know whether he goes through with the marriage. Interestingly it is he who is promoted to bombardier, a very soldierly role, when the previous incumbent leaves the unit.

The series may well have reminded men, then in their fifties and older, of the times they spent being entertained by their colleagues. Each man would have had a different experience, and perhaps some recounted to their families and friends what they thought about the female impersonators who so ably stepped up to perform the many roles in plays, acts, and musical numbers that required women. Or perhaps they kept their recollections to themselves. For some men, the hardships or particular relationships of those times were best forgotten.

Is it likely that such cross-dressing in performance will happen again when service personnel are engaged in conflict or peacekeeping roles away from home? Will men group together to perform in female roles for their colleagues who are separated from wives, girlfriends, and mothers? I think not. Those who identify as any gender now serve alongside each other at home and overseas. The US, British, Canadian, and Australian militaries have women in combat roles. Modern communication methods allow both real and virtual connections with family and friends to be expected and provided.

It is unlikely that all-male concert parties with men in drag will form again in wartime. But for many of those who served in the Allied forces in two world wars, it was fun at the time!

9

THERE IS NOTHING LIKE A DAME

For me, the dame needs to be a bloke—in a dress—playing it poor and old and down on her luck.

—SAM RABONE, PROFESSIONAL PANTOMIME DAME[1]

Old Mother Riley films were part of Sunday School treats when I was small. After the fish-paste sandwiches, the jellies, and the cakes, the superintendent would try to control fifty excited kids and get them to sit cross-legged and quietly on the floor. With little success. Sighing deeply, he would walk to the back of the hall to take command of the film projector. Carefully he adjusted the reel and turned out the lights, and the tall, angular Irish charwoman with the silly little hat strode across the wobbly screen, creating mayhem. The little boys loved it. We worldly small girls, all of five years old, sat in a disdainful group, informing the boys superciliously that of course she wasn't real; it was a man "dressing up." Not that the boys cared: they rolled about on the floor giggling at her antics. Old Mother Riley was a star.

Born as Arthur Towle, in Lincolnshire in 1885, he quickly established himself as a music hall comedian. Appearing in Dublin in 1913, he met and married sixteen-year-old Kitty McShane and changed his name to Lucan; together they developed a highly popular double act. In a sketch "Bridget's Night Out," he dressed in drag and began to develop the role of Old Mother Riley (with the full comedy name of Daphne Bluebell Snowdrop Riley), an Irish washerwoman and charwoman. It was a role he occupied for the rest of his career. His wife Kitty took on the role of his daughter. The duo continued to perform as Lucan and McShane in the halls, the theater, and the radio.

The act was so successful that it featured in the 1934 Royal Command Performance at the London Palladium, the most prestigious engagement for any British act. A long film career followed, and between 1936 and 1952, there were seventeen hugely profitable films; Lucan played Old Mother Riley in all but two. His comic character appeared in a radio series and even a strip cartoon that featured in the *Radio Times* and *Film Fun*. Lucan's character was the first and probably the most influential drag act on stage and screen. In his last film, *Mother Riley Meets the Vampire*, Lucan starred alongside Bela Lugosi (best remembered for the classic 1931 horror film *Dracula*) and the husky-voiced Dora Bryan, later to become one of Britain's best comedy actresses. Lucan's character became so much part of filmgoing life that the phrase "Old Mother Riley" was often heard as an alternative to swearing when someone was frustrated or angry.

I chose to use the character of Old Mother Riley as an initial example of cross-dressing "dames" in performance because all Lucan did to convey his character was to wear a long skirt, a shawl, and a small battered hat. There was no attempt to make his face into anything but the rather craggy masculine one that he possessed, or to pad his shape to womanly roundness. Why the sight of a man wearing the clothes of a middle-aged or elderly woman should be perceived as comic in our culture is an interesting question and one that is difficult to answer. A woman dressed as a middle-aged man would trigger no such response. Women, as we have seen, have crossed-dressed on the stage, certainly since Restoration times; however, they have never been seen as comic solely because of their masculine dress or demeanor. Dramatic impact, amusing or serious, comes from the parts they play, the songs they sing, and the monologues they deliver—not their looks. On the contrary, for men playing dames, the humor comes in the first place from their outfits, which signal that comedy is to be expected. Once in drag they can develop their characters using humorous dialogue and actions as they choose. They can be rude or worldly, satiric or motherly.

My definition of the term dame is any character played by a man who dresses usually as a middle-aged or older woman. While in women's clothes, he is obviously in drag. There is no illusion on the part of the audience; they know he is a man. But in drag he behaves in what the audience perceives as an unexpected way for a woman. Therein lies the comedy. Of course, such cross-dressing goes back a long way. From the ancient Greeks, through to Shakespeare and into the seventeenth century, men or boys played all the female roles, but most often seriously. In the late 1600s, women began to appear on stage in the theater, but these new actresses, often young themselves, often preferred to play the younger female roles. An older, usually comic, female part would be played by a mature man.

The British liking for watching men in "dame" roles may go back to Tudor times. The "Feast of Fools," presided over by the Lord of Misrule, was an unruly New Year's event, which involved much drinking and revelry, as well as role reversal. This may be a folk-memory that stayed in the collective British psyche and could be one reason why they are so receptive to a "Pantomime Dame," a role that seems culturally specific and is an enigma to most of those from other cultures. If most Brits now were asked what a theatrical dame is, the picture that would immediately come to mind for them would be a mature man in a pantomime dressed in exaggerated and comic female women's clothes. They know the character from childhood. Although in no way the character it has now become, the dame began to appear in the early nineteenth century, developing from the travesti tradition of theatrical cross-dressing. Since then, the Pantomime Dame role has become iconic. It is a key part of theatrical tradition, and many successful male comedians, from music hall, radio, and television, have developed a "dame" of some kind as part of their routines. For months over the Christmas period, they turn their attention to playing such roles as an Ugly Sister, Mother Goose, or Widow Twankey, in bowdlerized versions of fairy or folk tales.

But the other type of "dame" I find fascinating is that which evolved in the twentieth century, the male performer who took on a specific and sustained female persona. Such characters are in a comedic line of descent from Old Mother Riley to Brendan O'Carroll's character, Mrs. Brown, in the highly successful Mrs Brown's Boys. Some of these dames played their character in successive films or in TV series, like Old Mother Riley. Others developed a theatrical act in which their female character *was* the act, and the performer was known by the name of that character, even offstage. Barry Humphries, who subsumed his real-life personality into that of Dame Edna Everage, is typical. Many of these dames were able to perform across genres in their characters, for instance, in a television series, on stage, and in Christmas pantomimes. How Dame Edna and her like entertained the public on stage and screen from the late 1800s right through to the present day is worth analysis. But first let's look at the dame in pantomime.

Pantomime, or panto as it's usually called, is a very British tradition and, even more specifically, English. Practically every large theater, and indeed many small ones, put on a Christmas pantomime. Members of amateur companies the length and breadth of the United Kingdom spend all late autumn rehearsing their shows. For professional theaters, panto is often the biggest moneymaker of all their productions and allows theaters to produce less profitable and more experimental or new work for the rest of the year. The 2020 COVID-19 pandemic meant the cancellation of that year's panto and was a disaster for theater finances, which pushed many venues to a financial breaking point. Panto is as much part of a British Christmas as turkey, presents, and the Christmas tree. For children (and for many adults), it is an essential part of Christmas fun. Although a pantomime audience does contain many children, it is interesting to count how many adults it seems to take to accompany one child to a show. And a weekday matinee audience is often almost entirely adult. Other nationalities don't really "get" the attraction of pantomime, and it is rarely seen outside the British Isles except where pockets of settlers keep up the tradition.

Although it has its links to the mimes of Italy and France, particularly commedia dell'arte, according to pantomime historian Maureen Hughes,[2] the roots of what we recognize as panto now were firmly set in the early eighteenth century when *Italian Night Scenes* was staged in London. The production at Drury Lane by French troupes used dance and slapstick rather than words to convey misunderstandings, and these always resulted in a comedy brawl. Seeing the success of *Italian Night Scenes*, dancing master John Weaver presented his *Tavern Bikers*, in which he copied both the theatrical style and also appropriated Harlequin, a character that remained an important part of pantomime right up until the twentieth century. Weaver produced *The Loves of Mars and Venus* in 1717, which was actually billed as a pantomime—although not one we would recognize as such. But in the same year he joined John Rich to stage the first of the harlequinades at Lincoln's Inn. And it was Rich who had the idea of combining fairy tales with harlequinades. In the early eighteenth century, the Regency period, a significant part of a pantomime was a harlequinade. Harlequin would take the part of the persecuted lover; he was favored by the good fairy, who used a magic wand as she changed him and his beloved into Harlequin and Columbine. These lovers were aided by the Clown as they spent the rest of the drama attempting to escape from Pantaloon, the girl's father, and his bumbling servant, Pierrot. The idea of pantomime became popular with theatergoers. Well-known actor and theater manager David Garrick, not one to miss out on a successful idea, presented his own first pantomime production in 1750.

By the early nineteenth century, however, the harlequinade had significantly changed. By then the Clown was the principal character and the only speaking part. The most famous clown ever, Joseph Grimaldi, a favorite of Charles Dickens, began to play the role. Gradually, as extravaganza and burlesque took over, and music halls produced many young women singers and male comedians, these actors began to play pantomime roles. The productions started to include cross-dressing, and pantomime has kept up the tradition ever since. The parts of the Principal Boy (played by a young woman) and the Dame (played by a man) became more important than either the Harlequin or Clown.

Panto is a very predictable genre. Although the story lines are usually based on fairy stories or folk tales like *Cinderella, Aladdin, Mother Goose,* or *Jack and the Beanstalk,* they contain the same standard elements. The charm of the panto is that the audience is *not* surprised by any innovation; they know what will happen. Attempts to modernize panto into a less anarchic Christmas play have usually failed. Audiences come to the theater expecting to participate willingly in the action, and they respond enthusiastically and verbally to whatever is happening on stage. They anticipate mayhem in at least one scene. They know that there will be good and bad characters. They expect that the wicked Demon or Witch will come on from stage left and that the audience will boo their arrival. The Fairy Queen, the good nonhuman being, will enter stage right. Both will have pretty corny lines eliciting groans from the audience. There will be a love story, usually involving a poor girl and a prince or a princess falling in love with a boy who gains riches. Traditionally, although no longer as common, the male lead is a girl with long shapely legs and short shorts. Despite comments by traditionalists that it isn't "proper" pantomime, young male celebrities, usually singers, often now play the male lead in professional pantos. This provides an opportunity to feature current hit songs, which will secure the attention of teenagers and keep the families buying tickets. In a true pantomime, there must be periods of stage business, often a slapstick scene with lots of dirt, soap, and water, and a silly altercation between a comedy duo, resulting in a fracas. The audience also expects to join in a comedy ditty or a currently popular song, reading the words from a banner that is let down from the top of the stage. Traditionally led by the Dame, this communal song takes place in front of the curtain. This allows the stage hands time to set up the final walk-down scene, usually the most decorative, where all the cast parade on to the stage for their bow. For the song, the audience is divided into sections that compete with each other to sing the loudest. Sometimes the children in the audience are invited on to the stage to join the Dame. It is the Dame's role to organize the action, enthuse the audience, and control the children, encouraging the very shy ones or firmly keeping those who love the limelight from taking over. She then has to get them off the stage quickly when the backstage staff indicate that all is ready behind the curtain. Sweets are thrown out to the audience as the song ends and as the Dame and her entourage exit into the wings. There is a scramble of small children who are rather ineffectually retrieved by parents to watch the triumphant finale. All the main characters have special, usually wedding, costumes for this "walk down." The two lovers, Principal Boy and Principal Girl, are in wedding outfits, and the Dame wears her most extravagant, most outlandish clothes.

In 1812, Joseph Grimaldi cross-dressed to play Queen Ronabellyana in *Harlequin and the Red Dwarf* and later the Baroness in *Harlequin and Cinderella*. This is hailed as the birth of the pantomime dame,[3] and the role has become an integral part of pantomime since that time. No one watching a traditional pantomime, except perhaps the tiny children in the front row, thinks "she" is female. Dames usually dress outrageously in clothes that no real woman would dream of wearing: huge hats, the brightest of clashing colors, big baggy bloomers, and striped socks. They behave in a physical manner:

climbing ladders, doing prat falls, and often getting covered in soapy water, wallpaper paste, or mock mud.

Tradition has it that the Dame role should be played quite obviously by a man pretending to be a woman; however, the role is not just "a feller in a frock"; it is a nuanced cross-dressing role that many professional actors have embraced and made their own. Dames are given lines (or write their own) that contain topical and local references, political jibes, and sexual innuendo. These provide a subtext for the amusement of the adults in the audience while the children enjoy the mayhem. Thus, over many years, they have had to adjust their performances. They need to appeal to an increasingly sophisticated audience who have access to many forms of adult entertainment, and they must provide the children with enjoyable knockabout and silly verbal humor. And they succeed. In recent years, with the assimilation of drag "queens" into mainstream entertainment, some of the most famous appear as pantomime dames in professional Christmas shows, often dressed in fabulous gowns. These characters are often much less physical than their predecessors; they maintain their carefully created looks and let other roles cover the expected knockabout business. Traditionally, dames are old and cuddly and always down on their luck at the start. One current pantomime dame commented, "When a dame is dripping in diamonds, my problem is that it becomes less believable when she has to sell the cow because they are so poor (*Jack and the Beanstalk*). The dame is skint, down on her luck and always looking for a new man, and a new way to make money. For me the dame needs to be a bloke—in a dress—playing it poor and old and down on her luck!"[4]

There is still a role for actors who really enjoy playing the pantomime dame traditionally, who relish the knockabout and like to wear outrageous but unglamorous costumes. Sam Rabone is one of the new generation of dames for whom pantomime is a key part of their career. He started his career in an amateur dramatic society in stage management, but as such societies are often short of male acting members, one Christmas he played a henchman in their panto. The next year he was cast as the Dame and chose to keep his deep voice and not try what he calls a "Monty-Pythonesque" one. It worked. So, building up a wardrobe of frocks, he set about auditioning. Eventually Pantoni, a company specializing in producing pantomimes in the United Kingdom, gave him the break he needed, and he became a professional pantomime dame. Now he works for Evolution, another well-known company in the business, and currently he performs as a very popular dame at my local theater, the Garrick in Lichfield, each Christmas.[5]

In response to the question as to why the role of the dame character is so important to an audience, he replied, "Freedom! It gives the OK to them to laugh. Sometimes as a society we don't know if it's ok to laugh at things. . . . We are given the go-ahead to laugh as much as we want. The dame says things people want to say and can't. The dame is a commentator, she is not important in 90 percent of panto plots—she is there to comment on what's happening and sometimes bring light to a dark situation."[6] Sam says that children like the dame because she is colorful, playful, and reminds them of all their favorite women rolled into one—and says naughty things that they shouldn't say. The adults, on the other hand, are on the edge of their seats waiting for a joke that the kids won't get but they will. Some pantomime scripts use a great deal of innuendo, and certainly modern drag-queen dames make good use of it to amuse the adults. But innuendo is less apparent in the more traditional pantomimes, both professional and amateur, that proliferate in cities, towns, and villages over the Christmas season. Bad jokes are less controversial and allow the audience to "groan" as their contribution to the fun.

And why does pantomime not really work in other countries? The answer from Sam was thought provoking. It was nothing to do with the pantomime, he said, but everything to do with the audience.

Because it's not in the UK is the simple answer. The pantomime will work in all countries in one form or another; however, what it won't be in other countries is the art form we know it as. If we put it on anywhere else, people would laugh—people would have a good time—but they wouldn't know how to join in. For panto to work anywhere else in the world we would have to take half a UK audience with us for the first few years, to train audiences what to do. How would a Swedish audience know what to shout when the ghost is on stage [Look, he's behind you]*? Why would the French suddenly start booing the baddy? We need the audience in panto more than anyone would ever realise. They are one of the characters in the show and may not even know it!*[7]

10
THE OTHER DAMES

There is no more terrible fate for a comedian than to be taken seriously.

—BARRY HUMPHRIES[1]

"Stalking the stalls for prey, her standard opening gambit, the put downs on opening night were softer round the edges. Later, interrogating three hapless 'guests' from the audience in a chat show sequence, Edna's falsetto tone sounded almost wistful . . . until it was time to swivel the spotlight back on herself and send the trio packing. Deep down, she is still a volcano of vanity and liable to erupt at any time."[2] In 2019, Dame Edna Everage, still the most celebrated of stage dames, was on tour in Australia with her show, *Dame Edna: My Gorgeous Life.* And at eighty-five, her creator Barry Humphries, was still "defending to the ultimate his right to give deep and profound offence."[3]

Pantomime dames are a special breed, but like Santa and his reindeer, they only come out at Christmas. There are other "dames," of which Dame Edna is probably the ultimate example. These are the many female characters outside of pantomime played by men dressing up as women and played for comedy. Usually over-the-top characters, they are almost always mature or older women. While dressed as a woman, such a man is obviously in drag, and the audience knows it. He behaves in an unexpected way for a woman of that age or type, and therein lies the fun.

Such drag acts were staple elements in the acts of music hall comedians (Dan Leno's Mrs Kelly, for instance), and the concept continued to be successful in films (e.g., Old Mother Riley). Early film actors, including Charlie Chaplin and Stan Laurel, used female impersonation, as did later actors including Alec Guinness in *Kind Hearts and Coronets* (1949), Alastair Sim in the St. Trinians films of the 1950s, and Peter Sellers as Duchess Gloriana XII in *The Mouse That Roared* (1959), a role he claimed to have based on his grandmother. As far back as February 29, 1892, the comedy cross-dressing role of Lord Fancourt Babberley (who reluctantly impersonates a rich widow from Brazil, Donna Lucia d'Alvadorez) was played in the farce *Charley's Aunt* by W. S. Penley. The English actor, singer, and comedian achieved phenomenal fame as both the play's producer and star. This comic part has become a staple comedy role for many older actors.

More recently, famous actors have donned frocks and taken on film roles that portrayed them as funny, but "real" homely women: notably, Robin Williams in *Mrs. Doubtfire* (1993), Martin Lawrence as Big Momma in *Big Momma's House* (2000), and John Travolta in *Hairspray* (2007). These, however, were all disguise roles and temporary for the duration of filming. Often the roles were unusual choices for the actors to play and were often experiments. Some have never cross-dressed again in films.

The "dame" performances that dominated light entertainment from the 1960s to the 1990s, however, were quite different. Often beginning as stage acts, they became particularly numerous in the intimate genre of television. Danny La Rue, perhaps the most famous, was in many ways the last of the female impersonators similar to those of the music hall and vaudeville era. Like Bert Errol at the turn of the century, he impersonated a range of real, glamorous women in his act: Elizabeth Taylor, Zsa Zsa Gabor, Judy Garland, Margot Fonteyn, Marlene Dietrich, and, a rather bizarre choice, Margaret Thatcher. An excellent comic actor, he appeared on stage, in films, and on television. In 1982, he played the part of Dolly Levi in the musical Hello, Dolly! He even took over a woman's role in the West End theater when he replaced Avis Bunnage in Oh! What a Lovely War while she took a holiday. And like many comic actors before him, he played the role of Lord Fancourt

Babberley in Charley's Aunt. His version of the iconic part was seen in a BBC television "play of the month" in 1969. Like many of his contemporaries, he continued to be a regular performer as a dame in Christmas pantos well into old age. But he was always Danny La Rue. He called himself a "comic in a frock" and not a female impersonator. Parts of his act were performed in male clothes, and offstage he did not cross-dress.

Most comic actors have developed a range of characters as part of their careers, and most have at least one, highly recognizable, female persona. Dick Emery,[4] for instance, began his career entertaining troops in World War II. He created Vera Thin (the Forces' Sweetheart), loosely based on Vera Lynn, and much later in his own television show, that of Mandy, a busty peroxide blonde whose catchphrase, "Ooh, you are awful . . . but I like you!" was given in response to an innocent remark that she always took as a double entendre. "She" would then leave the stage with a shove to the "rude man" and a comic trip in her high heels. So cross-dressing is not unusual in comedy, nor ever has been. But the acts that I find most interesting are those in which male actors develop mature or older female personas by which they become known. For just a few of these, reality and performance blur for the audience and sometimes for the actors, and the characters are sustained both on and off the stage.

An early well-loved British television double act of the 1950s, Les Dawson and Roy Barraclough, created the roles of two elderly women, Cissie Braithwaite and Ada Shufflebotham. Barraclough's character Cissie had pretensions to refinement and corrected Ada's malapropisms or vulgar expressions. They spoke some words aloud, but Dawson mouthed others, particularly those pertaining to bodily functions and sex, often accompanied with a characteristic sideways look as though to check the pair wasn't being observed. A native of Lancashire in the industrial north of England, Dawson explained that the mouthing of words (or "mee-mawing") was a habit of Lancashire millworkers. Originally they used it to communicate over the loud noise of looms but then resorted to it in daily life for indelicate subects. Although dressed as ordinary working-class women and not as pantomime dames, there was a strong element of panto caricature in their appearance: the well-padded bosoms that were adjusted by hairy folded arms and Cissie's hair rollers under headscarves worn during the day. They used rapid-fire exchanges about their lives and husbands and delighted audiences with their mildly "blue" dialogue.

> CISSIE: I'm sure your Bert has hidden facets. When you went to Blackpool on you honeymoon, were you virga intacta?
> ADA: No it was just bed and breakfast.
> CISSIE: Were you interfered with? No chuck, what I meant was . . . did Bert ever suggest pre-marital relations?
> ADA: Well, I met his uncle Arthur. Little bald fella with a stick.[5]

Cissie and Ada were in a straight comedic line running from music hall star Dan Leno's Mrs Kelly through the 1950s "dame" act of Norman Evans and his *Over the Garden Wall* act. And like their predecessors, Dawson and Barraclough were actors for whom the cross-dressing Cissie and Ada characters were important, but not exclusive, roles in their careers.

Most female impersonators leave their well-known characters behind when they leave the theater or TV studio. But just a few have created characters that are sustained and segue into life offstage. An intriguing double act of such cross-dressers who came to fame in the 1970s through radio and television appearances was Hinge and Bracket. Unlike Les Dawson and his predecessors, the pair created just two female characters that they sustained over a long period. They were usually interviewed in character, and throughout their careers, their stage names were much better known to audiences than their real ones.

Dr. Evadne Hinge and Dame Hilda Bracket, two elderly intellectual female musicians, were the creations of George Logan and Patrick Fyffe, respectively. As genteel English ladies, the two young men sang songs and exchanged banter, often with double entendres. A classically trained pianist, Logan accompanied the songs and was able to adjust the music to suit their male voices. They created a complex backstory to their imagined lives to sustain the audience's belief in their act. Harking back to the interwar years, the "ladies" claimed that Dame Hilda was the daughter of Sir Osbert Bracket, who had left her the family estate at (the fictitious) Stackton Tressel, Suffolk. The women supposedly became firm friends while appearing in the Rosa Charles Opera Company, and Hinge lived in the east wing of Dame Hilda's mansion. They worked hard to convey the reality of ladies of a certain class in the 1930s. Patrick Fyffe claimed that his father had the most influence on his own characterization of Dame Hilda. "'He talked to me for hours about the 1930s in terrific detail,' he said. 'That's why Hilda is so authentic. She is not into tights or rinses. She wears lisle stockings on suspenders, and brushes a bit of henna through the grey, and always calls her albums gramophone records.'"[6]

Dressed in cocktail dresses and pearl necklaces, with neatly waved hair, they presided over musical evenings, in which the songs of "dear" Mr. (Ivor) Novello and Sir Noel (Coward) were particular favorites, although their main passion was reserved for Gilbert and Sullivan.

In the 1970s, Hinge and Bracket spent two years performing in London pubs and clubs including the Royal Vauxhall Tavern (a popular gay venue and a popular location for the more famous drag act, Lily Savage, in the mid-1980s). *An Evening with Hinge and Bracket* was the hit of the 1974 Edinburgh festival, and they transferred to London's Royal Court Theatre and then to the Mayfair for a three-month season. Their next show, *Sixty Glorious Years*, was equally successful. Hinge and Bracket were radio naturals, and for ten years, they broadcast regularly on BBC Radio 4 with *The Enchanting World of Dr Evadne Hinge and Dame Hilda Bracket* and other shows. In the early 1980s, they had their own television series, *Dear Ladies*, and their act was featured in two royal variety performances. They made many records. In 1983, they appeared in a televised Royal Opera House production of *Die Fledermaus*. After splitting up for a short time, they re-formed and, throughout the 1990s, toured with their own show, fully cross-dressed as the two ladies. They appeared in pantomime and acted in the Peter Shaffer play *Lettuce and Lovage*. Essentially, theirs was a very English sort of act, referring back to the music hall dowagers of George Robey and to Douglas Byng's regal revue impersonations.

According to Stephen Dixon of the *Guardian*,[7] "Their comic edge came from the hints of Evadne's wild youth, and such was the fidelity of the characterisations that some fans believed the pair really were elderly spinsters, rather than young men." Perhaps the most intriguing aspect of their success is that they were equally popular on radio as they were on stage and on television, and yet the whole comedy rested on the fact that these were two men masquerading as elderly women. I can only imagine that radio listeners were either fully aware of the real identities of Dr. Evadne and Dame Hilda or that they enjoyed the thought of two real old ladies having naughty conversations. When they could be seen, they paid immense attention to the details of their dress and behavior and certainly looked the part. But to enjoy the humor, it was necessary that the audience colluded with the joke. Both male and female impersonations depend largely for their effect on the fact that the audience knows that the actors are cross-dressing. Sara Maitland, the biographer of Vesta Tilley,[8] recalled that she once went to see Hinge and Bracket with someone who failed to grasp that it was a drag act—"God knows how"—and was therefore baffled and bored. She reflected that this was instructive for her but not much fun for him.

But some actors, notably Paul O'Grady as Lily Savage, Australian Barry Humphries as Dame Edna Everage, South African Pieter-Dirk Uys as Evita Bezuidenhout, and more recently Irishman Brendan O'Carroll's Mrs Brown, go much further. The public often recognize their assumed characters as real, despite knowing that the performers are in drag. The name of the actor in most cases is less well known than that of their alter ego. These "dames" are interviewed on television and by journalists as though they were the character they portrayed. Although, with notable exceptions, there seemed to be a lull in this type of "dame" act in the early 2000s, a time in the growth in mainstream popularity of more over-the-top drag queens, there is still a public taste for the older type. The most popular TV comedy in Britain at the time of writing is *Mrs Brown's Boys*, a broad Irish comedy with some elements both of pantomime and pathos. As in pantomime, the dame character, Mrs Brown, uses sexual innuendo—but it is much too rude for children.

So why do some male performers choose to cross-dress as middle-aged or older women, and what do they want to say in the role that can't be said as the person they really are?

Perhaps the most obvious reason for choosing the cross-dressing role is that it is a career choice, made by an actor after reviewing their options for a future in entertainment. Risqué or sexual comedy, certainly up to the end of the 1900s, seems to have been perceived as much funnier if a male comedian is dressed as a woman. Much more so than if the lines are delivered as a man—or by an actual woman. But more probably the success of a particular role is serendipity, a happy chance. Somehow the actor finds that one of the characters he creates is so popular with his public that he continues to develop that part of his performance portfolio more than others. Sometimes this is just for a limited period in a long career. For the last quarter of the twentieth century, Paul O'Grady was best known as Lily Savage, a role he developed on the London gay scene and took mainstream in the 1990s; however, he diversified away from the role in the early part of this century. Although O'Grady freely admitted in his autobiography that Lily Savage came about almost accidentally, he then used his visibility and popularity in the role for more than financial success; he became an outspoken champion of gay rights. Paul O'Grady's Lily Savage, however, was never a "dame" as I have defined it. Although by the time he abandoned Lily (after assuming the character for twenty years) and reverted to Paul O'Grady in performance, he was approaching middle age, and remained essentially a drag queen. His character was not an amusing older woman but remained a mouthy Liverpudlian of indeterminate age, with a huge blonde wig and tackily glamorous outfits.

It was the desire to change a political system that drove South African Pieter-Dirk Uys to assume his dame persona. In the 1970s, at the height of the apartheid era, and inspired by Australian Barry Humphries's character of Dame Edna Everage, Uys became Evita Bezuidenhout, a white Afrikaner socialite and self-proclaimed political activist. Uys gave Tannie Evita, Afrikaans for "Auntie Evita," the imaginary position of the former ambassadress of a fictitious black homeland located outside her home district in the affluent, formerly whites-only suburbs of Johannesburg. Moving from playwriting and acting to staging his one-man shows, Uys used the medium of comedy to criticize the South African government's apartheid policies. Somehow, in his comedic "dame" character, cross-dressed as a neatly attired white woman of indeterminate middle age, he was able to say the things, for which, as Pieter-Dirk Uys, he would probably have been imprisoned. As Evita, he was able to expose the absurdity of the South African regime and its leaders as well as the often-hypocritical attitudes of white liberals. Much of his work went uncensored and was tacitly sanctioned by ruling party politicians who were unwilling to criticize openly the government policies themselves—but nevertheless saw the need for change. Following South Africa's first nonracial elections in 1994, Uys interviewed Nelson Mandela in his assumed character as the coiffured, pearl-necklaced Evita.[9] The filmed interview shows how realistic his character was and how seriously it was taken. Since then, he has used his character to work in the field of HIV/AIDS activism and education.

But perhaps the best and most enduring example of such damehood is Dame Edna Everage, the creation of Australian actor Barry Humphries. Humphries's work and interests range widely; he is a theatrical star, film producer, writer, collector of art and rare books, and a talented landscape painter. In addition to being recognized as a highly accomplished comedian, he is best known for the comic, fully believable characters that he has created during his long career. These include such satirical characters as the "priapic and inebriated cultural attaché" Sir Les Patterson, a role Humphries much enjoys assuming; the gentle, grandfatherly gentleman Sandy Stone, which is the actor's favorite character; and archetypal Australian bloke Barry McKenzie. But it is Dame Edna that most audiences want to see. They love Dame Edna, the self-acclaimed megastar, known for her satirical comedy and ability to reduce big-name guests on her shows to mere side acts supporting her larger-than-life personality.

Humphries's character, unlike that of Hinge and Bracket or Lily Savage, did not emerge from the gay club scene. Still in his hometown of Melbourne after dropping out of university, newly married to the first of his four wives, and intent on a career in the theater, he joined the Union Theatre Repertory Company as a full-time actor. Just to amuse his fellow troupe members as they traveled between venues, Humphries invented Edna, the Melbourne housewife. The characterization expanded when in 1955 Humphries wrote a number of songs and sketches for a Christmas revue called *Return Fare*, and it was in one of these sketches that Mrs Edna Everage first appeared on stage. Quite unlike the imperious dame that she would later become, this Edna was "a simpering, painfully shy housewife offering accommodation in her lovely home to the foreign athletes who would soon be coming to Melbourne for the 1956 Olympic games."[10] She would only billet an athlete if he or she was white, clean, and spoke English—and was prepared to accept good "Australian food" rather than anything more exotic.

In the 1950s, Humphries played the character at comedy clubs, satirizing the atmosphere of that era's Melbourne suburbia, and then, in the early 1960s, he took the act to London. There was a lukewarm reception at Peter Cook's nightclub, the Establishment. Humphries had to wait some years for the great success he subsequently enjoyed in Britain. At this stage and into the early 1970s, Edna was titled Mrs Everage, not Dame Edna. But in 1972, Humphries worked as a scriptwriter on two films based on a character he had originally created as a comic strip, Barry McKenzie. In the Australian comedy films *The Adventures of Barry McKenzie* (1972) and its sequel *Barry McKenzie Holds His Own* (1974), Humphries plays the drag role of Barry's Aunt. At the close of the latter film, the Australian prime minister at that time, Gough Whitlam, in a cameo role, confers upon Edna the title of "Dame," henceforth to be known as "Dame Edna." Dame Edna Everage she duly became, and this title allowed her to change her character from an "average" Melbourne housewife to the larger-than-life character known for her lilac-colored or "wisteria hue" hair and cat eye glasses; her favorite flower, the gladiolus (gladdies); and her boisterous greeting: "Hello, Possums!"

As with British audiences when he first began, Humphries did not have much luck when he first took Edna over the Atlantic. Already successful in Australia and having won acclaim in Britain with his 1976 London production *Housewife, Superstar!* in London's West End, he decided to try his luck with the show in New York. It was a disaster. Humphries later summed up his negative reception by saying: "When *The New York Times* tells you to close, you close."[11] There were further forays into the United States in the late 1980s, and as an attempt to advertise Edna's invented megastardom across the Atlantic, Humphries wrote a very funny spoof "autobiography" of Dame

Edna, titled *My Gorgeous Life*. Published originally in Britain by Macmillan, the 1989 edition by New York's Simon & Schuster was billed as "at last the book America has been waiting for." The inside cover blurb announces, "In this book, my new American fans can read my own fearless story." This was indeed chutzpah. Three episodes of *Dame Edna in Hollywood* aired on American TV in 1991. Guests on the show included many major stars of the time: Cher, Jack Palance, Larry Hagman, Mel Gibson, Kim Basinger, Robin Williams, George Hamilton, Burt Reynolds, and Barry Manilow. She treated them with her customary risqué humor, and not all could cope with the probing of their intimate lives. But Cher certainly could. When Dame Edna asked her if men had been a disappointment to her, "On the odd night," was Cher's reply.

Although there was a growing fan base in the United States, it was almost twenty-five years after the first visit that real success came. In 2000, Humphries took his *Dame Edna: The Royal Tour* show to North America, winning the inaugural Special Tony Award for a Live Theatrical Event that same year. He also won two National Broadway Theatre Awards for Best Play and for Best Actor in 2001. Dame Edna's newfound success in the United States led to many media opportunities and an invitation to write for *Vanity Fair*.

But what was it that Humphries as Edna was trying to achieve, except for the fame and fortune that has come his way with the character? Although Edna describes her chat shows as "an intimate conversation between two friends, one of whom is a lot more interesting than the other," the character has been used to satirize the cult of celebrity, class snobbery, and prudishness. Humphries uses the shows to poke fun at the political leaders and fashions of the times. John Lahr, Humphries's official biographer, claims that the Edna character came into her own during the 1980s when the policies of Thatcherism in Britain,[12] and what he described as the "vindictive style of the times," allowed Dame Edna to sharpen her observations accordingly. He wrote that when Edna took Prime Minister Margaret Thatcher's "seemingly hypocritical motto" of "caring and compassion" for others and turned it on its head, Edna became the voice of Humphries's outrage. Edna's exuberant persona and scathing commentary on society and celebrity, as well as her habit of treating celebrities like ordinary people (on her television shows) and ordinary people like celebrities (in her stage shows) have become a key part of her act. On New Year's Eve 2020, fresh from yet another "last" tour of Australia and in a one-off BBC program, *Dame Edna Rules the Waves*, the eighty-five-year-old Humphries happily ripped into Edna's celebrity guests. Adam Sweeting, writing in the *i* newspaper that night, commented,

> *Resplendent in fire-alarm pink on a gilt throne, Edna chewed through her guests like a wood-chipping machine. First up was* Sharon Osbourne, *a woman feared for her volcanic temper and a vocabulary that would make* Snoop Dogg *blush, but reduced to simpering coyness in the presence of the Dame. Edna was taking no prisoners. "Of course I recognise you," she said sympathetically, "but you've been to the panel-beaters a few times, haven't you?" Osbourne admitted she'd had four facelifts, and was forced to agree that "an intimate part of her anatomy" has been surgically overhauled.*[13]

Humphries himself finds curious the process by which his Edna creation evolved from housewife to superstar to megastar. He states in his autobiography that Edna is "not an alter ego as some might like to suggest for I have absolutely nothing in common with this woman, except perhaps my legs."[14] He refers to acting the part of his most popular character as the perfect Method acting exercise, for the Method actor must fabricate his character's history when thinking about a new role. "He must invent its memories, relationships, previous existences, tastes and obsessions."[15] As he has "known" Edna well for so long, he can instantly assume her persona. He can do the same with his other stage creations, easily becoming Sir Les Patterson or Barry

McKenzie in the same way. He has created their elaborate lives outside the theater. "I try to give the impression in my shows that they have, as it were, accidentally *strayed* onto the stage so that what we see and hear in the theatre is a fragment of their total existence: the tip of the iceberg."[16]

I would have thought that a cross-dressing "dame" character fronting a mainstream television program would not be popular in the twenty-first century and would be thought to be rather old-fashioned. The likes of Les Dawson's Ada and Dick Emery's Mandy are remembered nostalgically by those television viewers who are of an age to recall the 1960s; however, the younger generation prefers different humor and drag acts have become harder edged and more openly sexual. But then in 2011 along came Mrs Brown.

The show *Mrs Brown's Boys* was aired for the first time on the BBC. While certainly not new at this time, Brendan O'Carroll, the show's creator, had enjoyed success with a radio play, *Mrs Browne's Boys* (the *e* was dropped later) as far back as 1992 on the Irish radio station RTE. This was followed by a film, *Agnes Browne* (1999) starring Angelica Houston in the title role. Success continued with adaptations of O'Carroll's stories, which were filmed and went straight to DVD release, and a series of Mrs Brown plays mostly performed in Ireland and on tour.

In 1999, O'Carroll decided to form his own family theater company to act his plays about the Irish mammy. The story goes that when the actress hired to play Mrs Brown failed to turn up, he dressed as a woman and took on the cross-dressing role of Mrs Brown. The rest, as the cliché goes, is history. After a shaky start at the Pavilion Theatre, Glasgow, where O'Carroll suggested that a two-for-one ticket price might help sell them, the shows became a hit, and the Pavilion became known as the "Home of Mrs Brown."

In 2009, O'Carroll was approached by BBC Scotland to create a television series of Mrs Brown; the first episode was transmitted in 2011. The widespread popularity of the series began with a 2011 Christmas Day special in Ireland and a day later on the United Kingdom's main channel, BBC1. The rest is performance history. The series and Christmas specials are repeated constantly, and DVDs of both series and specials continue to sell. Though the UK viewing figure of 4.6 million for the 2019/2020 special was well down from the 11.4 million in 2013, Mrs Brown also has fans in the United States, Canada, New Zealand, South Africa, Iceland, and Australia. And the character has even been adapted for French-speaking Quebec viewers as *Mme Lebrun* with Benoît Brière in the title role. "She" is definitely a dame from the comic tradition of music hall onward. The character of Mrs Brown is that of an Irish "mammy" who tries to control the doings of her family. She is foul mouthed, uses a great deal of verbal and physical innuendo, and interacts with the audience, coming through the fourth wall of the set in the studio to speak directly to the live audience and, seemingly, to the people watching on television.

Whether you love it or loathe it, and there are many in both camps, it is impossible to deny that *Mrs Brown's Boys* has been a great commercial success. Many critics are scathing. "The whole thing is predicated on viewers finding a man dressed as a foul-mouthed woman intrinsically funny. If you do, you're away in a hack, and the viewing figures are astronomical, but if you don't, and you think that died out with Les Dawson and Dick Emery, then it's a long half-hour," Bernice Harrison commented in the *Irish Times* on February 12, 2011.[17] Irish critics seem particularly enraged that Mrs Brown might somehow lower the tone of Irish culture. But outside Ireland, too, there are many poor reviews. Grace Dent, the *Independent* TV critic wrote, "Once seen it is rarely forgotten. To love Mrs Brown, one must be thrilled by a man in a hairnet and a dinner lady tabard saying the F-word once every ten minutes, egged on by a loyal studio audience so whipped to hysteria by him that one can hear pants being soiled and spleens exploding with mirth."[18]

I must admit that I am probably at one with the critics. But Brendan O'Carroll can afford to ignore them. The show appeals to viewers as is proved by the extremely high viewing figures. And O'Carroll and his family have enjoyed immense commercial success. *Mrs Brown's Boys* has won numerous awards, including a BAFTA television award in 2012, and for three consecutive years (2013, 2014, and 2015), the show won Best Comedy at the National Television Awards. O'Carroll is philosophical about the reaction to his character. "You write what makes you laugh," he says, "and you hope the audience agree, and so far they do. If you are writing comedy and try to please everybody, you'll please nobody." He claims that he doesn't know the secret of Mrs Brown, "but what I do know is that there are things that Mrs Brown says and does that Brendan O'Carroll couldn't get away with. I think maybe it's a leniency that they're with an old woman. It's the old woman thing. I think secretly we all want to be Joan Rivers."[19]

And maybe that's the key to the attraction of all the dames. As older women, they say what their alter ego males couldn't get away with. And audiences find that funny. We somehow expect our mothers, aunts, and grandmothers to be respectable, not rude, but we are so pleased when they aren't. Most of the cross-dressers of the dame type have always emphasized sexual themes as grounds for their humor, such as Les Dawson's Cissie with her pretense embarrassment at bodily functions; the suggestive and satirical interviewing of Dame Edna; the "mother being naughty," as in *Mrs Brown's Boys*; and, in the extreme, the "just avoiding the censor" patter of Lily Savage.

As the century progresses, there is an increased acceptance in mainstream performance of drag kings and drag queens, and of comedians who identify as men, women, or LGBT+, and of all age groups. Such drag queens and kings are prepared to say whatever they want to unshockable audiences. Traditional dame characters are less visible. Drag queens have taken over much of their role in amusing and challenging an audience. But are they female impersonators as many definitions claim? The ultimate in cross-dressers?

Or is this description of them outdated?

11
QUEENING IT

Look, you're born naked and all the rest is drag.

—RuPaul[1]

From the back of the stage appears a tall figure dressed head to toe in gold lame, hair piled high, teetering on stiletto heels. She sashays down to the front of the stage to be greeted by those who have arrived before her. One is ultra-slender, wearing a skin-tight catsuit and tattoos, another is mini-skirted, batting her long, long eyelashes. One sports a witch's headdress and black lipstick. They are joined by others equally eye-popping. These are drag queens, all competitors in *RuPaul's Drag Race*. When RuPaul, the most famous and successful of all modern drag queens, introduced his American show to the United Kingdom, with his "may the best woman win," his words suggested an assumption that drag queens impersonate women by cross-dressing. But is that altogether true in the twentieth century?

Already well established in the United States, his show is an international hit. It has been franchised, or the rights sold, in many countries including Chile, Thailand, Canada, Holland, Australia, and the United Kingdom. Each drag race features a number of outrageously dressed drag queens who compete to be the champion of the series and for the title of drag queen superstar. Dressed in spectacular, often bizarre outfits, they stride out, or even roller-skate on to the stage with the intention of making an instant impact. They glitter. They pose. No one would ever mistake them for women if they walked down the street. Each is a performer playing a role—that of a drag queen. Those selected to take part in the show are required to perform in various categories, and the two contestants ranked lowest at the end of the episode compete in a lip-synching competition (miming to a recording) to determine who goes and who stays. Generally, the contestant that the judges feel has displayed the most "charisma, uniqueness, nerve, and talent" (C.U.N.T.) is the one who stays. The show, as you would expect from that acronym, is raucous, rude, and brassy—and highly successful.

I thought long and hard before deciding whether drag queens are cross-dressing, and therefore a subject for this book. One dictionary definition of a drag queen is "a usually gay man who dresses as a woman and performs as an entertainer, especially to caricature stereotypically vampish women."[2] Mm! Perhaps that was true of early drag queens, but the nature, visibility, and look of such drag performers have changed and diversified a great deal in the last seventy or so years. We can ask two questions: Are modern drag queens cross-dressing? And if so, are they caricaturing particular types of women?

On the music hall and vaudeville circuits, drag performers were common and fully accepted by the public, although it was illegal in many countries to cross-dress offstage. The most famous female impersonators, among them Julian Eltinge, Bert Savoy, Douglas Byng, and Bert Errol, were big box office draws in the early part of the twentieth century. Eltinge was so successful that he was the best paid actor in the world at the time, paid even more than Charlie Chaplin. These performers dressed glamorously in female attire, sometimes aping the female stars of stage and screen of their day. Although some (but not all) were gay, they tended to emphasize their masculinity offstage to avoid censure. Eltinge was well known for getting into fights, which were probably planned. Things changed when, from 1920 to 1933, the United States was under Prohibition legislation, which outlawed alcohol production and consumption. By that time, both music hall and vaudeville were beginning to wane, and female impersonation went on to be linked with the gay culture. In the Prohibition era, gay men and some gay women used the underground clubs and speakeasies (illicit establishments selling alcoholic drinks) to express and enjoy themselves. Out of the sight of the law, gay men felt free to be themselves and some to dress as drag queens without persecution. For a short time from 1930 to the end of Prohibition, this gay subculture emerged into the mainstream of midtown Manhattan in what was termed the "Pansy Craze." However, after the end of Prohibition, tolerance waned. Any sympathetic portrayal of gay characters on screen was prohibited, and the law continued to criminalize gay people. Police cracked down on gay bars, and the drag scene moved underground. The State Liquor Authority and the New York Police Department regularly raided bars that catered to gay patrons. But even though it was illegal for them to be served alcohol in bars, or even to dance together, the gay community continued to flourish.

The gay bars that featured drag performances continued to operate well into the 1950s and 1960s, and soon drag queens began to make their presence felt in public, in defiance of the law. Drag queen Flawless Sabrina (born Jack Doroshaw), an American LGBT activist, actress, and drag queen organized multiple pageants across the United States in the late 1960s. Determined to champion gay rights, she made herself highly visible to the public and was invited to appear as a guest on television talk shows, unheard of at that time. Around the same time, the Stonewall bar in Manhattan's Greenwich Village became a hub of gay culture, and the famous Stonewall Riots of 1969 galvanized the gay community to action. Drag queens, most notably Marsha P. Johnson, protested against police raids on gay bars in New York City. There followed the creation of the Gay Liberation Front. The fight for acceptance and equality grew in profile over the 1970s and 1980s, with Harvey Milk becoming the first openly gay man to be voted in to public office in San Francisco in 1977.

In the early 1970s, LGBTQ people of color developed their "houses" in New York, in neighborhoods like Harlem and Washington Heights. The house "mothers," usually drag queens, collected around them "children," often young gay men who needed a home. They supported one another in this network of houses, and the house mothers and their children entertained each other by performing in costume. The drag "ball" culture was said to have developed from these early intense competitions between the houses. *POSE*, the American drama television series that debuted in 2018, was based on the documentary *Paris Is Burning* (filmed in the late 1980s), and the series faithfully represents this African American and Latino LGBT and gender-non-conforming ballroom culture. It has, as a backdrop, the AIDS epidemic, at its worst in the 1980s and early 1990s. Like *Paris Is Burning*, the drama features characters who are dancers and models who perform to compete for trophies and recognition at their balls. Actor Billy Porter, as Pray Tell, calls out the categories for each competition: "The category is—Best Dressed—High Class—in a Fur Coat. POSE!" The house members then take to the floor. Some are gay men in drag. They can be beautifully dressed and would definitely be taken as female if they walked down the street. Others dress in sexually exaggerated outfits, the audience accepting their female personas. Cross-dressing in performance is an accurate description here. The performers at the balls are similar to the actors in music hall and vaudeville who cross-dressed, sang, and danced to impersonate the opposite gender in what was then, at least on the surface, a binary-gendered world.

One of the most famous of the house mothers, Pepper LaBeija, talking to the interviewer in *Paris Is Burning*, was clear about how the nature of drag had changed during the two decades she had been a "mother." "When I started out going to balls," she said, "it was all about drag queens and they were interested in looking like Las Vegas showgirls—backpieces, tail pieces, feathers, beads. But when the '70s rolled around things started changing. They wanted to look like gorgeous movie stars, Elizabeth Taylor. . . . And then like models, Maude Adams, Iman, Christie Brinkley." She went on to explain that now (at the time of filming) the categories at the balls had widened to be more inclusive to encourage the new "children' to take to the floor. Along with categories such as "pretty," "good body," and "fashionable," the balls introduced others such as "school," "college," "town and country," and "executive." The young wanted to "push the old bulls out of the way."[3]

In a time of heightened antipathy to gay culture, looking as authentic as they could in representing the character they chose was more important than being showy. Those in drag wanted to blend in and not stand out. They wanted to look sufficiently authentic to be able to leave the ball and arrive home without losing their clothes or being covered in blood. The gay men, LaBeija said, wanted to be told by their peers that when they dressed in business suits at the balls they could be taken for "straight" men in the kind of jobs that at that time such gay men could not hope to attain. At that time, gender was assumed, even in such LGBT communities, to be binary. Mothers of the houses were transwomen, some having transitioned or in the process of doing so.

Decriminalization of homosexual acts began in Illinois in 1961, and slowly other states followed, although it took more than forty years for the Supreme Court to rule against such discrimination. Around the 1970s, too, as the rules relaxed, the drag culture segued into mainstream society, and drag queens, as well as continuing to multiply and appear regularly in clubs and other venues across the United States, were featured on national, network television and in films. At this point, drag queens were amassing large followings. Some of the first drag icons emerged. Divine, a striking three-hundred-pound drag queen from Baltimore, Maryland, worked with director John Waters and was the trashy, grotesque superstar of many cult films in the 1970s. In these, Divine would never be mistaken for a woman. A talented actress as well as drag queen, she eventually played the tragi-comic character Edna Turnblad in John Waters's film *Hairspray* (1988) to a much wider mainstream audience.

In the United Kingdom, there has been a lively LGBT nightlife for many years, and drag queens have been an integral part of it. After World War II ended, many men who had enjoyed performing in drag during the war became part of all-male revues that featured female impersonation. As in the United States, homosexuality, however, was considered dangerous to public safety and morale, and it was almost impossible to be openly gay. In 1952, Sir John Nott-Bower, commissioner of Scotland Yard, began to weed out homosexuals from the British government; at the same time, Senator Joseph McCarthy was conducting a witch hunt in the United States against homosexuals. Unable to feel safe because of such discrimination, drag queens found their home in underground clubs and bars in most cities of the United Kingdom. Many of these clubs, particularly those in London, became known to a wider audience than the LGBT community. The Black Cap and the Royal Vauxhall Tavern were two of the most popular among them.

However, there was some drag performance on television even in the late 1950s and 1960s. Rex Jameson, for instance, who had spent some time in a forces review show after the war and then in cabaret, developed his alter ego character, Mrs Shufflewick. She was a cockney woman who sat in her favorite pub, drinking port and lemon, and regaled the other regulars with filthy-in-disguise jokes. In the mid-1950s he appeared in early TV variety shows including Ralph Reader's *It's a Great Life*. In early 1970s, with his act rougher from years of drinking and his sexuality in the open after homosexuality was decriminalized in 1967, he found a new audience. As a drag queen, he performed on the London gay club circuit, notably at the Black Cap.[4]

Some drag performers, with acts just sufficiently cleaned up to amuse the increasingly more liberally minded public, emerged from the clubs. They appeared on television and in the more mainstream venues. Lily Savage, the alter ego of Paul O'Grady, developed his drag queen act on the London gay scene in the 1980s and went mainstream, extremely successfully, in the 1990s. Hinge and Bracket spent two years performing their act in clubs, including the Royal Vauxhall, before a visit to the Edinburgh Festival Fringe in 1974 gave them instant success and a long career on TV and radio.

Throughout the period from the 1970s to the 1990s, professional performers in various genres challenged gender stereotypes on stage by cross-dressing. Singers and band-members such as Freddy Mercury (Queen), David Bowie, Kurt Cobain (Nirvana), Marilyn Manson, and the Red Hot Chili Peppers also played with gender performance and sometimes dressed in drag on stage. The 1980s and 1990s too saw actors begin to appear in drag on television. They were mostly of the "dame" type. Dame Edna Everage and Hinge and Bracket were typical, but Lily Savage, as a loud-mouthed youthfully dressed woman, was less so. They were cross-dressers, each choosing a type of female character as their persona and becoming known in that role. All were consummate comedians, able to use their characters to amuse and challenge audiences with political, social, and particularly sexual banter and innuendo. But these were comparatively cozy versions of the drag queens to come.

By the 1990s, audiences in many countries were ready to receive drag queens into the mainstream like never before. Instrumental in that process was drag queen RuPaul, who made a name for himself in the late 1980s and early 1990s on the New York City club scene. His club act laid the foundation for his popularity, and he went on to achieve nationwide success. In 1993, he recorded a dance/house album, *Supermodel of the World*, and made an accompanying video. It was an unexpected hit in an era of grunge and gangsta-rap popular music. So began his rise to fame. Many more singles, videos, and albums followed, along with a modeling contract with MAC cosmetics, his own talk show, and an autobiography. In mid-2008, RuPaul began producing *RuPaul's Drag Race*.

Are the drag queens in the Drag Races cross-dressing? They are not just men dressing as women (i.e., crossing an imagined binary gender line), though most still use an accepted pronoun *her* to describe their fellow competitors. They are dressing and acting as drag queens and are competing as such. Most drag queens are gay men but certainly not all. Dame Edna Everage, perhaps one of the best-known mainstream "queens," is married to his fourth wife and has two daughters and two sons. San Franciscan Crème Fatale is female, as is Holestar, a British ex-soldier. Holestar describes herself as "a loud, opinionated, queer, kinky, ridiculous person who has performed all over the world in a wig and just happens to have a vagina."[5]

RuPaul, as well as being the most commercially successful drag queen in the United States, is also an actor, model, singer, songwriter, and television personality. He/she/they have strong opinions about what constitutes a drag queen persona. RuPaul does not consider himself to be impersonating a woman when in drag, although he looks fabulous in his many wonderful dresses and could easily be mistaken for one. He once said, "I do not impersonate females! How many women do you know who wear seven-inch heels, four-foot wigs, and skin-tight dresses?" And he is indifferent to gender-specific pronouns and well-known for the comment "You can call me he. You can call me she. You can call me Regis and Kathie Lee; I don't care! Just as long as you call me."[6] When he and other drag queens are acting as such on stage or screen, they are not claiming to be representing another specific and different gender; they are acting, performing as drag queens. RuPaul is an actor, among many other things, and has played male roles. In *The Brady Bunch* (1996), he took on a cameo role of a female schoolteacher; critics recognized his performance as a good, believable impersonation of a woman and not at all a parody. He makes public appearances in both male and female costume. When Divine, the best known of the early drag queens, took on the role of Edna Turnblad in *Hairspray* (1988), she maintained that the character of Edna could not be accurately described as that of a drag queen, proclaiming, "What drag queen would allow herself to look like this? I look like half the women from Baltimore."[7]

Ryan Roschke writes,

> In the 21st century, a drag queen is not just a man who wears women's clothes; a drag queen is an entirely separate entity. When so impeccably dressed and flawlessly painted, the person underneath the queen disappears almost completely. Oftentimes, I've heard drag performers describe their personas as though they were another person. They've plunged their hands deep down into their own psyches and pulled out the weirdest, fiercest, and most theatrical parts of themselves, then mashed them together to form something new. A character. An alter ego. A super-"she"-ro, if you will.[8]

Alongside these in-your-face queens, growing in number, who we see in clubs, films, and on television in the 2020s, there are also the drag queens who are transgender women. *POSE* has Mj Rodriguez in the leading role of Blanca Rodriguez-Evangelista. The actor playing Blanca is transgender, and the show features the largest cast of transgender actors as series regulars in a scripted series. Rodriguez's Blanca is a young woman who forms her own "house"—the House of Evangelista—after receiving a positive diagnosis for HIV. As the head of the House of Evangelista, she becomes a surrogate mother to several abandoned queer youths of color. Although originally an actor auditioning for male parts, Rodriguez was particularly successful when cast in the role of Angel, a young drag queen, in an off-Broadway production of the musical *Rent*.

After completing her time in *Rent*, she went through a transitioning period where she stepped out of the limelight for a time, emerging to state that she was now auditioning as a female actress. Since then she has appeared on stage and in films in different gender roles. Her performance as Ebony, a transgender woman, a supporting role in the independent film *Saturday Church*, earned her a nomination for Best Actress at the 2017 Tribeca Film Festival. And her performance in the straight female role of Audrey in *Little Shop of Horrors* at the Pasadena Playhouse in 2019 has showed again what a fine actor and singer she is. She has no need to limit herself to transgender roles. So far in her career Rodriguez has played male, transgender women, and straight female roles, and in none of them was she "crossing" genders. Other transgender actors, too, whether they have transitioned or not, are taking a variety of roles. What gender they claim in real life, if any, is irrelevant to their ability to perform; they are actors.

In a world that is increasingly accepting that gender is a social construct unlike sexuality, it is unsurprising that drag queens are varied in how they portray themselves. However they dress, from those who wear clothes that any cisgender woman might wear to the wildly creative outfits worn by RuPaul's competitors, they use their acts to entertain their audiences but also to challenge gender stereotypes.

As RuPaul says, and it is true of most drag queens in the twenty-first century, "I don't dress like a woman; I dress like a drag queen!"[9] And drag queens can be anything they want to be.

12
PRETTY WOMEN? HANDSOME MEN?

DAPHNE: Osgood, I'm going to level with you. We can't get married at all.

OSGOOD: Why not?

DAPHNE: Well, in the first place, I'm not a natural blonde.

OSGOOD: It doesn't matter. . . .

DAPHNE: I can never have children.

OSGOOD: We can adopt some.

DAPHNE: Oh, you don't understand Osgood. I'm a man!

OSGOOD: Well—nobody's perfect.

—*SOME LIKE IT HOT* (1959)[1]

Young men dressed as women were the hit of 1959. In one of the best-loved and funniest films of the twentieth century, *Some Like It Hot*, musicians Joe (Tony Curtis) and Jerry (Jack Lemmon) accidentally witness the 1929 St. Valentine's Day Massacre in Chicago. Fleeing from Mafia gangsters who want them dead, the boys decide that they have to get out of town. Their agent is looking for two musicians, a saxophonist and a double-bass player, to join a jazz band on tour, an ideal opportunity for the boys. The only problem is that it is an all-girl band. Dressing as women, Joe as Josephine and Jerry as Daphne, they join Sweet Sue and her Society Syncopators who are just about to leave for a gig in Miami. Their love affairs, Curtis with the singer and banjo player Sugar (Marilyn Monroe) and Lemmon with Osgood Fielding III (Joe E. Brown) are at the core of the movie. Who can forget Lemmon as Daphne, dancing wildly with maracas as she celebrates "her" engagement to Osgood, the elderly playboy? This was at a time when gay marriage in the United States would have been almost unimaginable. The end lines, too, "Oh, you don't understand Osgood. I'm a man! Well—nobody's perfect," are still, no matter how many times heard, unexpectedly comic.

It was a tried and tested story line. The French comedy film *Fanfare of Love* came out in 1935 and was followed in 1951 by the German version *Fanfares of Love* (*Fanfaren der Liebe*) directed by Kurt Hoffmann. *Some Like It Hot*, the same story in an American setting, was an immediate box office and critical success, receiving six Academy Award nominations, including Best Actor, Best Director, and Best Adapted Screenplay. In 1989, the Library of Congress selected it as one of the first twenty-five films for preservation in the United States National Film Registry for being "culturally, historically, or aesthetically significant." And in 2017, the film was selected as the best comedy of all time in a poll of 253 film critics from fifty-two countries conducted by the BBC.

The film was not only immensely enjoyable but also significant in legal history. It was distributed without the producers obtaining approval from the Motion Picture Production Code (Hays Code)[2] for its cross-dressing content and its suggestion of a gay relationship. The increasing tolerance in the 1950s for the subject of homosexuality had weakened the influence of the code, but it was still officially enforced until the mid-1960s. The overwhelming success of *Some Like It Hot* is considered to have been one of the final nails in the coffin for the Hays Code.

Of course, the tradition of men dressing as older and middle-aged women in comedy roles continued almost seamlessly from variety into films. There was a lot of slapstick humor to be garnered from the long and voluminous women's clothes of the early 1900s: witness Charlie Chaplin in *A Busy Day* (1914), playing a militant suffragette, or Wallace Beery in the *Sweedie* series of silent comedy films of 1914–1916. And the list goes on. From Terry Jones playing Brian's mother in *The Life of Brian* (1979) to Eddie Murphy in two female roles in *The Nutty Professor* (1996), Tyler Perry in *The Diary of a Mad Black Woman* (2005), John Travolta as Edna Turnblad in *Hairspray* (2007), and Rupert Everett in *St. Trinians* in the same year, many male actors have enjoyed a new comedy challenge. But in this chapter, I want to examine how so many men and women took on cross-dressing roles, not for the fun of seeing a man dress up, but in an attempt to portray a different gender as faithfully as possible. Why were there so few cross-dressing parts for actors from the 1930s up to the latter part of the twentieth century? Why have such roles proliferated since then? Why have so many recently well-known actors and actresses wanted to take on the roles?

Between the introduction of sound to the movies in the late 1920s and the full enforcement of the Hays Code in 1934, there was a brief period when there was limited oversight of films and their story lines. Movie content was restricted more by local laws, negotiations with the major studios, and popular opinion than by strict adherence to the Hays Code. Hollywood filmmakers often ignored it altogether. Aimed at censoring inappropriate content, the code took some while to take hold. During what is known as the pre-code period, some films with sexual themes such as homosexuality, promiscuity, and prostitution did reach the public cinemas; however, due to intense and increasing opposition from the Catholic Church in late 1933 and into 1934, the studios eventually had to change their filmmaking to support the accepted morality of the time. Such themes did not reemerge in American films until decades later. That short period in the early 1930s still reflected the "Roaring Twenties," the economic expansion of the United States, its hedonism, short-skirted women, and the jazz and club culture. Two of the popular films of the era—*Morocco* (1930) and *First a Girl* (1935)—center on a club singer. Both take on the themes of cross-dressing, the merging of masculine and feminine characteristics, and potential homosexuality. *Morocco*, starring Gary Cooper and Marlene Dietrich, is most famous for a scene in which

Dietrich, dressed in a man's tailcoat and bow tie, bends over and kisses one of the women diners, much to her embarrassment. Both the cross-dressing and the kiss were considered scandalous at the time. The film is an early attempt by the director, Josef von Sternberg, to examine how a woman can behave adventurously, quite differently from expectations. In a subtle allusion to the different aspects of sexuality, her impersonation of a man invites the attention of legionnaire Tom Brown, played by Gary Cooper.

First a Girl, a romantic comedy starring Jessie Matthews, tells the story of a shopgirl who dreams of a singing career. She meets an older man, a drag artist, Victor, sheltering from the rain. She is going to lose her job, and he, having lost his voice and unable to perform, has the idea of putting Elizabeth on stage in his place, pretending to be a female impersonator. Offstage, Elizabeth dresses as a man, Bill, and this leads to many complications. "He" attracts the attention of Robert, who, despite believing himself fully heterosexual, finds Bill attractive. Eventually, as you would expect from a romantic comedy, the deception is revealed, and Elizabeth and Robert motor off to a new life together. The film was based on a 1933 German film, titled *Viktor und Viktoria*, directed by Reinhold Schünzel and Roger Le Bon. At the same time, Schünzel made a French version of the film, *Georges et Georgette* (1934). The German film, written and directed by Schünzel, was shot during the Weimar Republic period in Germany, officially the German Reich, the German state from 1918 to 1933. This was a period when cabarets flourished in Germany. It is not surprising, then, that the original story of the film revolves around the cabaret scene. Cabaret was a French invention of the 1880s, and the most famous club, the Moulin Rouge in Paris, had prostitutes as dancers and waiters; however, cabaret became popular in Germany in the Weimar period. Patrons sat, drank, and ate at tables while singers, dancers, and comedians entertained them, often on a small stage. Such entertainment in Berlin, Munich, and other cities revolved around two themes: sex and politics. Jokes, songs, and dancing were laced with sexual innuendo, and anyone who has seen the film *Cabaret* (1972) can get the flavor. Although *Cabaret* shows a somewhat glamorized nightclub scene, "Two Ladies," a suggestive dance and song by Joel Grey as the master of ceremonies, and the nature of the all-male female impersonators of the dance band (dressed in drag, garters, top hats, and high heels) illustrate the type of ribald performances popular with cabaret patrons. As the 1920s progressed, this type of act gave way to open displays of nudity, to the point where most German cabarets had at least some topless dancers. Some shows were also patronized by homosexual men, lesbians, and transvestites who could relax in the permissive liberalism of the cabaret scene and allow them to be open and unapologetic about their sexual identities. In the British version of the film, the cabaret became the music hall.

Although the British Board of Film Classification (BBFC) was founded by the film industry in 1912 and was responsible for the national classification and censorship of films, *First a Girl*, unlike its German predecessor, was accepted as what it was purported to be, a comedy. It was a great hit. Although themes of gender and sexuality take center stage in the film, there seems to have been no condemnation of scenes that had female to male cross-dressing, or those where those seemingly of the same sex share beds. In a very explicit musical number, "Half and Half," chorus boys and girls show different genders in their half male, half female costumes. Perhaps it also helped that it seems unlikely that anyone could mistake Jessie Matthews, even with cropped hair, for a boy called Bill. It was hoped that the film starring the greatest British comedienne of the time would spearhead an entry of British films into the American market. But although it was good box office in the United Kingdom, the film had only moderate success in the United States. Almost fifty years later, however, in 1982, *Viktor und Viktoria* was adapted again, this time successfully, as *Victor and Victoria*, written and directed by Blake Edwards and starring Julie Andrews.

There was little cross-dressing or gender bending in films during the period from the beginning of World War II until the 1970s, and the first British movie dealing explicitly with homosexuality was the noir-suspense *Victim* (1961), which is believed to contain the first use of the word *homosexuality* in an English-language film. Before Dirk Bogarde accepted the role of the gay hero, Hollywood stars Jack Hawkins, James Mason, and Stewart Granger had already turned it down. Most likely they saw it as a threat to future casting in the very masculine roles in which they specialized. Although some scenes were removed, it still proved highly controversial on its release in the United Kingdom. The BBFC gave the film an X rating, which was "recommended for adults only," a classification then usually given to erotica or horror films. In the United States, the Hays Code assessors refused to give their seal of approval, but just a year later, in 1962, the Hollywood Production Code agreed to lift the ban on films using homosexuality as a plot device. A few years later, the code was replaced by the Motion Picture Association of America (MPAA) film rating system, which introduced an age-appropriate classification system for films. In 1982, when attitudes to sexuality had become much more openly discussed and liberal, the VHS version of the film was rated as PG-13 (i.e., children over the age of thirteen could see it with parental approval).

But until the 1960s, the general consensus, or at least that which was endorsed publicly on film, was that men were men and women were women, and that they were two significantly different genders determined by birth sexuality. They were portrayed as fulfilling very different roles in society. There were many British films of the 1930s and early 1940s with a wide variation of theme. Along with comedies, romances, and musicals, there were mysteries (*The Lady Vanishes*, 1938), history (*Henry VIII*, 1933), adventure (*Gunga Din*, 1939), drama (*Ourselves Alone*, 1936), and even sci-fi (*The Mask of Fu Manchu*, 1932). But all, even those that examined difficult interpersonal relationships firmly emphasized heterosexuality.

When the war started and during World War II, the film industry was an important source of communication to the people in all the warring countries. Cinema was an extremely popular form of entertainment, and along with its role of keeping up morale with comedy and drama, it was used to distribute propaganda and to influence the public to support the war effort in their everyday lives. Films such as the drama/documentary film *They Also Serve* (1940) directed by a woman, a rarity in British filmmaking of the time, is such an example. It shows how a housewife performs various good deeds to keep her family, neighbors, and hence the country, running during the early days of the war. These films paralleled the many films or film documentaries about the airmen, sailors, and soldiers who were fighting the enemy: *Spitfire* (1942), *The Silver Fleet* (1942), and *The Big Blockade* (1942) are typical. *The Gentler Sex*, a 1943 romantic comedy, showed seven young women during World War II driving lorries and manning ack-ack batteries.

When the war ended, however, even though women in the war took on many of the physically and mentally exacting jobs that had been thought the domain of men, their roles were assumed to be temporary. The UK government tacitly encouraged the return to strict gender role separation. The 1942 Beveridge Report on Welfare, which aimed to improve the lives of everyone in postwar Britain, and indeed did so, implicitly assumed a clear separation of male and female roles. "In the next thirty years housewives as Mothers have vital work to do in ensuring the adequate continuance of the British Race and of British ideals in the world."[3] The warriors were back from the fray, and their role now was to work and provide for families; the role of women was to support the men by staying at home or taking less onerous jobs. Surprising maybe to our modern ears, after six years of bombs and shortages, many women bought into this view of postwar life with relief.

Cross-dressing films were restricted to those that showed a male actor dressing up as a middle-aged or older woman in a comedy role. In 1949, Alec Guinness played eight roles in the film *Kind Hearts and Coronets*, one of which was Lady Agatha D'Ascoyne, and in 1954, Alastair Sim amused a huge cinemagoing audience as the permissive headmistress Millicent Fritton in *The Belles of St. Trinians*.

In the United States, too, partly due to the Hays Code, in the period from the late 1930s to the late 1950s, it would be hard to find a film portrayal of cross-dressing or any exploration of gender roles. The industry was expected to self-censor its output following the code's set of moral guidelines. Censorship began to be more rigidly enforced in 1934. The list of things that could not be represented did not include cross-dressing as such, although the phrase "Any inference of sex perversion" would have given producers, directors, and screenwriters food for thought. So too would a subsection that demanded that care should be taken in the manner in which subjects were treated "to the end that vulgarity and suggestiveness may be eliminated and that good taste may be emphasized."[4] What exactly was "good taste" is not specified. The film industry followed the guidelines set by the code well into the late 1950s, but by then the influence of the code had weakened due to television and the influence of foreign films. Some directors ignored the code, and there was minimum enforcement by assessors. In 1968, the Production Code was replaced by the Motion Pictures Association of America (MPAA) film rating system, which assessed age-appropriateness. It appears from the hundreds of films that emerged from the US film industry during the 1940s and 1950s that none, certainly no memorable ones, showed women or men stepping out of rigid gender roles until *Some Like It Hot* in 1959.

It wasn't only the restrictions of the code that would have deterred filmmakers from tackling stories involving cross-dressing. In the late 1940s and early 1950s, McCarthyism took hold in the United States. Senator Joseph

McCarthy instituted a campaign spreading fear of communist influence on American institutions. Primarily the target was to identify and flush out supposed communists from the State Department, but later from other places employing large workforces, including Hollywood. In 1947, Hollywood actors as well as directors, screenwriters, and producers were blacklisted. Ten writers and directors, the Hollywood Ten, were subpoenaed to appear before a committee where they refused to cooperate in admitting their political beliefs or naming other communists. In 1950, in the pamphlet Red Channels, many entertainment industry professionals were named as potential communists and sympathizers and barred from employment for some years afterward. On the basis of lies and what later would be accepted as illegal procedures, a great deal of fear was created in the industry. People lost their jobs, livelihoods, and in some cases took their own lives as pressure became too intolerable.

Parallel to McCarthyism was the "Lavender Scare," which portrayed gay men and lesbians as national security risks and led to persecution of homosexuals. This witch hunt, which McCarthy used to link homosexuality and a susceptibility to communist influences, caused harm to far more people than even the "Red Scare." In the postwar period, a visible homosexual subculture had emerged, particularly in big cities such as Washington, and this was seen as a threat to previously held puritanical ideas about gender. As families reunited, a national narrative, which included stories told in American films of the time, promoted ideals of the nuclear family and traditional gender roles. From the 1945 film Brief Encounter, in which the attraction of the nuclear family triumphs over temptation, to the 1953 Calamity Jane, where the erstwhile gutsy Indian scout is finally reduced to wearing a skirt and clutching a feather duster as she cleans the cabin for her man, no hint of gender impersonation is allowed.

So, it is not surprising that with all the legal, political, and social pressures of the 1950s, there was no appetite to produce films and plays that might be seen as undermining the family and the heterosexual mores of the time. Story lines that questioned rigid gender stereotyping with cross-dressing roles were avoided, and actors, male and female, were keen to take on parts that demonstrated unquestionably their masculinity or femininity.

But *Some Like It Hot*, which ignored the Hays Code and dealt—albeit as a comedy—with issues of men in women's clothes and a potential gay relationship, began a period in which there was an explosion of male and female cross-dressing and, more recently, less gender-specific acting. Story lines have been written to include cross-dressing characters, not just for the fun of seeing a man or woman dress up but in an attempt to portray a different gender or genders as faithfully as possible. More recently, directors have chosen to ignore the given gender of a role and have encouraged the actor to concentrate on its psychological characteristics. Actors such as Frances de la Tour and Maxine Peake have played Hamlet with critical success. Well-known actors, far from avoiding them, have been keen to take on such cross-dressing and transgender roles. Some of these movies have long since been forgotten, but a few remain in the collective memory as marking seminal moments in the way in which society regarded gender. They exemplify the range of cross-dressing roles taken by well-known actors in the late nineteenth and early twentieth centuries. Many movie fans will have their favorites, and my choices may not be theirs—but where to begin?

In 1982, Dustin Hoffman took on the title role of *Tootsie* in the American romantic comedy directed by Sydney Pollack. It is typical of the many story lines in movies in which a character masquerades as a different gender to achieve a particular purpose. *Tootsie* tells the story of an actor, Michael Dorsey, whose reputation for being difficult forces him to take on a new identity as a woman to secure work. He reinvents himself as the feisty Dorothy Michaels. The film was a major critical and financial success, and in 1998, the Library of Congress deemed the film "culturally, historically, or aesthetically significant." In an interview for the American Film Institute,[5] Dustin Hoffman recalled his feelings when playing a woman. He had not been prepared to take on the role, he said, unless he could be made to look sufficiently authentic as a woman to be able to walk down the street and not be seen as "a man in drag." To prepare for his role, he watched the (then) recent film *La cage aux folles* (1978), which featured a man in disguise, and had many makeup tests. He would not ask the audience to suspend belief. Quite emotionally, he recalled that he was surprised that, despite their best efforts, the makeup artists were unable to turn him into the beautiful woman he had expected. He felt that when in the role of Dorothy Michaels, he was an interesting woman, and yet, as she was not a beauty, he, the real Dustin Hoffman, would not have approached such a woman at a party or engaged her in conversation. As a result, he admitted, he realized that he had missed out on knowing many interesting women. Hoffman did not consider the film a comedy, and at a time when women's roles, especially in the workplace, were changing rapidly, the film certainly invited audiences to look more deeply into what gender equality really meant.

In the same year that *Tootsie* was such a success, *Victor/Victoria*, the remake of *Viktor und Victoria*, came to the big screen. Later it was adapted as a Broadway musical and premiered on stage in 1995. Although a very successful comedy, and to some extent a typical "male impersonation" story, the film examined lightly, but directly, gay sexual relationships. By this time, more explicit cross-dressing, bed scenes, and homosexuality elicited no adverse comment from critics. Indeed, "Driven by a fantastic lead turn from Julie Andrews, Blake Edwards' musical gender-bender is sharp, funny and all-round entertaining," was an aggregate comment from Rotten Tomatoes.[6] It won many award nominations, and Julie Andrews won the Golden Globe Award for Best Actress—Motion Picture Comedy or Musical.

In contrast, the British period drama *Orlando* (1992), with Tilda Swinton in the title role, examined the transition of a man to a woman, not an impersonation. Based on Virginia Woolf's novel of the same name, the story begins just before the death of Queen Elizabeth I in 1603 and ends in the present day (1992 in the film; 1928 in the novel). The dying queen was played wonderfully and appropriately by the cross-dressing Quentin Crisp. A few years after his performance in the film, writer and actor Quentin Crisp, at the age of ninety, said that he realized that he was not a gay man but a trans woman. At the start of the film, Elizabeth promises Orlando, a young nobleman played by an androgynous Tilda Swinton, a great inheritance. But in return Orlando has to make an unusual promise: not to fade, not to wither, not to grow old. Centuries later, still young, he travels to Constantinople as the English ambassador where he is badly injured and almost killed. Waking up a week later, he finds he has transformed into a woman. Back in England, and finding that, as a woman (now Lady Orlando), "she" has no rights to the property bequeathed by Queen Elizabeth, she spends the next two centuries up to the present day fighting for her rights. Eventually and philosophically, she achieves a tranquil existence alongside her daughter (a son in the book).

At the time, the film received a varied response. Tilda Swinton's handling of maleness and femaleness was praised, but there seems to have been little discussion of how the film handled the transgender issues; however, twenty-five years later, the contribution of the film to examining issues of gender and sexuality was acknowledged. The film was screened as part of a multimedia arts project titled *Orlando: The Queer Element*, which explored issues of science and gender through history. The performance, using five actors, some from the LGBT community, took place on March 24, 2017, at the BFI Flare London LGBTIQ+ Film Festival accompanied by a screening of the film.

There are many films involving cross-dressing roles of all kinds and many famous actors playing them. But for me, one of the most impressive and serious films involving cross-dressing was *The Crying Game* (1992), featuring an unknown actor, Jaye Davidson. Set at the time of the "Troubles" in Northern Ireland, the complicated story explores themes of nationality, race, and gender, and it has been much discussed. The main character, Fergus, a Provisional IRA[7] volunteer, establishes a tenuous relationship with a soldier, Jody, while guarding him as a prisoner of the Provisionals. Jody begs Fergus to protect his love interest, Dil (Davidson) if he were to die. Finding that Dil is a truly beautiful woman, Fergus falls in love. Fergus is initially shocked to discover Dil is transgender, as are most viewers who see the film for the first time; however, the relationship survives, and eventually Fergus protects Dil from arrest for murder by taking the blame. The film ends with Dil visiting Fergus in prison as he serves a long prison sentence.

The film company needed funding for the project and sought it in the United States but failed because funders wanted a woman to play Dil. They did not believe that a male actor could play a convincing female. But without the full-frontal male nude scene when Dil reveals that she has male genitalia, the film would have lacked its shock element. It would also have removed one of the key issues in the film, that of Fergus's complex sexuality. The original plan was retained. Released in 1992, the film had little initial success in the United Kingdom, probably due to its scenes showing pub bombings and its sympathetic portrayal of an IRA fighter. Undeterred, the distributor Miramax decided to promote it in the United States where it was a great financial and critical success. It was nominated for six Academy Awards, including best supporting actor for Davidson; the film was rereleased to great acclaim in Britain and Ireland and won success around the world.

Davidson, American born but brought up in Britain, did not stay long in the acting profession; he preferred modeling. He is gay, not transgender, and said his androgynous look as a young man alienated him within the gay community as gay men usually preferred more masculine men. Later in life he adopted a more traditionally male appearance with a shaved head and tattoos, and he developed a more muscular physique. His was a short life as a cross-dressing performer, but his performance in the film contributed significantly to the debate on transgender issues.

Jaye Davidson as Dil was totally believable as a woman; however, other attempts to impersonate women have been successful in varying degrees. In films made in the Western world, those where men cross-dress are mostly those where the plot involves disguise. Moviegoers are expected to suspend belief. It is not always necessary for the actor to be able to "walk down the street" as a believable woman, as Dustin Hoffman insisted. The audience can accept that the actor is cross-dressing temporarily, however unconvincingly, to confuse a situation. He will revert to his male gender before the end of the story. Of course, what makes a man appear to be female and not obviously in drag, depends on many things. Clothes, stance, build, walk, the voice, and makeup all have a part to play—so, too, does the observer's idea of femininity. If a small, slim person is your idea of feminine, then a statuesque person with size twelve shoes might not fit the bill no matter how soft the face. At the same time, if a curvy shape is considered important for verisimilitude, then a slim, lithe young man may not convince.

Cross-dressing can be hard work. Young boys in Shakespearean plays were squeezed into wooden cages to give them a rounded shape. Tony Curtis in *Some Like It Hot* had to learn how to hold his arms to hide muscle. Dustin Hoffman practiced different makeups for *Tootsie*. It takes effort. Perhaps one of the reasons why there have been proportionally far more attempts to turn male actors into attractive women in the movies than on the stage is because such effort is more possible in films than the theater. The period during which a movie is filmed is usually long, and scenes are often shot separately. This allows detailed but short-term attention to aspects of the face, the walk, the voice, and such, which would be less sustainable in a stage performance.

Cross-dressing by a woman as a man is more problematic as there can be less reliance on makeup. Perhaps that is why many of the more successful male impersonations have been in historical movies. In *Orlando*, Tilda Swinton was totally believable in the title role when being a man, just as Quentin Crisp in full royal regalia as Queen Elizabeth I was a totally acceptable female. Swinton's character wore typical period clothing representing that worn during the four centuries of his/her life. In *Albert Nobbs* (2011), a British-Irish film set in Dublin at the end of the nineteenth century, Glenn Close and her costar Janet McTeer played women who lived long term as men. Although the film itself received mixed reviews, Close and McTeer were nominated for Academy, Golden Globe, and Screen Actors Guild awards for their portrayals of Nobbs and Hubert Page, respectively. Perhaps also relevant to their success was the film's nomination for the Academy Award for Best Makeup. It is more difficult for women attempting to look like men if the role is a modern rather than historical figure. But there seems to be agreement that one role, although short, was a great cross-dressing success. In *I'm Not There*, the 2007 film in which different characters illustrate aspects of Bob Dylan and his life, the fourth character, Jude, was praised as authentic by many critics. Played by Cate Blanchett, Jude is the personification of the early Dylan when, in 1965, he alienated many fans by changing from acoustic to electric guitar. Blanchett manages to convey to perfection the slim, angular, and rather androgynous look of Dylan at that time of his life.

Many men and women have crossed-dressed in performance to play the "other" gender in plays and films, which, until the latter part of the twentieth century, had themes assuming a binary version of gender. Men impersonated women, and women impersonated men; however, the last thirty years have seen an acceptance and, increasingly, a celebration of LGBT+ lifestyles. And while heterosexual relationships remain an important basis of theatrical and film story lines, there are now acclaimed movies with characters representing other genders. And it is in these films where good actors often best achieve believable impersonations of genders that are not their own. Whether comedies or dramas, these films continue to explore the differences of gender and sexuality represented in our societies and often provide a catalyst for open discussion of such issues.

The Crying Game was one of the earliest of such movies, and its themes have been much discussed, especially those of the reactions to trans people. Juliet Jaques,[8] in a short essay on the film, states that *The Crying Game*

> subscribes to the trope of presenting happiness and satisfaction as impossible
> for trans people. In this sense, The Crying Game *is of its time, but, despite
> its faults, it presents Dil (a trans woman) as someone with genuine agency
> and strength, a generous spirit who nonetheless has the freedom not just to be
> imperfect, but outright bad, whether she has to be, or just wants to. How-
> ever, much of the film reverts to the "straight" white man's gaze, it allows
> a trans woman to love and be loved, by both the male protagonist and the
> audience—something rarely shown on the screen before of such films.*

The Birdcage (1996), a remake of *La cage aux folles* (1978), again celebrates variousness in gender. Nathan Lane plays Albert, an effeminate and flamboyant man who is the life partner of club owner Armand Goldman (Robin Williams). Refusing to pretend to be a straight man, he dresses as a woman to help Goldman convince his future daughter-in-law's parents that they live a heterosexual lifestyle. The film was praised by the Gay and Lesbian Alliance against Defamation (GLAAD) for showing opposition to hiding difference. It also praised the film for going beyond the stereotypes to see the characters' depth and humanity.

Such films and plays have often been used to highlight issues of change in society. *Taking Woodstock*, a 2009 comedy about the Woodstock Festival of 1969 and directed by Ang Lee, was not a box office success. Nevertheless, it is notable for how the actor Liev Schreiber, known for theater and screen performances of villains and tough guys, played the part of Betty von Vilma, a gay transvestite. Fifteen years previously he played Chris in *Mixed Nuts*, a 1994 American Christmas comedy film directed by Nora Ephron. The film was panned by critics; Rotten Tomatoes[9] gave it a 10 percent "rotten" rating. Yet Schreiber's portrayal of transgender Chris was praised: "Liev Schreiber, in his first film role, is a transvestite with a real heart and soul, a surprisingly sensitive portrayal given the rest of the film and the time period this is made."[10]

Much more recently the immensely enjoyable musical *Everybody's Talking about Jamie*, which started at the Crucible Theatre in Sheffield, has wowed the West End of London. The musical is inspired by the 2011 television documentary *Jamie: Drag Queen at 16* directed by Jenny Popplewell; the story follows a sixteen-year-old teenager as he overcomes prejudice on his way to becoming a drag queen. In his four-star review in the Daily Telegraph, Dominic Cavendish wrote, "I can't think of a musical that has set me spinning right round (like a record, baby) quite as much as this funny, outrageous, touching but oh-my-word PC flag-waving show. . . . The show sends you out on a feel-good bubble of happiness. Think about it too much, though, and the bubble gets pricked."[11] No doubt the issues in the musical will continue to be discussed and find their way into many a PhD thesis dealing with cultural change.

Themes of sexuality and of lesbianism were part of the film *I Shot Andy Warhol*, a 1996 American-British independent film about the life of author and radical feminist Valerie Solanas and her relationship with artist Andy Warhol. Stephen Dorff plays Candy Darling, the American actress, best known as a Warhol Superstar and transsexual icon. Dorff is just as believable as a young transgender woman as his character Candy Darling was in reality. And in *Rage* (2009), "Jude Law certainly got in touch with his feminine side for his new role," commented one reviewer.[12] The thirty-six-year-old (at the time) actor wore a jet-black wig and heavy makeup to play the part in which Minx talks directly to the camera. The character of the supermodel worried about ageing, once a pretty small boy who played with dolls much to his mother's dismay, comes over very clearly.

Film, too, has been used to explore gender issues related to psychological conditions. A cross-dressing role is used to explore the unusual dissociative identity disorder in *Peacock* (2010), an American psychological thriller. Cillian Murphy plays the role of John Skillpa, a quiet bank clerk living what appears to be a perfectly normal life; however, he has a secret that is threatening to be discovered. Suffering from multiple personality disorder, he disguises one half of his personality under the character of "Emma," a woman who cooks and cleans for him every morning. Critics and audiences liked the film without overpraise, but Cillian Murphy's portrayal of John/Emma was highly regarded. While not at all a similar plot, the film recalls the theme of Alfred Hitchcock's *Psycho*, in which Norman recreates his dead mother in his own mind as an alternate personality. He dresses in her clothes of his jealous and possessive mother to murder the women he finds attractive.

But perhaps the most open and often joyous dressing up by men in what are regarded as women's clothes is to be found in the numerous films, plays, and musicals that feature drag queens among their characters. One of the earliest and arguably the most famous is *The Adventures of Priscilla, Queen of the Desert* (1994). The Australian film tells the story of two drag queens (played by Hugo Weaving and Guy Pearce) and a transgender woman Bernadette, played by Terence Stamp. "Tick" (Weaving) who uses the drag pseudonym Mitzi Del Bra, accepts a booking to perform at a casino in Alice Springs and persuades Bernadette and Adam (Pearce), a younger drag queen with the stage name Felicia Jollygoodfellow, to join him on a trip from Sydney to the resort. They set off across the desert in a bus they name Priscilla. Along the way, the party has many adventures and is subject to much generosity but also abuse and violence. For instance, their tour bus is vandalized with homophobic graffiti. Undeterred, they paint the bus lilac and continue. The film was a surprise worldwide hit, and its positive portrayal of LGBT individuals helped introduce LGBT themes to a mainstream audience. Rotten Tomatoes[13] reported the critical consensus at 95 percent: "While its premise is ripe for comedy—and it certainly delivers its fair share of laughs—*Priscilla* is also a surprisingly tender and thoughtful road movie with some outstanding performances." *Priscilla* subsequently provided the basis for a musical, *Priscilla, Queen of the Desert,* which opened in 2006 in Sydney before traveling to New Zealand, the United Kingdom, Canada, and Broadway.

Less commercially successful was the American drag queen road movie *To Wong Foo, Thanks for Everything! Julie Newmar* (1995). Similarly to *Priscilla, Queen of the Desert,* it tells the story of two established drag queens, Noxeema Jackson (Wesley Snipes) and Vida Boheme (Patrick Swayze) and their adventures. In this film, the two main characters jointly win a trip to Hollywood to take part in the "Miss Drag Queen of America Pageant." They set off in an old Cadillac convertible, taking with them the younger novice, drag princess Chi-Chi Rodriguez (John Laguizamo) and a photo of Julie Newmar, filched by Vida from a restaurant wall. A predictable set of adventures—some heartwarming, some homophobic—and a happy ending make the film amusing but not challenging in any way. Roger Ebert of the *Chicago Sun–Times* wrote, "What is amazing is how the movie manages to be funny and amusing while tippy-toeing around (a) sex, (b) controversy and (c) any originality in the plot."[14]

The film gave an insight into the New York drag scene, however, by using many real drag queens, including RuPaul, in the parts of the movie set in the city. The casting of the film also emphasized the fact that being cast in drag parts was, in 1995, not only acceptable but also desirable. Playing such roles did not affect the public perception of actors known for playing virile he-man roles. There was intense competition to play the part of Vida; Patrick Swayze beat more than a dozen established actors to the part, including Robert Downey Jr., Gary Oldman, Mel Gibson, Johnny Depp, Tom Cruise, and Robin Williams. The film was given a seal of approval too by American celebrity actors who played cameo roles, including Julie Newmar herself, Robin Williams, Naomi Campbell, and Quentin Crisp.

But well before *Priscilla* or *To Wong Foo*, American Harris Glenn Milstead, better known by his stage name Divine, had appeared in many now infamous and cult films for the independent filmmaker John Waters. Divine was a gay American actor, singer, and drag queen. Usually performing female roles in both the theater and on film, he adopted a female drag persona for his music career. In 1985, not wanting to be stereotyped as a female impersonator, he played the gay male gangster Hilly Blue in *Trouble in Mind*. Although perhaps best known as a drag queen and still a cult figure, he was primarily a comedy actor. In the first film of *Hairspray* (1988), he took on two roles, one male and one female. Set in Baltimore during the 1960s, the story is about a plump teenager, Tracy Turnblad, as she pursues a show business career. In the film, Divine plays Tracy's mother, Edna Turnblad, as well as the racist television station owner Arvin Hodgepile. Reviews of the film were predominantly positive, with Divine in particular being singled out for praise; several commentators expressed their opinion that the film marked Divine's breakthrough into mainstream cinema. Unfortunately, his career ended prematurely as he died in 1988, the year of *Hairspray*'s release.

Such films are just one way in which drag queens and, to a much lesser extent, drag kings have come to play a significant part in the mainstream entertainment business. In many movies with drag queen characters, however, they are played successfully by heterosexual male actors; good examples are the roles Hugh Weaving and Guy Pearce take in *Priscilla*, and the three lead actors in *Wong Foo*. Actors playing drag queens, unlike drag performers playing themselves, are adopting a persona that is not their own and are using clothes and makeup traditionally used by women to create that character.

Perhaps this is the key to whether those who dress in drag in films are cross-dressing. Yes, if the film assumes a fixed view of gender and the actor intends to be accepted as a different gender than they usually claim? But perhaps it is time, in the 2020s, to assess whether the term *cross-dressing* is any longer valid to describe the multiplicity of gendered roles played by actors on stage and screen.

Things have changed.

13

CROSS-DRESSING — AN OUTDATED CONCEPT?

For last year's words belong to last year's language
And next year's words await another voice.

—T. S. Eliot, "Little Gidding"[1]

As soon as performers step on to the stage or face a camera, they are different people. If playing a role, they work hard to take on the characteristics of the person they are trying to represent. Some study appropriate behaviors to copy; others try to "get into the skin" of the character, trying to work out how the person would be feeling and thus how they would act. Even when entertainers such as stand-up comedians are on stage as themselves, they exaggerate their usual behaviors. And to add another visual layer to the subterfuge, all actors spend time donning their costumes and applying makeup before they emerge on to the stage or start filming.

For more than twenty-five hundred years in Western society, the male actors who were representing women have tried to portray behaviors traditionally considered feminine, such as affection, sensitivity, and intuition. And, since they were allowed to tread the boards, at different times in different countries, actresses have impersonated acceptedly male characteristics, such as assertiveness, dominance, and protectiveness. Early authors and playwrights wrote parts predicated on such assumptions, and actors behaved accordingly; however, the assumption of such fixed differences between men and women have come into question. People are much more complex, and their personality characteristics and resulting behaviors exist on a spectrum that is little to do with gender. Any directors and actors who want to portray characters as faithfully as possible will discuss what a particular role involves and together develop the mix of visual and aural clues that will best convey the character to their audience.

Although sex depends on the anatomy and the majority of people are born with male or female sexual characteristics, gender depends on the society or culture to which we belong. Sex characteristics do not vary substantially between different human societies, but gender characteristics certainly do. In society at large, there are some who identify with a different gender than that ascribed to them at birth. Issues relating to gender are increasingly important to modern living. Opinions of the LGBT+[2] community are frequently expressed in all aspects of the media. Changing views on gender are reflected in the performing arts: in the subject matter of plays, films, operas, and such; in recruitment of members to the profession; and in the different ways in which actors represent characters once firmly defined as masculine or feminine. If gender is less important, more fluid than in the past, is *cross-dressing* still an appropriate term to describe the shift of gender in performance? Do we need such a term?

The prefix *cross* became part of the concept of "cross-dressing" when society considered that gender was binary; that there were just two genders based on sexual characteristics. Gender and sexual orientation were considered synonymous. A person was male or female sexually and, therefore, of a masculine or feminine gender. The prefix *cross*, however, suggests a move from one fixed state to another, a leap across a divide rather than a choice of destinations or of various ways to get there.

And dress? The term *cross-dressing* was coined at a time when it was the norm to identify as either a man or a woman in Western society and dress accordingly. Men wore certain types of clothes, usually with pants of some kind, and women wore skirts. From the Greeks to the mid-twentieth century, cross-dressing performers could rely on dress conventions to create belief in their stage characters. A long frock, which "dragged" on the floor, was enough to communicate to an audience that the actor was impersonating a woman; this was, most likely, the origin of the term *drag* (although another suggested source of the word is the acronym *DRessing As a Girl*). When it was unthinkable for a woman to wear trousers in public, and doing so would incur censure, adopting male attire on stage would immediately state that the performer was impersonating a man.

A cross-dresser in ordinary life, sometimes referred to as a transvestite, is most typically a man who derives pleasure from dressing in clothes primarily associated with the opposite sex; however, those who dress like this on stage are usually doing so to entertain. Throughout performance history, entertainers have taken to drag for this purpose. The difference is in the intention. The general word *drag*, which refers to wearing such clothes in the *performance* of masculinity, femininity, or other forms of gender expression, may now describe gender impersonation more appropriately than the term *cross-dressing*.

In modern or modernized plays, operas, musicals, or dance, dress is no longer sufficient to signal gender differences. Many everyday and working clothes are unisex. Observe the military and the police, as well as rail and postal workers. Go to factories and supermarkets. There is little or no gender difference in the uniforms that workers wear. In some schools in Britain, where schoolchildren usually wear a uniform, both boys and girls can wear trousers, and often the uniform includes a necktie. They can wear skirts, and many girls do—and occasionally some of the boys demand to do so, too. Watch a group of teenagers at a skateboarding park—gender is almost indistinguishable. And accessories no longer signal gender roles in the same way as they did in the past. Shoulder bags and briefcases are carried by all. Nor do hairstyles give an accurate indication. Those of any gender can sport whatever hairstyle they like, increasingly without comment. On stage and on screen, directors wanting to suggest different gender roles in performance cannot, in the twenty-first century, rely on visual conventions to convey difference. Falling tresses from a cap in a Restoration comedy no longer announce definitively to an audience that "he" has now become a "she." We increasingly see gender-neutral clothes worn by actors. Jeans, shirts, and jackets are typical in contemporary plays. Loose trousers and robes often obscure sexual characteristics in historical productions.

If *cross-dressing* is no longer a true descriptive term for how performers represent gender on stage and on screen, what are the ways we can describe such different representations?

There is no doubt that on stage and screen we will see more performers experimenting by representing those of a different gender from that which they have chosen in their offstage life. Of course, many of these roles will still be heterosexual men impersonating women or vice versa. Pantomime will still have its share of "fellers in a frock," famous female actors will want to play the big male Shakespearean roles, and male actors will try their hand at being women. Dress is often used when men take on female comedy roles. Brendan O'Carroll as Mrs Brown in *Mrs Brown's Boys* immediately signals his caricature of an Irish mother with a curly wig, a wrap-around apron, and cardigan.

Many intentional cross-dressing performances are successful and add deeper insights to the characters, but others raise questions about why cross-dressing seemed appropriate when the play was being cast. At the Vaudeville Theatre in 2015, for instance, David Suchet took on a role that many of the finest British actresses—Edith Evans, Judi Dench, and Maggie Smith, for example—have played: Lady Bracknell in *The Importance of Being Earnest*. His success in the part, as well as the reason for his casting, divided critics. The *Daily Telegraph*'s Dominic Cavendish disliked the play as a whole but praised Suchet's handling of the role.

Now we've got David Suchet causing a cross-dressing commotion by donning a corset and braving Lady Bracknell—the first time we've had a male Lady B in the West End. Watching Suchet in action, I was put in mind of some magnificent figurehead on an ancient sailing-ship that seems to be strangely listing. . . . Whenever Suchet is in sight, you're less inclined to notice—or care—about this lacklustre state of affairs. . . . I can't imagine this gift of a gorgon role being better handled by another male actor. Rather than over-emphasising his feminine side, or stooping to the crasser, panto-dame end of female-impersonation, Suchet locates the mannishness in this haughty, formidable creature. Character and player meet in the middle—you see the join but it barely matters, and it helps cement the work's delight in inverted norms, assumed identities and double lives.[3]

Cavendish was very aware of the cross-dressing element in the production, referred to it, and thought it worked. The *Guardian*'s Michael Billington liked Suchet's performance, too, but reviewed Suchet as an actor playing a part and not as a man playing a woman. "Even if occasionally the mood seems closer to *Charley's Aunt* than Oscar Wilde this is a thoroughly enjoyable production and, at its centre, lies a superb performance by Suchet that reminds us that even Lady Bracknell contains a certain impishness beneath her elegantly frocked hauteur."[4]

But critic and actor Stephen Collins disagreed. He tackled head-on the question of whether cross-dressing worked in the production.

The simple truth is that a man in a dress, no matter how fine an actor the man might otherwise be, just cannot succeed in the role of Lady Bracknell unless the man plays her as a woman—not as a Wagnerian drag queen with stentorian lips, prissy affectations, and an overwhelming "look at me" sensibility. Lady Bracknell is not the starring role in the play and it is a schoolboy error to so regard her. . . . Does David Suchet make an excellent Lady Bracknell? No, he does not.[5]

Collins also questions the motives for such casting. Suchet freely admitted that he was looking for a good comedy role and had never played a woman on stage before in his forty-six years in the business. And it could not be ignored that Suchet would be a box office magnet. Collins goes on to comment,

> *But should that be enough reason to take a plum role from a worthy woman?*
> *. . . There are not that many fabulous parts for woman of a certain age, but*
> *Lady Bracknell is one of them. There will be many other worthy, wondrous*
> *actresses . . . who could play the role with great distinction. It's not like the*
> *play is presented with the frequency of, say, Hamlet, which centres on a part*
> *which younger actors feel the need to tackle: they want "to give" their take on*
> *the Prince of Denmark, just as older actors want to give their Lear or Willy*
> *Loman or Malvolio. Why shouldn't actresses be given first dibs at giving their*
> *Lady Bracknell when a production of* The Importance of Being Earnest *is*
> *being mounted, especially in the West End?*[6]

So, changing roles in a different gender from that written by the playwright can sometimes be controversial. The assessment of success would seem to be whether doing so adds value. Do we perceive new, interesting aspects of the character that original gender casting would not have revealed?

But with the acceptance by most Western cultures, at least officially, that gender is not binary, and often irrelevant to what needs to be portrayed, is acting as a person of a different gender any different than taking on other characteristics of the role? Is it not just good acting? Does this particular aspect of a character need to be separated out as something to be wondered at? Increasingly there are many plays, films, and musicals with LGBT characters. There is, however, increasing debate about whether such characters should be played by LGBT actors or open to those of any gender. Lesbian and gay part casting seems to be much less controversial than trans roles.

Suranne Jones, a straight actor, played the role of Gentleman Jack in the BBC series of that name. It tells the story of the aristocratic Anne Lister who was an open lesbian long before the term was coined, when homosexual acts were illegal but sexual relationships between women were largely unacknowledged. In 1834, Anne returned to the family estate in Yorkshire to rescue the family fortunes. She loved many women and described her life in great details in coded diaries. I am not aware of any insistence from the LGBT community that she should have been played by a lesbian actor. However, in 2020, American actor Scarlett Johansson dropped out of a role in which she was going to play a transgender man following a backlash from the LGBT community. She was due to play 1970s Pittsburgh crime boss Dante "Tex" Gill, who was born Jean Gill, in *Rub and Tug*. The original announcement was met with intense criticism from those who said the role should have gone to a transgender actor, and that it showed the limited opportunities given to transgender actors.

In spring 2021, there was a backlash over the casting of a cisgender man in the transgender role of Bernadette in a UK tour of *Priscilla, Queen of the Desert*. It generated the penning of an open letter to many venues, signed by transgender and nonbinary theatermakers, urging them to turn away shows in which cisgender performers are cast in transgender roles. The letter complained that transgender roles were not being offered to transgender actors, and that they were thought to be not good enough to play themselves. The producers countered by saying that they had auditioned transgender performers but had not found anyone suitable for roles in their production. The debate is set to continue.

If acting skills are what is required, there seems to be no reason why any actor who has the ability to transform themselves visually and is also able to convey the character of the person concerned should not be cast. As one

LGBT actor rather testily told me when discussing the various roles he had played, including the female persona he had successfully adopted for many years, "I'm an actor. I once played a duck." However, if the profession is keen to right wrongs and increase opportunities for actors of any ability, color, or gender, and if this is an avowed intention, then perhaps the playing field has to be leveled by positive discrimination. Trace Lysette, an actor who stars in the Amazon series *Transparent*, said it was representative of a wider problem in Hollywood. "I wouldn't be as upset if I was getting in the same rooms as Jennifer Lawrence and Scarlett for cis roles, but we know that's not the case," she tweeted. "A mess."[7] The film was quietly killed off, but in 2020, work started on a TV series. The trans writer Our Lady J was commissioned to write a pilot for New Regency Television, and there was a commitment to cast a trans actor in the main role.

Many roles, particularly minor ones, although gender specific when written can be cast as any gender or none. The actors are not cross-dressing; the roles themselves are gender neutral. Writers who penned plays when gender was taken as binary and most professions were closed to women assumed that their created roles of soldiers, courtiers, doctors, and lawyers would be played by men. Detectives and police were always male. Nurses and cleaners were female. Now in Western society we expect as many women to be doctors as men, and vice versa we know of many men who are nurses. Audiences are no longer likely to comment on the unusualness of such casting on stage. Theaters want to mount the best productions they can. They want the best of talent on stage. Changing the gender of roles or ignoring color and gender means more scope for good choices and more equality of opportunity for actors. Such roles and a myriad of others are often cast gender neutral; in theory, whoever auditions best for the part, gets it. In a National Theatre Live production of Alan Bennett's *The Madness of King George*, from the Nottingham Playhouse, the doctors were women, and even though the action is set in the Georgian era when this would have been impossible, no one turned a hair. Many reviewers, however, still comment on the fact that a play contains gender-blind casting before going on to appraise the acting. But it is becoming less frequent. As time goes on, we should expect less emphasis on the gender, color, age, or physical ability of players and more concentration on what actors bring to their roles.

There are more women directors across all performance genres, and they are having a significant impact on the casting debate. The shift to equitable career prospects, irrespective of gender, is gaining ground. Michelle Terry, the artistic director at Shakespeare's Globe, says she is committed to a fifty-fifty gender split in casting; however, not all artistic directors feel able to balance the allocation of roles. The Royal Shakespeare Company's artistic director, Greg Doran, has refused to enforce a fifty-fifty gender casting, insisting the plays were written "for a group of blokes." In 2018, he stated, "In terms of re-gendering roles, Michelle Terry at the Globe has made a very bold statement about re-gendering so it is going to be 50:50 right across the board. . . . I don't want to impose that on directors as such, that would mean that we couldn't do an all-female production. I want to keep it much more fluid and organic."[8] He refused to accept quotas for female thespians.

True gender-blind casting is a popular aim in the profession but not always easy. How an audience perceives characters on stage or screen is not only affected by how well the actor can show appropriate feelings, attitudes, and behaviors. Culture, particularly sexual politics at the time, can change how an audience will react. Watching the film *Tootsie* now, almost forty years after it was first shown, it is difficult not to notice elements of inappropriate behavior by the men to the women in the workplaces. Behaviors that, at the time, would be annoying but typical would now be classed as harassment and have the MeToo campaigners rightfully objecting. Current cultural perceptions also affect how audiences see a woman playing a male character in what is intended to be a heterosexual relationship. Some members of the audience may not be able to suspend belief and will perceive the characters as the same gender and in a lesbian relationship.

Story lines also sometimes change with an attempt at gender-neutral casting. When the National's *Treasure Island* was produced in 2014, the two stars were, according to reviewers, the magnificent, original set, and the young actress Patsy Ferran. The Jim Hawkins of the book was transposed into an androgynous girl, rebelling against gender roles. "Be you boy or be you girl?" "That be my business." Ferran's performance was highly praised. But for me the relationship between Jim and Long John Silver, an important feature of the story, is glossed over in the production. Or at least it becomes something different. In the book, Jim's father has died, and Jim finds himself in a proxy-son relationship with the complicated Mr Silver. Jim reminds Silver of the young, handsome man he once was. The relationship becomes one of real affection between them. But the alternating hero worship and disillusion felt by the younger man, clear in the original story, is perforce missing when Jim is played by a girl.

But perhaps it doesn't matter. It was a Christmas production with many children in the audience, and even if the writer of the new version, Bryony Lavery, "plays fast and loose with both gender and plot line in an epic production where the set, designed by Lizzie Clachan, out-acts the actors and the pitch is somewhere between *Harry Potter* and panto,"[9] it was a box office success. What matters when directors break away from established gender roles and cast differently is whether it works. From the actors' viewpoint, the measure of success could be whether the casting increases the opportunities for more actors to play the part. For an audience, it must be whether the casting adds something that old gender casting does not. Does it expand and deepen our understanding of the character or increase our enjoyment?

Cross-dressing? Perhaps it's an outdated combination of words in the modern profession, and maybe we need different ones now to describe the different approaches to gender change in performance. Or should we just ignore gender, avoid any adjectives to describe such roles, and concentrate on how well a character is represented and how good the actor is?

Challenging cultural gender norms in performance can be controversial, and it will never suit all critics or all audiences. But words and norms change over time, and we should all salute those who for the last two thousand years have been prepared to challenge such norms and stride out into the spotlight to entertain us.

ACKNOWLEDGMENTS

Exploring the issues in this book has been both enjoyable and enlightening. Many people have helped. In particular, professional pantomime dame Sam Rabone contributed his ideas on being a "feller in a frock"; David Reed, the archivist of the British Music Hall Society provided much information and a great selection of photographs; and Julie Brown at the New Art Gallery, Walsall, allowed the use of a rare Roman actors mask in their collection. A whole host of people who write about theater, ballet, opera, and films have contributed much to this work, albeit unknowingly. I would like to thank them all and hope I have acknowledged all the comments that I have quoted.

My editor at Rowman & Littlefield / Globe Pequot, John Cerullo, has guided me kindly and efficiently through my role in the publication process, and Barbara Claire has patiently liaised with me to organize the images for the book.

My partner Keith Alldritt, who loves theater, opera, and all the arts, has been a continuing presence during the writing of the book, offering suggestions and insights as well as access to his great stock of opera performances.

Thank you all.

NOTES AND REFERENCES

Chapter 1

1. Gilbert Murray, trans., *The Medea of Euripides* (New York: Oxford University Press, 1912), 11, Kindle.

2. Maddy Costa, "Medea: The Mother of All Roles," *Guardian*, October 2, 2012.

3. Decimus Junius Juvenalis, known in English as Juvenal, was a Roman poet active in the late first and early second century CE. He is the author of the collection of satirical poems known as *The Satires*.

4. Juvenal, *The Sixteen Satires*, 3rd ed. (London: Penguin, 2004), 16.

5. Juvenal, *The Sixteen Satires*, 17.

Chapter 2

1. William Shakespeare, *Hamlet* (1611), act 2, scene 2, line 340. Rosencrantz is describing to Hamlet the group of child actors that compete with the adult troupes of players.

2. A double date comes from the transition from the Julian calendar to the Gregorian calendar. According to the Julian calendar, the first day of the year was March 25, and each year was 365 days and six hours long. Not all areas accepted the change to the Gregorian calendar at the same time, however. For this reason, many people wrote dates falling between January 1 and March 25 with double dates. The first year in a double date given is the Julian calendar, and the second given is the Gregorian calendar.

3. Miguel de Cervantes, *Don Quixote* (Ware, Herfordshire: Wordsworth Editions, 1993), pt. 2, 69.

4. Hannah Mankelow, "Do You Not Know I Am a Woman? The Legacy of the First Female Desdemona," in *Shakespeare in Ten Acts*, ed. Gordon McMullan (London: British Library, 2016), chapter 4.

5. Max Beerbohm, "Macbeth and Mrs Kendall," review of *Macbeth*, *Saturday Review of Politics, Literature, Science and Art* (London), October 1, 1898.

6. William Shakespeare, *As You Like It* (1623), act 2, scene 7, lines 139–42.

7. Peter Thompson, "English Renaissance and Restoration Theatre," in *The Oxford Illustrated History of the Theatre*, ed. John Russell Brown (New York: Oxford University Press, 2001), chapter 6.

8. William Shakespeare, *Twelfth Night* (1602), act 1, scene 1, line 48.

9. Shakespeare, *Twelfth Night*, act 5, scene 1, line 272.

10. William Shakespeare, *The Two Gentlemen of Verona* (1623), act 2, scene 6, lines 39–54.

11. Shakespeare, *Hamlet*, act 2, scene 2, line 340. Rosencrantz is describing to Hamlet the group of child actors that compete with the adult troupes of players.

12. Patricia Reynolds, "Kidnapped to Order," *National Archives* (blog), May 12, 2016, https://blog.nationalarchives.gov.uk/kidnapped-order-child-actors-shake speares-day/.

13. Bart van Es, *Shakespeare in Company* (Oxford: Oxford University Press, 2013), 195–231.

14. Reynolds, "Kidnapped to Order."

15. Frank Romany, introduction to *The Complete Plays* by Christopher Marlowe, ed. Frank Romany and Robert Lindsey (London: Penguin, 2003), loc. 127, Kindle.

Chapter 3

1. John Dryden, *Secret Love, or The Maiden Queen* (1667), act 5, scene 1.

2. Thomas Jordan (for the King's Company), prologue to the first performance of *Othello* with a woman as Desdemona, quoted in Zoe Wilcox, "Who Was the First Shakespearean Actress?," *English and Drama Blog*, May 7, 2016, https://blogs.bl.uk/english-and-drama/2016/05/index.html.

3. Jordan, quoted in Wilcox, "Who Was the First Shakespearean Actress?"

4. Peter Martin, *Samuel Johnson: A Biography* (London: Phoenix, 2009), 214.

5. Wikipedia, s.v. "*Histriomastix*," last modified April 26, 2021, 18:47, https://en.wikipedia.org/wiki/Histriomastix.

6. Peter Thompson, "English Renaissance and Restoration Theatre," in *The Oxford Illustrated History of the Theatre*, ed. John Russell Brown (New York: Oxford University Press, 2001), chapter 6.

7. Peter Thompson, *The Cambridge Introduction to English Theatre, 1660–1900* (Cambridge: Cambridge University Press, 2006), 10.

8. Samuel Pepys, diary entry of October 26, 1667, in *The Diary of Samuel Pepys: Complete Edition*, ed. Henry B. Wheatley (London: George Bell, 1893), Kindle.

9. Thompson, "English Renaissance and Restoration Theatre," 208.

10. John Dryden, *The Tempest, or The Enchanted Island*, in *Delphi Complete Works of John Dryden* (Hastings, UK: Delphi Classics, 2013), loc. 37131, Kindle.

11. Pepys, diary entry of March 2, 1667, in Pepys, *Diary of Samuel Pepys*.

12. Pepys, diary entry of August 5, 1667, in Pepys, *Diary of Samuel Pepys*.

13. George Farquhar, *The Recruiting Officer* (1706), act 3, scene 1.

14. A cathedral city in the west midlands of England, known as the birthplace of David Garrick and Samuel Johnson, as well as the home of Erasmus Darwin.

15. Elizabeth Inchbald was an English novelist, actress, and critic. The quote is from the remarks in prompt book for *The Constant Couple* by George Farquahar (London: Longman, Hurst, Rees and Orme, n.d.,), loc. 1, Kindle.

16. Mrs. Dorothea Jordan, an Anglo-Irish actress and courtesan, was the mistress and companion of the future King William IV of the United Kingdom for twenty years (1791–1811) while he was Duke of Clarence. Together they had ten illegitimate children, all of whom took the surname FitzClarence.

Chapter 4

1. Dominic Dromgoole was the director of the Globe Theatre, London, from 2005 to 2016.

2. Dominic Dromgoole, *Hamlet: Globe to Globe* (Edinburgh: Canongate Books, 2017), 205.

3. William Shakespeare, *Hamlet* (1611), act 3, scene 1, lines 585–90.

4. Ian McIntyre, *Garrick* (London: Allen Lane, Penguin, 1999), 411.

5. Mrs. Siddons (Sarah Siddons nee Kemble) 1755–1831. Best known tragedienne of the eighteenth-century English stage.

6. McIntyre, *Garrick*, 411.

7. Shakespeare, *Hamlet*, act 1, scene 2, line 129.

8. Sylvia Morris, "The Divine Sarah Bernhardt's Hamlet," *Shakespeare Blog*, September 5, 2015, http://theshakespeareblog.com/2015/09/the-divine-sarah-bern hardts-hamlet/.

9. Unsigned review of *Hamlet*, *Athenaeum*, June 17, 1899.

10. Unsigned review of *Hamlet*, *Birmingham Gazette*, June 1899.

11. Wikipedia, s.v. "Sarah Bernhardt," last modified November 2, 2021, 14:10, https://en.wikipedia.org/wiki/Sarah_Bernhardt.

12. Edward P. Vining, *The Mystery of Hamlet* (Philadelphia: Lippincott, 1881), chapter summaries 6 and 7.

13. Professor Tony Howard, Warwick University.

14. Michael Billington, "Doing a Man's Job," review of *Hamlet*, Half Moon Theatre, London, *Guardian*, October 20, 1979.

15. Ian Shuttleworth, "The Roaring Girl's [*sic*] *Hamlet*," *City Limits Magazine*, February 1992, http://www.cix.co.uk/~shutters/reviews/92014.htm.

16. Michael Paulson, "She Gave Up a Lot to Play Othello," *New York Times*, September 4, 2020.

17. Charles Spencer, review of *King Lear*, Leicester Haymarket Theatre, *Telegraph*, March 1997.

18. Paul Taylor, "Second Opinion / Paul Taylor Defends Fiona Shaw's *Richard II* from the Baying Critics," *Independent*, June 13, 1995, https://www.independent.co.uk/arts-entertainment/second-opinion-paul-taylor-defends-fiona-shaw-s-richard-ii-from-the-baying-critics-1586371.html.

19. Michael Billington, "What I Like about Cross-Dressing," *Guardian Theatre Blog*, September 7, 2007, https://www.theguardian.com/stage/theatreblog/2007/sep/07/whatilikeaboutcrossdressin.

20. Susanna Clapp, "*Hamlet* Review: Maxine Peake Is a Delicately Ferocious Prince of Denmark," *Observer*, September 21, 2014, https://www.theguardian.com/stage/2014/sep/21/hamlet-maxine-peake-royal-exchange-review-delicate-ferocity.

21. Peter Bradshaw, "Maxine Peake as Hamlet Review—Fast, Fluent and Revelatory," *Guardian*, March 19, 2015, https://www.theguardian.com/film/2015/mar/19/maxine-peake-as-hamlet-fast-and-fluent-with-a-new-edge.

22. Michael Billington, "*Julius Caesar*—Review," *Guardian*, December 5, 2012, https://www.theguardian.com/culture/2012/dec/05/julius-caesar-review.

23. Charles Spencer, "*Julius Caesar*, Donmar Warehouse, Review," *Telegraph*, December 5, 2012, https://www.telegraph.co.uk/culture/theatre/theatre-reviews/9722122/Julius-Caesar-Donmar-Warehouse-review.html.

24. Jayne Bennett, review of *Hamlet*, Festival Players Theatre Company, *Glasgow Evening Times*, July 27, 2016.

25. Ben Brantley, "How Mark Rylance Became Olivia," *New York Times*, August 14, 2016, https://www.nytimes.com/2016/08/15/theater/how-mark-rylance-became-olivia-onstage.html.

26. Brantley, "How Mark Rylance Became Olivia."

27. Brantley, "How Mark Rylance Became Olivia."

28. Mark Shenton, "Review: *Henry IV* at the Sam Wanamaker Playhouse," *London Theatre*, November 22, 2019, https://www.londontheatre.co.uk/reviews/review-henry-vi-at-the-sam-wanamaker-playhouse.

29. Michael Billington, "*King Lear* Review: Glenda Jackson Makes a Triumphant Return to the Stage," *Guardian*, November 5, 2016, https://www.theguardian com/stage/2016/nov/05/king-lear-review-glenda-jackson-old-vic.

30. Dominic Cavendish, "*King Lear*, Old Vic, Review: Glenda Jackson's Performance Will Be Talked about for Years," *Telegraph*, November 5, 2016, https://www.telegraph.co.uk/theatre/what-to-see/king-lear-old-vic-review-glenda-jacksons-performance-will-be-tal/.

31. Mark Shenton, "*King Lear*: A Tour de Force," *Stage*, November 5, 2016, https://www.thestage.co.uk/reviews/glenda-jackson-in-king-lear-review-at-the-old-vic--a-tour-de-force.

32. Paul Taylor, "*King Lear*, Old Vic, London, Review: Glenda Jackson Got a Fervent Standing Ovation," *Independent*, November 7, 2016, https://www.independent.co.uk/arts-entertainment/theatre-dance/reviews/king-lear-glenda-jackson-old-vic-review-deborah-warner-morfydd-clark-a7402206.html.

33. Ben Brantley, "Review: Glenda Jackson Rules a Muddled World in *King Lear*," *New York Times*, April 4, 2019, https://www.nytimes.com/2019/04/04/theater/king-lear-review-glenda-jackson.htmlhttps://www.nytimes.com/2019/04/04/theater/king-lear-review-glenda-jackson.html.

Chapter 5

1. Octavian as Mariandel in Richard Strauss, *Der Rosenkavalier*, act 3.

2. Wolfgang Amadeus Mozart, *The Marriage of Figaro* (1786), act 1, scene 5.

3. Mozart, *The Marriage of Figaro*, act 1, scene 7.

4. Charles Gounod, *Faust* (1859), act 3, scene 1.

5. A "Falcon" is a rare type of soprano voice that takes its name from the singer Marie Cornélie Falcon (1814–1897), a French soprano who sang at the Opéra in Paris.

6. In becoming the *Un ballo in maschera*, which we know today, Verdi's opera (and his libretto) underwent a significant series of changes, caused by a combination of censorship regulations in both Naples and Rome, as well as by the political situation in France. The censorship concerned possible political and homosexuality themes in the plot. Based on the Scribe libretto and begun as *Gustavo III* set in Stockholm, it became *Una vendetta in domino* set in Stettin, and finally *Un ballo in maschera* set in Boston during the colonial era. It became one of the most frustrating experiences of Verdi's career.

7. Le Comte D'Ory, DVD recording by Glyndebourne Festival Opera for Channel 4 Television, 1997.

8. Henry Purcell, *Dido and Aeneas*, with René Jacobs and the Orchestra of the Age of Enlightenment, 2006, Harmonia Mundi #2991683, compact disc.

9. Elizabeth Holland, "A Strategy for Historically-Informed Role-Allocation in the Twenty-First Century" (PhD thesis, University of Sheffield, 2002), http://british postgraduatemusicology.org/bpm5-strategy.html.

10. Mark Swed, "Music Review: L.A. Phil Premieres Gerald Barry's Sensational Opera *The Importance of Being Earnest*," *Los Angeles Times*, April 8, 2011, https:// latimesblogs.latimes.com/culturemonster/2011/04/music-review-los-angeles-phil harmonic-premieres-gerald-barrys-sensational-opera-the-importance-of-being-ear nest.html.

11. George Hall, "Emma Rice's Misjudged Production," review of *Orpheus in the Underworld*, *Stage*, October 6, 2019, https://www.thestage.co.uk/reviews/orpheus -in-the-underworld-review-at-london-coliseum--emma-rices-misjudged-production.

12. Mark Brown, "*The Marriage of Figaro* Returns to Royal Opera House with a Twist," *Guardian*, June 28, 2019, https://www.theguardian.com/culture/2019/ jun/28/marriage-of-figaro-returns-royal-opera-house-with-a-twist.

Chapter 6

1. Dean Speer, "Les Ballets Trockadero de Monte Carlo: Flocking to the Trocks," *Critical Dance*, February 13, 2019, https://criticaldance.org/les-ballets-trockadero -de-monte-carlo-flocking-trocks/.

2. Christie Beaver, "The All-Male Ballet Company Defying Stereotypes," *Irish Times*, September 29, 2018, https://www.irishtimes.com/culture/stage/ the-all-male-ballet-company-defying-stereotypes-1.3640889.

3. Speer, "Les Ballets Trockadero de Monte Carlo."

4. Beaver, "The All-Male Ballet Company Defying Stereotypes."

5. Selby Schwartz, "Dance History according to Drag," *Dance*, June 2007, https://dancersgroup.org/2007/06/dance-history-according-to-drag/.

6. Richard Move as Martha Graham, interview by Matthew Bourne, "BBC Television: Bourne to Dance," YouTube video, accessed November 3, 2021, https:// www.youtube.com/watch?v=ioH380u20tk.

7. Move, "Bourne to Dance."

8. Walter Terry was a dance critic for the now-defunct *New York Herald Tribune* and the *Saturday Review* and an internationally known champion of dance through his books and lectures.

9. Catherine Bravo, "Richard Move as Martha Graham," ArtsConnection, accessed October 7, 2021, https://teens.artsconnection.org/2583/.

10. Wikipedia, s.v. "Modern Dance," last modified October 27, 2021, 03:53, https://en.wikipedia.org/wiki/Modern_dance.

11. Patricia Boccadoro, Culturekiosque, 2016, http://www.culturekiosque .com/dance/reviews/de_keersmaeker966.html. (URL is no longer active.)

Chapter 7

1. Dorothy Parker, *Complete Poems* (London: Penguin Classics, 1999), 206.

2. Lyrics and music by Harry B. Norris, 1900; performed by Vesta Tilley.

3. Charles Dickens Jr., quoted in S. D. Trav, *No Applause, Just Throw Money* (New York: Farrar, Straus & Giroux, 2005), loc. 1644, Kindle.

4. Fern Riddell. British historian specializing in gender, sex, suffrage and Victorian culture.

5. Laura Ormiston Dibbin Chant was an English social reformer and writer. She lectured on social purity, temperance, and women's rights. In 1894, she started attacking music halls as temptations to vice.

6. "What Did She Know about Railways?," lyrics and music by C. G. Cotes and Bennett Scott (1897); sung by Marie Lloyd.

7. Although gay, Hindle married and divorced briefly. Then, in 1886, she married her dresser, Annie Ryan, while on a tour through the Midwest. Hindle dressed herself in male clothing and gave her name as Charles; a local Baptist minister performed the wedding ceremony. Later, after Annie's death, she married another woman, Louise Spangehl.

8. "The Army of Today's Alright," lyrics and music by Fred W. Leigh and Kenneth Lyle, 1914.

9. Sara Maitland, *Vesta Tilley* (London: Virago Pioneers, 1986), 118.

10. "A Bit of a Blighty One," lyrics and music by Herman Darewski and Arthur Wimperis, 1918.

11. E. Carlton Winford, *Femme Mimics* (Dallas, TX: Winford, 1954), quoted in "More Bert Savoy," Queer Music Heritage, June 2004, http://queermusicheritage .com/jun2004b.html.

12. "Eve Golden / Queen of the Dead: Bert Savoy," *LA Daily Mirror*, October 30, 2012, https://ladailymirror.com/2012/10/30/eve-golden-queen-of-the-dead-bert-savoy/.

13. Douglas Byng, "Sex Appeal Sarah" (1929), YouTube video, accessed November 4, 2021, https://www.youtube.com/watch?v=ijCwkFPe8dU.

14. Laurence Senelick, "Lady and the Tramp: Drag Differentials in the Progressive Era," in *Gender in Performance*, ed. Laurence Senelick (Hanover, NH: University Press of New England, 1992), 29.

15. Trav, *No Applause, Just Throw Money*, loc. 384.

16. Trav, *No Applause, Just Throw Money*, loc. 465.

17. The first published edition of "Miss Lucy Long" is uncredited in an 1842 songster called *Old American Songs*. Billy Whitlock of the Virginia Minstrels later claimed the song in his autobiography: "I composed . . . 'Miss Lucy Long' (the words by T. G. Booth) in 1838" (Wikipedia, s.v. "Miss Lucy Long," last modified December 13, 2020, 20:00, https://en.wikipedia.org/wiki/Miss_Lucy_Long).

18. Trav, *No Applause, Just Throw Money*, loc. 913.

19. Senelick, "Lady and the Tramp," 29.

Chapter 8

1. Excerpt from introductory song to all episodes of *It Ain't Half Hot Mum*; unattributed.

2. Lisa Z. Sigel, "Best Love: Female Impersonation in the Great War," *Sexualities*, January 24, 2016; quoted in Lauren Oyler, "A Farewell to Pants: The Role of Cross-Dressing during WWI," *Vice*, November 26, 2016, https://www.vice.com/en_us/article/ypa8qy/a-farewell-to-pants-the-role-of-cross-dressing-during-wwi.

3. Private Dudley Cave, quoted in Peter Tatchell, "A Gay Soldier's Story," BBC, June 1, 2004, https://www.bbc.co.uk/history/ww2peopleswar/stories/36/a2688636.shtml.

4. Stephen Bourne, *Fighting Proud* (London: Bloomsbury Academic, 2019), 17.

5. Cave, quoted in Tatchell, "A Gay Soldier's Story."

6. Patrick B. O'Neill, "The Canadian Concert Party in France," *Theatre Research in Canada* 4, no. 2 (1983), https://journals.lib.unb.ca/index.php/TRIC/article/view/7462.

7. Laurence Senelick, *The Changing Room: Sex, Drag and Theatre* (New York: Routledge, 2002).

8. J. G. Fuller, *Troop Morale and Popular Culture in the British and Dominion Armies 1914–1918* (Oxford: Oxford University Press, 1990).

9. Emma Vickers and Emma Jackson, "Sanctuary or Sissy? Female Impersonation as Entertainment in the British Armed Forces, 1939–1945," Research Online, accessed October 7, 2021, http://researchonline.ljmu.ac.uk/id/eprint/9543/4/Sanctuary%20or%20sissy%20Male%20to%20female%20cross%20dressing%20as%20entertainment%20in%20the%20British%20Armed%20Forces%2C%201939-1945.pdf.

10. Clare Makepeace, *Captives of War: British Prisoners of War in Europe in the Second World War* (Cambridge: Cambridge University Press, 2017), 116.

11. Vickers and Jackson, "Sanctuary or Sissy?"

12. Source transcript of interview with Charles Pether on *Conduct Unbecoming* (Channel 4, 1996) in Makepeace, *Captives of War*, 8.

13. Danny La Rue, *From Drags to Riches: My Autobiography* (London: Penguin, 1988).

14. La Rue, *From Drags to Riches*, 57.

15. Bourne, *Fighting Proud*, 72–73.

16. Katy Cowan, "Soldier Studies: Fascinating Photographs of Cross-Dressing in the Third Reich's Army," Creative Boom, November 1, 2018, https://www.creativeboom.com/inspiration/soldier-studies-fascinating-photographs-of-cross-dressing-in-the-third-reichs-army/.

17. Sigel, quoted in Oyler, "A Farewell to Pants."

18. Makepeace, *Captives of War*.

19. O'Neill, "The Canadian Concert Party in France."

20. *The Goon Show* (originally *Crazy People*) was a British surreal and absurdist radio comedy show produced and broadcast by the BBC Home Service from 1951 to 1960. Spike Milligan was its chief creator and main writer. It was heard regularly from the 1950s in Australia, South Africa, New Zealand, India, and Canada, although these versions were frequently edited to avoid controversial subjects. NBC began broadcasting the program in the United States on its radio network from the mid-1950s.

21. La Rue, *From Drags to Riches*, 58.

22. Stuart Jeffries, "Some Like It Hot," *Guardian*, February 3, 2003, https://www.theguardian.com/world/2003/feb/03/race.stuartjeffries.

Chapter 9

1. Sam Rabone, e-mail interview with author, June 2, 2020.

2. Maureen Hughes, *A History of Pantomime* (Barnsley: Pen and Sword History, 2013), 16–17.

3. Hughes, *A History of Pantomime*, 127.

4. Rabone, e-mail interview with author, June 2, 2020.

5. At time of writing, due to the COVID-19 pandemic, theaters have just reopened but with social distancing. Pantomime is, however, likely to be canceled as it cannot be staged without singing, contact, and a big, enthusiastic audience. Sam Rabone was booked for 2020 in *Peter Pan*.

6. Rabone, e-mail interview with author, June 2, 2020.

7. Rabone, e-mail interview with author, June 2, 2020.

Chapter 10

1. Barry Humphries, *My Life as Me: A Memoir* (London: Penguin, 2004), 58.

2. Simon Plant, "Dame Edna's Gladdies Still Flying High," *Herald Sun*, October 24, 2019, https://www.heraldsun.com.au/lifestyle/melbourne/dame-ednas-glad dies-still-flying-high/news-story/75b0aec5703cca2a6d3f2ea63c57d242.

3. Simon Hattenstone, "Barry Humphries: 'I Defend to the Ultimate My Right to Give Deep and Profound Offence,'" *Guardian*, July 11, 2018, https://www .theguardian.com/culture/2018/jul/11/barry-humphries-interview-offence -dame-edna-everage-sir-les-patterson.

4. Richard Gilbert Emery (1915–1983) was an English comedian and actor. His self-titled television series ran from 1963 to 1981.

5. Les Dawson and Roy Barraclough, "Cissie and Ada—Honeymoon Memories," YouTube video, accessed November 4, 2021, https://www.youtube.com/ watch?v=ZjVQOjBPJ_o.

6. Patrick Fyffe, quoted in Stephen Dixon, "Patrick Fyffe," *Guardian*, May 15, 2002, https://www.theguardian.com/news/2002/may/15/guardianobituaries1.

7. Dixon, "Patrick Fyffe."

8. Sara Maitland, *Vesta Tilley* (London: Virago Pioneers, 1986), 24.

9. Nelson Mandela, interview by Pieter-Dirk Uys (in character of Evita Bezuidenhout), November 17, 1994, YouTube video, accessed November 4, 2021, https://www.youtube.com/watch?v=tjUhwYr48vE.

10. Humphries, *My Life as Me*, 138.

11. Wikipedia, s.v. "Barry Humphries," last modified October 25, 2021, 19:33, https://en.wikipedia.org/wiki/Barry_Humphries.

12. The term *Thatcherism* describes the political and economic policies advocated by former Conservative prime minister Margaret Thatcher. These included attempts to promote low inflation, the small state, free markets, privatization of national industries, and constraints on the labor movement. She believed in the individual and not society.

13. Adam Sweeting, "*Dame Edna Rules the Waves*, BBC1, Review: Dame Edna Was Resplendent in Fire-Alarm Pink on a Gilt Throne," *i*, December 31, 2019, https://inews.co.uk/culture/television/dame-edna-rules-the-waves-bbc1-review-380418.

14. Humphries, *My Life as Me*, 214–15.

15. Humphries, *My Life as Me*, 215.

16. Humphries, *My Life as Me*, 215.

17. Bernice Harrison, "It's Not That 'Mrs Brown' Is Too Mainstream: It's Just Not Funny," *Irish Times*, February 12, 2011, https://www.irishtimes.com/culture/tv-radio-web/it-s-not-that-mrs-brown-is-too-mainstream-it-s-just-not-funny-1.570578.

18. Grace Dent, "Grace Dent on TV: *Mrs Brown's Boys*, BBC1," *Independent*, December 29, 2012, https://www.independent.co.uk/arts-entertainment/tv/reviews/grace-dent-on-tv-mrs-brown-s-boys-bbc1-8432020.html.

19. Alex Fletcher, "Brendan O'Carroll Interview: 'We All Want to Be Joan Rivers,'" October 7, 2011, https://www.digitalspy.com/tv/a344331/brendan-ocarroll-interview-we-all-want-to-be-joan-rivers/.

Chapter 11

1. RuPaul, interview by Oprah Winfrey, YouTube, accessed November 4, 2021, https://www.youtube.com/watch?v=9RPDSdRCDYs.

2. *Merriam-Webster*, s.v. " drag queen (n)," accessed October 7, 2021, https://www.merriam-webster.com/dictionary/drag%20queen.

3. Pepper LaBeija, interview in *Paris Is Burning*, directed by Jennie Livingston (Liverpool: Academy Entertainment, 1990).

4. Dan Jones, *50 Drag Queens* (London: Hardie Grant Books, 2020).

5. Jones, *50 Drag Queens*, 84.

6. Wikipedia, s.v. "RuPaul," last modified November 2, 2021, 22:05, https://en.wikipedia.org/wiki/RuPaul.

7. Wikipedia, s.v. "Divine (Performer)," last modified October 25, 2021, 05:24, https://en.wikipedia.org/wiki/Divine_(performer).

8. Ryan Roschke, "Sashay through the History of Drag Queen Culture," Popsugar, May 27, 2018, https://www.popsugar.co.uk/news/History-Drag-Drag-Queen-Culture-44884827.

9. "The Fabulous History of Drag," BBC Bitesize, accessed November 4, 2021, https://www.bbc.co.uk/bitesize/articles/zbkmkmn.

Chapter 12

1. Final lines spoken by Jack Lemmon as Daphne and Joe E. Brown as Osgood in *Some Like It Hot* (1959).

2. The Motion Picture Production Code, known as the Hays Code, is named after Will H. Hays, the president of the Motion Picture Producers and Distributors of America (MPPDA) who served from 1922 to 1945.

3. "Beveridge: Married Women Change 6," Beveridge Report, November 1, 1942, section 117, https://www.sochealth.co.uk/national-health-service/public-health-and-wellbeing/beveridge-report/beveridge-married-women-change-6/.

4. Wikipedia, s.v. "Motion Picture Production Code," last modified October 30, 2021, 15:56, https://en.wikipedia.org/wiki/Motion_Picture_Production_Code.

5. American Film Institute, "Dustin Hoffman on *Tootsie* and His Character Dorothy Michaels," YouTube video, December 17, 2012, https://www.youtube.com/watch?v=xPAat-T1uhE.

6. "*Victor/Victoria*," Rotten Tomatoes, accessed October 7, 2021, https://www.rottentomatoes.com/m/victor-victoria. Rotten Tomatoes is an American review-aggregation website for film and television.

7. The Irish Republican Army was an Irish republican revolutionary paramilitary organization.

8. Juliet Jaques, quoted in a booklet accompanying the BFI 2017 DVD release of *The Crying Game*. Juliet Jaques is a British journalist, critic, and writer of short fiction, known for her work on the transgender experience, including her transition as a trans woman.

9. "*Mixed Nuts*," Rotten Tomatoes, accessed October 7, 2021, https://www.rottentomatoes.com/m/mixed_nuts.

10. Rotten Tomatoes, "*Mixed Nuts*."

11. Dominic Cavendish, "Sends You Out on a Feel-Good Bubble of Happiness," *Daily Telegraph*, February 14, 2017, https://www.telegraph.co.uk/theatre/what-to-see/everybodys-talking-jamie-sheffield-crucible-review/.

12. Lizzie Smith, "Jude Law the Russian Transvestite . . . Coming to a Mobile Phone Near You," *Daily Mail*, October 2, 2009, https://www.dailymail.co.uk/tvshowbiz/article-1217184/Jude-Law-shows-feminine-transvestite-film-role-goes-straight-mobile-phone.html.

13. "*The Adventures of Priscilla, Queen of the Desert*," Rotten Tomatoes, accessed October 7, 2021, https://www.rottentomatoes.com/m/adventures_of_priscilla_queen_of_the_desert.

14. Roger Ebert, "*To Wong Foo, Thanks for Everything! Julie Newmar*," Roger-Ebert.com, September 8, 1995, https://www.rogerebert.com/reviews/to-wong-foo-thanks-for-everything-julie-newmar-1995.

Chapter 13

1. T. S. Eliot, "Little Gidding," in *Four Quartets: Collected Poems 1909–1962*, 3rd ed. (London: Faber & Faber, 1966), lines 120–21.

2. LGBT+ is an acronym standing for Lesbian, Gay, Bisexual, Trans, +. The + sign represents the countless other groups of sexual and gender minorities that would make the acronym too long for practical use. There are many other terms people now identify with, giving us the acronym LGBTQQIAAP. The ten terms cover the different ways people define their gender and sexuality, but the list is not exhaustive: *L* (lesbian) describes a woman who is attracted to other women. *G* (gay) describes a man who is attracted to other men or, more broadly, people who identify as homosexual. *B* (bisexual) describes a person who is attracted to both men and women. *T* (transgender) describes a person whose gender identity is different from the sex that is recorded on their birth certificate. *Q* (queer): Originally it was used as a hate term; some people want to reclaim the word, while others find it offensive. It can be a political statement, suggest that someone doesn't want to identify with "binaries" (e.g., male versus female, homosexual versus straight), or suggest that they don't want to label themselves only by their sexual activity. *Q* (questioning) describes a person who is still exploring their sexuality or gender identity. *I* (intersex) describes a person whose body is not definitively male or female. This may be because they have chromosomes that are not XX or XY or because their genitals or reproductive organs are not considered "standard." *A* (allies) describes a person who identifies as straight but supports people in the LGBTQQIAAP community. *A* (asexual) describes a person who is not attracted in a sexual way to people of any gender. *P* (pansexual) describes a person whose sexual attraction is not based on gender and may themselves be fluid

when it comes to gender or sexual identity. Some people may also identify with more than one of these descriptions.

3. Dominic Cavendish, "*The Importance of Being Earnest*, Vaudeville Theatre, Review: A Trial," *Telegraph*, July 1, 2015, https://www.telegraph.co.uk/culture/the atre/theatre-reviews/11711048/The-Importance-of-Being-Earnest-Vaudeville-The-atre-review-a-trial.html.

4. Michael Billington, "*The Importance of Being Earnest* Review—David Suchet's Lady Bracknell Is Majestically Funny," *Guardian*, July 1, 2015, https://www .theguardian.com/stage/2015/jul/01/david-suchet-importance-earnest-lady-brack nell-oscar-wilde.

5. Stephen Collins, "Review: *The Importance of Being Earnest*, Vaudeville Theatre," BritishTheatre.com, July 2, 2015, https://britishtheatre.com/review-the-im portance-of-being-earnest-vaudeville-theatre-3stars/.

6. Collins, "Review: *The Importance of Being Earnest*."

7. *Hollywood Reporter* (@THR), Twitter, July 5, 2018, https://twitter.com/thr/status/1014862233153785859.

8. Rod Ardehali, "RSC Refuses to Cast Plays with Equal Numbers of Men and Women, Insisting Shakespeare Wrote for Men," *Daily Telegraph*, September 12, 2017, https://www.dailymail.co.uk/news/article-4878710/Royal-Shakespeare-Com pany-refuse-equal-gender-split.html.

9. Suzanne Hawkes, "*Treasure Island*," *British Theatre Guide*, April 16–23, 2020, https://www.britishtheatreguide.info/reviews/treasure-island-national-theatr-18950.

INDEX